Table of Contents

Acknowledgements—iv
Preface—v
Introduction: Why write this book?—vi

Chapter 1—Encounters with revival—1
Chapter 2—What is revival?—7
Chapter 3—Ten signs of true revival—16
Chapter 4—How did we get here?—42
Chapter 5—Prayer: the fire that ignites revival—72
Chapter 6—Whatever happened to sin?—88
Chapter 7—Revival leadership—100
Chapter 8—The top ten ways the church opposes revival—112
Chapter 9—Return to the ancient path—129
Chapter 10—Jeremiah: the prophet of revival—139
Chapter 11—The point men and women that lead revival—149
Chapter 12—The watchmen on the wall—162
Chapter 13—Revival power—172
Chapter 14—Count the cost—185

Acknowledgements

Nothing of any consequence is accomplished in this life without a little help from our friends. Ringo Starr and Joe Cocker, famous rock singers, knew this and recorded songs to remind us all.

In any valued endeavor in life there are individuals that appear at appropriate times in order to lend encouragement and support. This truth was especially hammered home during the writing of this book.

I gratefully acknowledge the help of many of my friends that offered support at opportune times. I could have never finished the task without the heroic efforts of Jim Poulson who spent many hours reading my manuscript and offering suggestions. My special thanks is extended to friends like Max and Carolyn Seisser, Jim and Noemi Greer, Gary and Judy Hackworth, Pastor Steve Sheridan and his family, Mike and Michelle Chapman, Todd and Jennifer Engel, John and Francesca Hillman, Dr. James Morgan, Jim Fore and Rick and Chris Will. All of them encouraged me to continue the project.

I also want to mention the love and support that I have always received from my family. Joshua, Louise, Mack, Alexandra and Marianne have always been there. I thank God for them and for my grandchildren, Joshua Jr. and Lily. They hold a special place in my heart.

May God bless this book and use it to advance the revival that He has always called His people to seek.

Pray for revival.

Preface

It was the 1970s and I was a new Christian. The Jesus Movement was spreading throughout California touching off both revival and controversy.

I did all the things that a young Christian did in those days----I attended "end-times rapture" Bible studies; I attended Friday night concerts at Calvary Chapel Costa Mesa; I wore Jesus T-shirts with catchy slogans; and I made weekly pilgrimages to the dozens of intercessory prayer meetings all across the state. It seemed that no one slept in those days and everyone was wound as tight as a drum. I get tired even now when I remember it all.

It was at that time that I first met Brother Willis. He was in his nineties and was the only person that I ever knew that was converted in the 1904 Welsh Revival. The man was a gospel machine. He dressed the part—black suit, turned-back collar of an Anglican priest, the biggest Bible I ever saw and a voice that rolled across a room like a tidal wave. His favorite topic was the Lord Jesus Christ and he mentioned Him in every sentence he uttered in that thick Welsh accent.

When Brother Willis was asked about Evan Roberts and the 1904 Welsh Revival he lit up like a Christmas tree. His stories of those exciting days were as vivid as a newsreel. Midnight prayer meetings, churches busting at the seams, thousands of sinners coming to Christ and entire towns aflame with the fire of God. Brother Willis' stories burned the word "revival" within my spirit like the finger of God on those tablets of stone on Mt. Sinai.

Revival. The subject has captivated my heart and soul for more years than I wish to remember. Revival. I see the word afire and blazing in my thoughts, consuming all my mundane pursuits of daily life. Revival. How can any Christian with a pulse not be excited about such a wonderful blessing sent from the Throne of God?

Is There No Balm in Gilead? is my attempt to put in writing the subject that consumes me like the ancient fire on the Temple altar. My deepest desire is that my readers will catch a glimpse of this profound topic and join the ranks of Christians that lived and breathed revival across the centuries. Reach for the torch they bore and hand it on. Join the timeless relay that brings the fire of God.

—ROBERT ALLAN

Pray for revival.

Why write this book?

After subduing vast lands and kingdoms, King Nebuchadnezzar of Babylon fastened his gaze on tiny Israel. The Prophet Jeremiah, deeply concerned about the ominous threat building on Israel's borders, cried out to God:

"My sorrow is beyond healing, my heart is faint within me. Behold, listen! The cry of the daughter of my people from a distant land. Is the Lord not in Zion? Is her king not within her?"

God's response addressed a perplexing question—Israel's chronic rebellion against God's prohibition of idol worship. God said, *"Why have they provoked me to anger with their graven images, with foreign idols?"*

Jeremiah, mindful of the seriousness of the situation, continued his plea: *"Harvest is past, summer is ended, and we are not saved. For the brokenness of the daughter of my people I am broken. I mourn, dismay has taken hold of me.* **Is there no balm in Gilead?**[1] *Is there no physician there? Why then has not the health of the daughter of my people been restored?"* (Jeremiah 8:18-22).

Jeremiah's intercession moved God to offer forgiveness and restoration to His wayward people. This deliverance, however, was contingent on Israel's repentance. The two-edged offer was simple: **Resist God and perish! Repent and be restored!** Only a fool would reject such an offer of grace.

History records that the fools prevailed. God's call for repentance was ignored by prideful Israel, and judgment fell upon the land. Nebuchadnezzar's armies laid waste to Jerusalem and thousands died. The survivors entered captivity. The truth was etched in stone: ***A Rejection of God's call for repentance has grave consequences. Without revival our present rejection of God's call for repentance is sealing our fate.***

Although King Nebuchadnezzar is long dead and Babylon lies deserted in the Iraqi desert, new and more diabolical enemies are attacking America from within and without. Vicious Islamic terrorists are murdering thousands and building upon their victim's spilled blood a demonically inspired Caliphate.[2] Christians are being butchered around

---

[1] **Balm:** A balm was an aromatic, medicinal substance derived from a plant, the exact plant is unknown. It was used by ancient physicians to heal various diseases and ailments. This balm was a product of Gilead, an area east of the Jordan River famous for its spices and ointments. When Jeremiah asks God "is there no balm in Gilead?" he is pleading for the Lord to heal Israel of its sin of rebellion that was driving it toward God's wrath and judgment. The phrase has taken its place in popular culture to mean "a plea for a healing answer to a destructive circumstance." It is a plea that we should be offering up to God in our own time.

[2] **Caliphate:** A form of Islamic government led by a caliph, a person considered a political and religious successor of the Islamic prophet, Mohammed, and a leader of the entire Muslim community. The Caliphate is ruled by Sharia law, a strict Islamic dictatorship designed to

the world as we speak. Iran, a rogue, terrorist nation is building nuclear bombs, with our own government's assistance, to incinerate western civilization. Malevolent gangs roam our streets in every major city implementing a reign of terror while protected by liberal politicians saturated in the deception of "political correctness." Drugs, rebellion and perverted sex are revered by our youth while God has been banned from our schools. Reprobate social engineers are demanding that all Americans participate in soul-destroying acts of blasphemy. Once biblically founded Christian denominations are rejecting God's Word and becoming just another secular social club like the Elks or the Eagles. The insidious threats are of such stunning dimensions that stout hearts are failing. The parallels between ancient Israel's position and ours are eerily similar.

Like Jeremiah, I plea for God's intervention. I believe it is exactly what we need to give our country a chance to make a course correction before we fall over the precipice into oblivion. Like Jeremiah, I seek the balm in Gilead (a call for national revival). And like Jeremiah, I am stunned by the indifference and resistance that permeates our modern culture.

I am a revivalist. I offer no apology for my belief that revivals are welcome experiences of divine intervention. There is, however, a question that perplexes me. Why do so many of my fellow Christians hold the opinion that revivals should be avoided?

After much thought, I believe the reasons are multi-faceted. They range from a simple ignorance of the subject to a fear of the unknown and on to an outright rejection of the effort that the pursuit of revivals will require.

Many of my Christian friends have explained that their reluctance to embrace revival is based on the stories concerning the questionable behaviors that have been exhibited by revival participants. To be honest, there are historic accounts describing how some people, when encountering a genuine move of God, have become highly emotional and have exhibited strange behaviors. The great revivalists have all given eyewitness testimonies concerning these manifestations of the flesh. But this begs the question: *Should the extraordinary successes of revivals— thousands being saved and delivered, churches, cities and countries on fire for God, entire denominations and ministries birthed out of genuine revivals, and great advances made for the gospel—be discounted because of the questionable actions of a few?* In my opinion, the positive effects of revival far outweigh the fleshly responses of some revival participants. Unfortunately, the fear of the unknown is often

---

implement total control of the populace through any means necessary. Under Sharia law the most evil and bloodthirsty acts of murder are held up as the will of Allah.

insurmountable, motivating many sincere Christians to reject what they do not understand.

A pastor of a Seattle mega-church and I had developed a friendship. Once over breakfast I asked him for his opinions concerning revival. He poured me some coffee and then explained how his particular church had been birthed out of a revival back in the 1960's and had made a major impact in the Seattle area. He noticed that I was smiling and nodding in agreement when he decided to throw me a curve. He said, *"Bob, I can see that you're excited about my revival testimony."*

I answered, *"Absolutely, I love hearing about revival."*

"Maybe you won't be as excited when you hear my testimony in its entirety" he said.

"What do you mean?" I asked quizzically.

He answered, *"Well, I was a revival supporter back then, but now I see revival as a liability."*

I almost fell off my chair. I cleared my throat and said, *"But how can you say that revivals are a liability, especially when a revival directly brought your own church into existence?"*

He smiled and then said, *"Bob, I do acknowledge that a revival blessed my early ministry. I'll always remember that fondly...but..."*

"But what?" I asked. He paused and gathered his thoughts before answering.

"Actually, a lot has changed since then," he said. *"When I first began my ministry, I believed that revivals are blessings. But since I've become involved in the church-growth movement[3] I've realized that revivals are a bit messy and definitely uncontrollable."*

I must have looked like I was just hit by a car. He folded his hands and looked at me in the same way that my doctor did when expressing his concern over my health.

"Bob, you've got that strange look like you're ready to pass out," he said with concern.

"I'm still dealing with the 'revivals are messy and uncontrollable' comment. Give me a moment to recover," I said.

"C'mon Bob, revivals are messy and uncontrollable. You've said that yourself."

---

[3] The Church Growth (Seeker Sensitive) Movement focuses on "numerical success" by using "slick marketing techniques" to sell the church to those "church shoppers" looking for a church that caters to their perceived needs. The movement is designed to advance the same marketing and advertising programs that are used in successful secular businesses. Critics of the movement see the foundational premises of the participating churches as a degradation of the gospel message in two key areas: First, the spiritually shallow church shoppers become the evaluative yardstick of the success and/or failure of the church's ministry and secondly, the resultant church becomes nothing more than a social club that has no semblance to the historically powerful churches led and directed by the Holy Spirit that have always upheld the Lord's high standards.

"Sure I did," I answered. *"But I never meant to insinuate that they should be discarded because of a few problems. Revivals are unpredictable, but they're still acts of God that we have no right to ban because of our discomfort."*

He laughed. *"You're acting dramatic, Bob. After all, programs are cleaner and safer,"* he said.

"Programs? You're saying that programs are cleaner and safer?" I must have looked like a fish out of water.

"Yes, programs. Oh, I resisted at first, but now I've enthusiastically embraced the fact that we are now a program church. We develop programs and follow them. Programs are safe, predictable, and not considered a threat by our members. Revivals, although sometimes beneficial, can disturb the church members that are suspicious of any excess. We try to avoid them as much as possible to keep our membership happy."

My jaw fell to the ground and I sat there in stunned silence. The pastor, recognizing my bewilderment, decided to expand his explanation. He continued: *"C'mon Bob, after all, people change. It's evolution, Bob. The old, revival tent evangelists are a thing of the past. As a church-growth adherent I recognize that a genuine revival is unpredictable and can cause discomfort in a congregation. I'm not willing to take the risk of causing discomfort in our membership that may cause them to go elsewhere. I'll stick to the safe and controllable programs and insure that we can continue paying our bills."* He noted my distress and added: *"Cheer up Bob...maybe our methods are a bit slow and plodding for your taste, but we still do some damage to Satan's program."*

His explanation spoke volumes. His church, once a fiery weapon in the hand of God, had abandoned its revival roots and was developing some programs that might cause a little damage to Satan's programs! I visualized a huge poster that read: God's programs vs. Satan's programs! It sounded like a boring and uneventful chess match. Realizing that his position was all too common, I sat in stunned silence. He smiled and poured me another cup of coffee. He then asked me if I was available for golf.

I will admit that revivals can be unpredictable, but rejecting a revival because of a lack of "controllability" is a different matter. Who in their right mind would even consider trying to control God? Consciously suppressing an authentic move of God for any reason disturbs me deep within my spirit...and should disturb all sincere Christians.

With all that said, I must make it clear that my support for revival rests on two major points: First and foremost, true revivals are sent by God Who obviously feels that they are needed. Faced with this undeniable fact, I believe that Christian resistance to a God ordained revival is an act of disobedience that must be thoroughly rejected. Discounting God's plans and purposes for any reason is repugnant to me, and I will not entertain the thought.

And secondly, revivals have always multiplied the effect of the Christian church many fold and turned it into a formidable weapon against the works of darkness. True revivals, unpredictable or not, have powerfully transformed the church on every front. Because I know this is true I will not rest until I see revival sweep this land.

My decision to write this book was a sobering one. Weighing all the pros and cons I decided that I will take the risk of being a target of those who will get out their red editing pencils and find fault with whatever I say.

In this book I attempt to make it clear what revival is, how it occurs and what it does. I mix in a lot of other points such as—when will revivals occur, why do they cease and most importantly, why revivals are sparse in America in our time. I know that my comments concerning the failure of some church leadership and the subsequent cooling of the spiritual ardor in their churches and denominations may seem callous to those who demand peace at all costs, but I truly love the Lord's church and will not be silent in the face of a forfeiture of our orders to speak truth. Remember, the Lord Jesus was not a "peacenik" that embraced every wind of doctrine and behavior in order to buttress some semblance of peace. His words are set in stone:

"Do not think that I came to bring peace on the earth; I did not come to bring peace, but a sword. For I came to set a man against his father, and a daughter against her mother, and a daughter-in-law against her mother-in-law; and a man's enemies will be the members of his household." (Matthew 10:34-36).

A rejection of revival as a viable act of God for the advancement of His kingdom should never be considered by those who bear His name. The Apostle Paul's statement concerning God's blueprint is apropos:

But we should always give thanks to God for you, brethren beloved by the Lord, because God has chosen you from the beginning for salvation through sanctification by the Spirit and faith in the truth. It was for this He called you through our gospel, that you may gain the glory of our Lord Jesus Christ. So then, brethren, **stand firm** *and* **hold to the traditions which you were taught,** *whether by word of mouth or by letter from us.* (II Thessalonians 2: 13-15)

The debate on revival has continued for two thousand years. The sides have drawn clear lines in the sand and see it as their solemn duty to not be moved from their positions. My prayer is that my fellow brothers and sisters will not reject the revivals that are sent by God, but will actively embrace the outpouring of grace from our blessed Savior and Lord. I pray that we will permit the Lord to move us.

Pray for revival.

Robert Allan
Omaha, Nebraska
May 30, 2017

Chapter One
Encounters with Revival

"Oh, that you would rend the heavens and come down, that the mountains would tremble before you." -Isaiah 64:1

It was in 1960 when the American public was first exposed to the Hollywood film **Elmer Gantry**[4] starring Burt Lancaster and Jean Simmons. The film was made from a 1927 book written by avowed atheist Sinclair Lewis and was anti-God, anti-Christian and anti-revival. The "sophisticated" liberal progressive crowd loved the book and the subsequent film, for it supplied them with the ammunition to help them attack the influence of the Christian church. In their opinion, their assault on the Christian church was a public service.

Lewis' plot was centered on religious charlatan Elmer Gantry, a con-artist masquerading as a man of God that easily manipulated all that fell prey to his lies and deceptions. After a life of drunkenness, sexual debasement, thievery and shameless blasphemy, Gantry met the naive female evangelist, Sister Falconer, and wormed his way into her life and ministry.[5] The despicable Gantry used the unwitting Falconer to advance his nefarious plans to defraud the people of God. To Gantry, the sexual conquest of the gullible Sister Falconer, was an added bonus.

With acrimonious precision, Lewis painted his picture of unabashed corruption and hypocrisy. In his opinion, Brother Elmer Gantry was the typical sociopathic evangelist unashamedly fleecing the gullible public and Sister Sharon Falconer was the typical ignorant do-gooder bent on blind obedience to some non-existent God while easily acquiescing to Gantry's fleshly seductions.

The pagan filmmakers, closely following Lewis' theme, produced what they considered as a much-needed expose´ of blatant religious hucksterism. I sat in the movie theater and watched transfixed as they methodically advanced the impression that all evangelists and preachers were thieves and sexual predators manipulating the unsophisticated rabble. Their position that all revivals were fool's errands—led by fools and followed by fools—was drilled into my adolescent mind with the force of a pneumatic jackhammer. It is no stretch of the imagination

---

[4] **Novel** written by Sinclai Lewis (1927) Harcourt Trade Publishers.
  Broadway Play by Patrick Kearney opened on Broadway on 7 August 1928 at Playhouse Theatre where it ran for 48 performances.
  Film (1960) starring Burt Lancaster as Gantry, Jean Simmons as Sister Sharon Falconer, Arthur Kennedy and Shirley Jones. Nominated for five Academy Awards in 1961, including for Best Picture and Best Score, winning the other three; Best Actor for Lancaster, Best Supporting Actress for Shirley Jones and Best Adapted Screenplay. Directed by Richard Brooks.
[5] Sinclair Lewis admitted that he had patterned his Sister Falconer character on the famous female evangelist, Aimee Semple McPherson, a popular Christian leader of the time. Sister McPherson had been subject to many criticisms during her life and ministry and was easily targeted by antagonists.

when I confess that the film Elmer Gantry became a major excuse for my spiritual rebellion. With the cinematic image of Burt Lancaster's lascivious grinning face and drooling lips burned into my subconscious, I decided to never become merchandise in the hands of some sleazy religious huckster and plunged, headlong, into the sewer of sin. I became just another statistic on Satan's chalkboard while Burt Lancaster won the academy award for his efforts to assist in Hollywood's twisted attack on Christianity. I didn't win an academy award but instead received a spiritual beating that crippled my life.

Many dark and lonely years followed.

Rescued by a revival

It was not until the 1970s that revivals started to interest me. The reason was simple. After a life of brazen immorality I had become a Christian in 1971 during a revival called the Jesus Movement that exploded in California and spread across the world—bringing many to Christ. My conversion, far from being the exercise of futility described by Sinclair Lewis, was a supernatural reality that touched my life in ways that can only be understood as a miracle. Filled with God and reinforced by His Word, I ceased abiding in the moral sewer. With my mind freed from the oppressive control of the world's mentality, I began to focus on the call of God.

And that call was revival.

1970s California was inundated with the Charismatic Renewal[6]— the closest thing to a genuine revival that has occurred in my lifetime. With hundreds of new Spirit-filled churches popping up across the country, the topic of revivals was prominent in every Christian coffee shop in America. Since my friends and I were still young enough to want to be part of something new and world-changing, we began to seek each and every opportunity to learn more about revivals. It was then that I was introduced to the ministry of Keith Green.[7]

I first experienced Christian musician and evangelist Keith Green when he was invited to speak at the church I was attending. Before encountering Jesus, Keith had been a popular rock musician that had spent his time smoking dope while sitting cross-legged in ridiculous yoga poses.

---

[6] **The Charismatic Renewal** was a revival movement that spread across many historically mainstream denominations and churches. The movement was centered on the receiving of the Holy Spirit's power for ministry, the use of spiritual gifts to advance the kingdom, an intense Spirit-driven worship, a love of Bible study, an infectious evangelism, a return to biblical orthodoxy, and a rejection of the apostate liberalism that had gripped the mainline denominations and churches. Among Protestants, the movement began around 1960. Among Roman Catholics, it originated around 1967.

[7] **Keith Green** was a musician that conducted an evangelistic ministry during the 1970s until his death in a plane crash in 1982. Green was the author of many Christian worship songs that are still popular today. Like a modern John the Baptist he called many young people of his generation to Jesus Christ and urged them to share their faith.

Converted from a life of sin and rebellion, Keith Green combined his piano playing and singing with a powerful message focusing on Jesus Christ and His call to revival. He made it crystal clear that the call to revival was directly from the lips of Jesus and that we Americanized Christians needed to repent of our resistance and get it done. Keith knew only one way—attack Satan's kingdom head on and proclaim the kingdom of Christ with great intensity. The man was a ball of fire.

When Keith finished his last song he leapt to his feet, almost toppling the piano bench in the process. He locked on the crowd with his piercing eyes, paused a few seconds and then said: *"Unlike the rest of the world we American Christians all have Bibles and we've all heard hundreds of sermons challenging us to respond to God's Word. As American Christians with such great access to spiritual information we are all without any valid excuse for ignoring God's call on any subject. Now I'm telling you that the call of God is for revival...true revival...real revival."* He paused a moment and then said, *"So what are you going to do? Sit on your backsides and ignore the call for revival or stand to your feet and pray for God's anointing to get it done? The ball is in your court."*

Challenged by his words, I jumped to my feet and called out to the Lord, asking Him for forgiveness for my self-centered approach to Him and His Word. I then asked the Lord to ignite a revival fire inside my heart and use me to pass the fire on to others. Within a few moments a strange warmth filled my heart and I knew that I would never be the same.

With revival fire burning in my belly, I began telling everyone I met about the sacrifice of Jesus Christ for the salvation of the world. Realizing that I needed to learn how to better proceed in my task, I began to read everything I could find on the subject of revival. It was then that I discovered the writings of Leonard Ravenhill.

Who was Leonard Ravenhill?

Leonard Ravenhill (1907-1994) was a British Christian evangelist and author who focused on the subjects of prayer and revival. He was a mentor to evangelist Keith Green and taught at Keith and Melody Green's *Last Days Ministry* in Texas.

Born in Leeds, in Yorkshire, England, Ravenhill was educated at Cliff College in England and sat under the ministry of Samuel Chadwick—a theologian, lecturer, powerful evangelist and pastor that authored the book *The Way to Pentecost.*[8]

Ravenhill was a serious student of church history with an intense interest in Christian revival. Realizing that modern liberalism[9] had

---

[8] **The Way to Pentecost** by Samuel Chadwick (1932) 64 page e-book in PDF format.

[9] Liberalism in the church is a form of extreme apostasy. The leaders in this movement methodically substitute their theories and opinions for the revealed doctrines of historical Christianity. Many

poisoned the evangelical church, he took every opportunity to unmask its toxicity and clearly define its danger to God's people. He patiently detailed the steps of the liberal apostasy that is attempting to turn the American church into a body of social engineers trying to build a world without the biblical Jesus Christ. He drew a line in the sand and stated clearly that the liberal progressives were the modern false prophets that the Holy Bible warned about.

But false prophets also arose among the people, just as there will also be false teachers among you, who will secretly introduce destructive heresies, even denying the Master who bought them, bringing swift destruction upon themselves. Many will follow their sensuality, and because of them the way of the truth will be maligned; and in their greed they will exploit you with false words; their judgment from long ago is not idle, and their destruction is not asleep (II Peter 2:1-3).

The cooling of the church toward evangelism and revival coupled with its loss of interest in intercessory prayer drove him to begin his lifelong call for the re-awakening of the church. With great fire and exuberance he crisscrossed England and the European continent crying out for a return to the foundations of the early church. In 1950, Ravenhill was called by God to America where he began his attempt to re-light the revival fires that once burned on the North American continent.

Ravenhill was immovable in his opposition to the deadness of the modern church of his time. He clearly addressed the disparities he perceived between the New Testament church and the American church and called for a return to its revival roots. Everywhere that Ravenhill went he spoke out against the lethargy that had crippled the church.

Ravenhill, like the prophets of old, was relentless in his opposition to those who distorted God's Word to sell a false gospel. This clear declaration of war against apostasy and rebellion prompted the famous evangelist and pastor, A.W. Tozer to state his support: *"Those who know of Leonard Ravenhill recognize in him the religious specialist, the man sent by God to battle the priests of Baal on their own mountain top, to shame the careless priests at the altars, to face down the false prophets, and to warn the people who are being led astray by them. Such a man is not an easy companion. He insists on being a Christian all the time and everywhere which marks him as difficult. Why do we have men of such fiery swords as Ravenhill? They are sick inside when they see the*

---

historic denominations once aflame with evangelistic fire have jettisoned the Word of God and developed a secular religion mixed with bits and pieces garnered from a dozen other religions and philosophies. In essence, liberalism is the religion of denial—denying every biblical doctrine revealed within the Word of God.

children of heaven acting like the sons of earth. To such men as these, the church owes a debt too heavy to pay."[10]

The first Ravenhill book I read was ***Why Revival Tarries***.[11] The book was as subtle as a car wreck I read it until the cover came off and then went to purchase another copy so I could re-read his words. Over the years I have purchased many copies of this profound book and given it away to anyone that expressed an interest in understanding the machinations of revival. A friend that had accepted this book from me as a gift commented, *"Bob, the publishers should give you a stipend for all the Ravenhill books you have purchased and given away."*

There was no middle ground with Leonard Ravenhill. Intensely infectious, he breathed revival and spoke with an authority hard to find in our modern era. He was a man both greatly loved and greatly loathed with no room in the middle. By his very presence he could divide a room. Those who have discovered his sermons on the internet are confronted with a man that is literally aflame with the fire of God.[12] How can any Christian with a pulse not like a man who uttered things like the following?

- *My main ambition in life is to be on the Devil's most wanted list.*
- *The church used to be a lifeboat rescuing the perishing. Now she is a cruise ship recruiting the promising.*
- *Today's church wants to be raptured from responsibility.*
- *The man who can get believers to praying would, under God, usher in the greatest revival that the world has ever known.*
- *When there's something in the Bible that churches don't like they call it legalism.*
- *You can't live wrong and pray right.*
- *How can you pull down the strongholds of Satan if you don't have strength to turn off the TV?*
- *Our God is a consuming fire. He consumes pride, lust, materialism, and other sin.*
- *Someday someone is going to pick up this book (The Bible) and believe it, and put us all to shame.*
- *Someone asked me, "Do you pray for the dead? I said, "No. I preach to them!" I think every pew in every church is death row.*

---

[10] **A.W. Tozer:** Pastor within the Christian and Missionary Alliance Denomination famous as an author and evangelist. Author of many books and publications he is best known for two books: "The Pursuit of God" (1948) Harrisburg, PA Christian Publications and "The Knowledge of the Holy" (1961) New York: Harper & Row

[11] **Why Revival Tarries:** by Leonard Ravenhill (1959) (Expanded edition Bethany House Publishers 1979) Also by Leonard Ravenhill:
Revival Praying: Bethany House Publishers (1981)
Revival God's Way: Bethany House Publishers (1986)

[12] The interested reader can listen to Ravenhill's sermons on YouTube. Be prepared for a soul-stirring message that was designed to extract you from your lethargy.

> *Think about that! They're dead! They sing about God; they talk about God, but they're dead! They have no relationship (with God).*

- *A sinning man stops praying, a praying man stops sinning.*
- *If Jesus had preached the same message that ministers preach today, He would have never been crucified.*
- *The only reason we don't have revival is because we are willing to live without it.*
- *Revival is when God gets so sick and tired of being misrepresented that He shows Himself.*
- *The only time we can say "Christ is all I need," is when Christ is all we have.*

Being a Christian with a pulse, it was not difficult for me to choose my side in the Ravenhill debate. Like him, I wanted revival, true revival, and like him, I believed that "business as usual" within the church was just a euphemism that meant no dynamic growth, no contagious witness, no world-changing thrust, no prayer, no power and no revival. It was my humble opinion that rejecting the message of a Leonard Ravenhill was nothing short of a full embrace of spiritual mediocrity.

And an agonizing slide into spiritual mediocrity and death.

A list of those influenced by Leonard Ravenhill reads like a Who's Who of Christian evangelism and revival. Ray Comfort, Ravi Zacharias, Tommy Tenney, Steve Hall, Charles Stanley, Keith and Melody Green, Paul Washer and David Wilkerson are just a few of the names that shine forth from the pantheon of heaven's heroes as lights of evangelism and revival. Thousands, and maybe millions, have come to Christ through the efforts of these men and women and many like them that learned from the anointed words of Leonard Ravenhill.

To thousands of thirsty believers, Leonard Ravenhill was revival's lion. He preached under the anointing of the Holy Spirit and radicalized an entire generation of God seekers. His message was an alarm bell. Simple and to the point, Leonard Ravenhill's call for revival is forever imprinted on my soul.

Thank you, brother Ravenhill, for sounding that alarm.

Pray for revival.

Chapter Two

What is Revival?

Restore us, O God of our salvation, and cause Your indignation toward us to cease. Will You be angry with us forever? Will You prolong Your anger to all generations? Will You not Yourself revive us again, that Your people may rejoice in You. –Psalm 85: 4-6

When I was a boy the local Foursquare Church[13] had a yearly event they called a "revival." A traveling evangelist came to town and conducted the weeklong series of meetings for the express purpose of reaching the town's lost. Many members of that Foursquare Church knew, however, that the real targets were the unsaved husbands of the faithful women that attended the church.

A huge banner would be attached to the church, usually across the roof of the church building or around the steeple. The banner would say something like the following: Revival Tonight! Or Revival Week! The members of that particular church were so excited about their event that they papered every inch of the town with handbills, placing them in every mailbox and under every car's windshield wiper.

The residents of the town streamed into the church on "kickoff night" prepared for a workout that rivaled an NFL training camp. There was a week of singing, praying, shouting, clapping, jumping, crying, sweating and unbridled emotions that peeked on the last night when those wayward husbands finally gave in and came forward.

After the evangelist left town the excitement subsided and things got back to normal. Church became church, with all of its boredom and repetition. The wayward husbands went back to their wayward ways and their besieged wives began interceding again for their salvation.

With all due respect to many in the church that think that revivals are nothing more than a weekend visit by a traveling evangelist, calling something a revival when it is not, no matter how good it might be, misses the mark. A revival is a revival and a church meeting is a church meeting. Anyone who has spent a few hours in a church meeting knows the difference. A revival exudes life, forgiveness and power that spreads out to an entire culture while a typical church meeting can slay even the hardiest soul.

I will agree that anything that a traveling evangelist can do to re-direct the church toward a stronger walk with Christ is welcome and needed, but a weekend visit by the evangelist is not a revival on the same

---

[13] The International Church of the Foursquare Gospel or "Foursquare Church" is a Protestant Pentecostal denomination founded in Los Angeles, California in 1923 by evangelist Aimee Semple McPherson. As of 2000 it had over 8,000,000 members in 144 countries. It is known as a scripturally based fundamental church with a dynamic outreach style and method.

magnitude of a genuine revival. Again, I will say it: A revival is a revival and a church service is a church service.

But again, God bless the traveling evangelist. They do much good. With that said, I present what I believe is a true definition of revival:

Revival defined

True revival is defined as a spiritual reawakening launched by a fresh outpouring of God's Holy Spirit that transforms the lives of God's people. This outpouring is prompted by intense prayer offered up by individuals that have rejected the spiritual deadness and apathy of the existing church. The Holy Spirit's outpouring directly confronts the following spiritual conditions:

- *The dissipation of a genuine love for God.*
- *A lazy response toward God and His call for true discipleship.*
- *The lack of holiness within God's people.*
- *The neglect of prayer and true worship exhibited by a suffocating malaise within the church.*
- *The lack of passion for evangelism and personal witness toward non-believers.*
- *The neglect of the study of God's Word.*
- *The ignoring of God's call for personal repentance and restoration.*
- *The weak attempt of desperate leadership to draw people into their congregations through the use of secular business techniques and not by biblically ordained fasting and prayer and personal evangelism.*

The pattern of a true revival is universal and proceeds as follows: — A renewal of the believers through repentance and restoration that births a fresh and intense new commitment to Christ. Those affected by a true revival have a renewed, heightened love for God that results in obedience to the Lord in all areas of their lives. There is a deep repentance from sin and a pursuit of God that is many times beyond what these persons ever experienced before. A true revival transforms society by way of a spiritual transformation that first explodes within the church and then moves outward to transform cities, regions, and countries. A true revival causes the church to fulfill its God-ordained mission—the bringing of the gospel to the world. In essence, when God shows up everything changes[14]

---

[14] A revival will only occur when a person or persons recognizes that the church is too weak to confront a corrupt culture that has sunk to the lowest levels imaginable. That person or persons will understand that nothing can derail Satan's plans to destroy the church's influence except a direct intervention of God Himself. That person or persons led by the Holy Spirit will enter a time of intense prayer and fasting and call out to God and plead for that intervention. That person or persons have become a catalyst that prepares the way for the appearance of God.

In a true revival the Lord literally shows up and overturns the status quo.[15] His tangible presence is inescapable to anyone that makes any attempt to discern and understand what is occurring. When the Lord shows up He will accomplish a number of significant things that are clearly detailed within the Word of God. His presence is of such irresistible power that situations and conditions that had appeared to be impossible melt away and are transformed. When God shows up everything changes.

When God shows up

- **Nature is healed:**

    Until the Spirit is poured out upon us on high, and the wilderness becomes a fertile field, and the fertile field is considered as a forest. (Isaiah 32:15).

    And,

    The wilderness and the desert will be glad, and the Arabah will rejoice and blossom (Isaiah 35:1).

- **The sick and lame are healed:**

    Then the eyes of the blind will be opened and the ears of the deaf will be unstopped. Then the lame will leap like a dear, and the tongue of the mute will shout for joy. (Isaiah 35:5, 6).

    And,

    Bless the Lord, O my soul, and forget none of His benefits; Who pardons all your iniquities, Who heals all your diseases. (Psalm 103:2, 3).

- **Prayers are answered:**

    You (the Lord) have given him (the prayer petitioner) his heart's desire. And You have not withheld the request of his lips. (Psalm 21:2).

- **God's people will shout for joy:**

    Shout for joy, O heavens! And rejoice, O earth! Break forth into joyful shouting, O mountains! For the Lord has comforted His people and will have compassion on His afflicted. (Psalm 49: 13).

- **Those committed to evil will flee:**

    For the Lord of hosts will have a day of reckoning against everyone who is proud and lofty (those who are evil) and against everyone who is lifted up, that he may be abased...The pride of men will be humbled and the loftiness of men will be abased; and the Lord alone will

---

[15] Although it is clear that God is always present and does not physically disappear, there is a sense of God's presence that is felt by His people when a true revival occurs. This sense is deep and profound and removes all doubt that God is real. In the word we will find many descriptions of the changes that occur when God shows up.

be exalted in that day. But the idols will completely vanish. Men will go into caves of the rocks and into holes of the ground before the terror of the Lord and the splendor of His majesty, when He arises to make the earth tremble. (Isaiah 2:12-19).

- **Those desiring God will come to His presence:**

    Ho! Everyone who thirsts, come to the waters (waters = the Holy Spirit); and you who have no money come, buy and eat. Come buy wine and milk without money and without cost. Why do you spend money for what is not bread, and your wages for what does not satisfy? Listen carefully to Me, and eat what is good, and delight yourself in abundance. Incline your ear and come to Me. Listen, that you may live; and I will make an everlasting covenant with you, according to the faithful mercies shown to David. (Isaiah 55:1-3).

- **God's glory will be clearly seen and felt:**

    Lift up your heads, O gates, and be lifted up, O ancient doors, that the King of glory may come in! Who is the King of glory? The Lord strong and mighty, the Lord mighty in battle. Lift up your heads, O gates, and lift them up, O ancient doors, that the King of glory may come in! Who is this King of glory? The Lord of hosts, He is the King of glory. (Psalm 24:7-10).

And,

He said to me, "You are My servant Israel, in whom I will show My glory." (Isaiah 49:3).

- **God's unmerited favor (grace) is abundant:**

    He predestined us to adoption as sons through Jesus Christ to Himself, according to the kind intention of His will, to the praise of the glory of His grace, which He freely bestowed on us in the beloved. In Him we have redemption through His blood, the forgiveness of our trespasses, according to the riches of His grace. (Ephesians 1:5-7).

- **True worship becomes a weapon of spiritual warfare:**

    Let the high praises of God be in their mouth (God's people), and a two-edged sword in their hand. To execute vengeance on the nations and punishment on the peoples (God haters). To bind their kings with chains and their nobles with fetters of iron (spiritual warfare). To execute on them the judgment written; this is an honor for all His godly ones. Praise the Lord! (Psalm 149:6-9).

And,

> *They (Israel) rose early in the morning and went out to the wilderness of Tekoa; and when they went out, Jehoshaphat stood and said, "Listen to me, O Judah and inhabitants of Jerusalem, put your trust in the Lord your God and you will be established. Put your trust in the prophets and succeed." When he had consulted with the people, he appointed those who sang to the Lord and those who praised Him in holy attire, and they went out before the army and said, "Give thanks to the Lord, for His lovingkindness is everlasting." When they began singing and praising, the Lord set ambushes against the sons of Ammon, Moab and Mount Seir, who had come against Judah; so they were routed.* (II Chronicles 20:20-22).

- **God's righteous judgment brings restoration:**
> *Hear a just cause, O Lord, give heed to my cry; give ear to my prayer, which is not from deceitful lips. Let my judgment come forth from Your presence; let Your eyes look with equity. You have tried my heart; You have visited me by night; You have tested me and You find nothing; I have purposed that my mouth will not transgress. As for the deeds of men, by the word of Your lips I have kept from the paths of the violent. My steps have held fast to Your paths. My feet have not sl ipped.* (Psalm 17: 1-5).

- **God's people are united in Christ:**
> *He made known to us the mystery of His will, according to His kind attention which He purposed in Him with a view to an administration suitable to the fullness of times, that is, the summing up of all things in Christ (unity), things in the heavens and things on the earth.* (Ephesians 1:9, 10).

And,

> *Therefore if there is any encouragement in Christ, if there is any consolation of love, if there is any fellowship of the Spirit, if any affection and compassion, make my joy complete by being of the same mind, maintaining the same love, united in spirit, intent on one purpose. Do nothing from selfishness or empty conceit, but with humility of mind regard one another as more important than yourselves;* (Philippians 2:1-3).

Some important facts concerning revival

- Revival occurs when God's people desperately seek it and pray for it to occur. **Unrelenting, pervasive prayer is the driving factor.**[16]
- Although prayer opens up the doors of revival, it must be said that a true revival is not controlled by man and is a pure work of the Holy Spirit. We pray and ask for revival. God answers, but He always holds total control of its direction and outcome.
- Revival causes a deep repentance within the hearts of those who experience it. A "revival" without deep repentance being exercised by the individuals involved cannot fulfill the definition of a true revival. In fact, a revival without repentance is nothing but a show.
- Revival occurs when the church and God's people are at their lowest. It is time for revival when our anemic churches are lying dead in the water, the bottom falls out of our plans and designs and we are at the end of our rope. It is only then that God will send forth His power and presence and rescue us from ourselves.
- Revival promotes a re-establishment of true biblical authority exhibited through called men and women that are defined by their inner spirituality and not by academic degrees.
- Revival is often missed by church leadership who may actively oppose it. The reasons for their opposition can be theological, fear of the loss of control, contentment with the status quo, or just plain laziness. Whatever the reason may be, the sad truth is that revival is often resisted by established Christian leadership.
- Revival is never "owned" by any particular church or denomination, but is owned by God Who sends it, directs it, empowers it and infuses it with His presence. There is nothing more pathetic then watching a church or denomination attempting to use revival to advance their own designs. If and when a church or denomination may attempt to use a revival for its own advancement the revival will cease. This is an example of the prohibition of the mixing of the seed in the field as mentioned in Leviticus 19: 19.[17]

---

[16] This point is probably the most contested in the revival controversy. Many churches and denominations resist the fact that prayer is the key and instead believe that revivals are random events that occur only when God chooses to send it without any prayer input. In my opinion, this is nothing but a human generated theological position and not one that is readily discerned in the Scriptures.

[17] Many theologians have agreed that this prohibition concerning the mixing of various things such as seed is a caution about adding to God's Word and statutes any human word or reasoning. The Lord's Word must stand alone without additions or subtractions. No mixing of the profane and the holy. The prohibitions against adding to and/or subtracting from God's Word appears in various places in the Bible (Deuteronomy 4:1, 2; Revelation 22:18, 19).

- Revival pulls down the barrier walls of denominationalism and brings a greater unity amongst the people of God. This is often resisted by church leadership who may not want relationship with other churches and denominations. One possible reason for their reluctance to embrace relationship: *the fear of losing tithing members to those whom they see as competition.*
- Revival will cause deep changes within the hearts of those who experience it. These inflamed souls will never forget what they have seen and heard. After a revival has waned, those Christians who have experienced it will long for its return and will never be satisfied with business as usual within the church. In essence, the power and majesty of revival will forever "ruin" them for the expression of mundane, mediocre "Churchianity."
- Revival will stop when men attempt to use it for their gain or agenda. Like Uzzah, who touched the Ark of God in order to keep it from falling, any attempt to "help" God or use His work for ulterior motives will result in a disaster.

They spoke with eloquence

The comments I have listed below are from some of history's great preachers and revivalists. They may use different words, but all reflect what is genuine about revival:

"An awakening is ready to break on the dismal scene when Christians have a deep, profound spirit of prayer for an awakening." -Lewis Drummond

"Revival is that strange and sovereign work of God in which He visits His own people—reanimating, and releasing them into the fullness of His blessing. -Stephen Offord

"Revival is falling in love with Jesus all over again." -Vance Havner

"Revival is not the discovery of some new truth. It's the rediscovery of the grand old truth of God's power in and through the cross." -Sammy Tippit

"Nothing short of an outpouring of God's Spirit will revitalize and empower an impotent and anemic church to display once again God's glory to a lost world." -Del Fehsenfeld Jr.

"Trying to run a church without revivals can be done when you can run a gasoline engine on buttermilk" -Billy Sunday

"Perhaps the greatest barrier to revival on a large scale is the fact that we are too interested in great display. We want an exhibition. God is looking for a man who will throw himself entirely on God. Whenever self-effort, self-glory, self-seeking or self-promotion enters into the work of revival, God leaves us to ourselves." -Ted Rendall

"A baptism of holiness, a demonstration of godly living is the crying need of the day." -Duncan Campbell

"Revival is a renewed conviction of sin and repentance followed by an intense desire to live in obedience to God. It's giving up one's will to God in deep humility." -Charles Finney

"God's time for revival is the very darkest hour, when everything seems hopeless. It is always the Lord's way to go to the very worse cases to manifest His glory." -Andrew Gih

"A revival almost always begins among the laity. Ecclesiastical leaders seldom welcome reformation. History repeats itself. The present leaders are too comfortably situated as a rule to desire innovation that might require sacrifice on their part. And God only falls on sacrifice. An empty altar receives no fire." -Frank Bartleman

"There has never been a spiritual awakening in any country or locality that did not begin in united prayer." -A. T. Pierson

"There is a growing conviction everywhere, and especially among thoughtful people, that unless revival comes, other forces will take the field, that will sink us still deeper into the mire of humanism and materialism." -Duncan Campbell

The knowing

Something is wrong and we know it. We can feel it when we enter our churches. Something is missing. We may try to cover it up, keep a positive attitude, or ignore it altogether, but the truth just sits there...confronting us...not going away. Something is wrong and we know it.

What we sense is a spiritual vacuum. It is the lack of holiness, power, purpose and anointing that only comes when we experience revival. No matter how hard some Christians try to pretend that revival is not necessary we know that something more is out there waiting for us to reach out and grasp it. We know that our very lives and lives of our children are at stake and that a response is required for our survival.

And we know it.

It does not take a Bible scholar to know that the cultures of the world are cesspools of hate, sin, unbelief and immorality. Fear stalks our neighborhoods and rules the night. Killers stalk our streets and all of us are targets. No one is exempt: old men, old women, young men, young women, children, infants, all are "fair" game to the predatory animals that hunt for victims. America has lost its moral bearings.

And we know it.

Our beloved country, once a lighthouse of hope, has descended into the pit of rationalism and despair. The committed servants of God that once raised the spiritual temperature of the nation have shed their mortal coil and are gone. With their passing we are bereft of their fire and glory and are now plagued with ineffectual spiritual politicians running for office each Sunday. They are empty and weak.

And we know it.

The patriotic leaders of our past are only memories, dead and turned to dust. Sadly, our country is now led by shameless opportunists, men and women who are filled with a desire for power and control and empty of any godly virtue and faith. The thieves and scoundrels are in charge and we are in trouble.

And we know it.

The faint trumpet call of the revivalists can be heard on the mountains. The sound, although barely discernible, is echoing in our hearts. Yes, we are in trouble and we know it. We are in trouble and only God can rescue us. We are in trouble.

And we know it...

Pray for revival.

Chapter Three

Ten Signs of True Revival

"Do not put out the Spirit's fire; do not treat prophecies with contempt. Test everything. Hold on to the good. Avoid every kind of evil." I Thessalonians 5:19-22

Calling something a revival when it is not is like driving the church bus off the cliff with the congregation on board. The results will not be good…and you will lose your driver's license.

In this chapter I have distilled the signs of a true revival down to ten. I know that there are other signs, probably just as important that I have not included, but in the spirit of brevity, I chose the following ten:

1. True revivals give Jesus Christ the preeminent place.

All true revivals will focus on the Person of the Lord Jesus Christ. Any focusing on human beings, human personalities, specific churches and denominations or other factors make the "revival" highly suspect and subject to dismissal. Notice the potent lesson presented in the Gospel of Luke.

*…He (Jesus) took Peter, John and James with Him and went up onto a mountain to pray. As He was praying, the appearance of His face changed, and His clothes became as bright as a flash of lightning. Two men, Moses and Elijah, appeared in glorious splendor, talking with Jesus. They spoke about His departure, which He was about to bring to fulfillment at Jerusalem. Peter and his companions were very sleepy, but when they became fully awake, they saw His glory and the two men standing with Him. As the two men were leaving Jesus, Peter said to Him, "Master, it is good for us to be here. Let us put up three shelters— one for You, one for Moses and one for Elijah." (He did not know what he was saying.) While he was speaking a cloud appeared and enveloped them, and they were afraid as they entered the cloud. A voice came from the cloud saying, "This is My Son, whom I have chosen; listen to Him." When the voice had spoken they found that Jesus was **alone*** (Luke 9:28-36).

As the Lukan verse so powerfully portrays, nothing can be added to Jesus.[18] He is **complete** and stands **alone**. Moses, who represented the Law in his appearance with the transfigured Christ, although important, is not Jesus and is not to be viewed as an equal. Elijah, who represented the prophets, although important, is also not equal to Jesus. The Father made His position crystal clear by stating: *"This is My Son, whom I have*

---

[18] The principle advocates of "liberal Christianity" act embarrassed when speaking of Jesus. They universally embrace the attempt to accommodate other religions by demeaning the importance of Jesus to bring Him down and thus making Him equal among many or elevating the importance of other religious concepts to again include Jesus amongst "equals." This is undoubtedly an antichrist position designed to demean the unique Lord Jesus Christ. **FACT: Jesus and only Jesus is Lord.**

chosen; listen to Him." There can be no mistake. Jesus is the unique object of faith. It is Jesus + nothing.

The Son of God's role as the object of faith

The Word of God sets forth two important points concerning the Son of God's role as the object of faith:

First, Jesus Christ is the divine Messiah Who died for the sins of the world (Romans 5:8). It is true that the Triune God was involved in the redemptive act of Jesus Christ (Isaiah 53:10; Hebrews 9:14), but the Father and the Holy Spirit did not die on the cross for mankind—only the Son (Romans 2:23). This makes the Son the sin-bearer Who is the only mediator between God and man (I Timothy 2:5, 6). This unique position is possible because Jesus of Nazareth is both God and man. [19]

Secondly, it is the Father's will that mankind's salvation be predicated on the acceptance of the Son. This means that a person does not receive salvation by believing in the Father or in the Holy Spirit. It is Jesus, the second Person of the Triune God, Who is the object of faith,

*"Let it be known to you all, and to all the people of Israel, that by the name of Jesus Christ of Nazareth, whom you crucified, whom God raised from the dead, by Him this man stands here before you whole. This is the stone, which was rejected by you builders, which has become the chief cornerstone. Nor is there salvation in any other, **for there is no other name under heaven given among men by which we must be saved."*** (Acts 4:10-14; see also I John 5:10-13).

The uniqueness of Christ and His position as the object of faith was not a recent New Testament addition, but part of the original plan found in both Testaments (Isaiah 53 with Acts 8:26-35). One example presents the clearest connection between the Old and New Testaments. It is the story of the serpent on the pole found in Numbers 21:4-9,

They (the Hebrews) traveled from Mount Hor along the route to the Red Sea, to go around Edom. But the people grew impatient on the way; they spoke against God and against Moses, and said, "Why have you brought up out of Egypt to die in the desert? There is no bread! There is no water! And we detest this miserable food!" Then the Lord sent venomous snakes among them; they bit the people and many Israelites

---

[19] **The dilemma:** All human beings are sinners by nature (Romans 3:10-18; 3:23) and cannot offer a sacrifice to gain forgiveness from God (all our righteous deeds are like a filthy garment—Isaiah 64:6). This dilemma was solved by two acts of God. First, God determined that Jesus, the eternal Son, was to be born of a Virgin (Matthew 1:18-25; Luke 1:26-38). This birth, called the incarnation (putting on human flesh) was how the divine Jesus became a human being (John 1:14). And secondly, Jesus, although human retained His divine nature (Colossians 2:9). His unique condition as both God and man made Him qualified to be the sacrifice for our sins (Hebrews 2:14-18). This qualification was based on the fact that as a man He was able to die for mankind, and as God He was sinless making Him the perfect sacrifice (Exodus 12:1-7; Leviticus 22:17-20; John 1:29; I Peter 1:18-20). He was and is the "only begotten" (John 1:14) which means "monogenes"—one of a kind. Jesus is thusly 100% man and 100% God. He was both God and man—a startling reality and a truth that is by itself unique.

died. The people came to Moses and said, "We sinned when we spoke against the Lord and against you. Pray that the Lord will take the snakes away from us." So Moses prayed for the people. The Lord said to Moses, "Make a snake and put it on a pole; anyone who is bitten can look at it and live." So Moses made a bronze snake and put it up on a pole. Then when anyone was bitten by a snake and looked at the bronze snake, he lived. (Numbers 21:4-9).

The New Testament connection:

Just as Moses lifted up the snake in the desert, so the Son of Man must be lifted up, that everyone who believes in Him may have eternal life. (John 3:14, 15).

The connection is not difficult to understand. The snakes represented the sin that was killing the rebellious Israelites. To be healed of this destructive sin the Israelites were given a simple command: Look at the bronze snake lifted up on the pole and be healed. The New Testament gospel message, paralleling the Numbers 21 account, also includes a simple command: Look to Jesus Christ and be healed (John 19:37; I Peter 2:24). It is clear that the incident in Numbers was a sign pointing toward Christ and the plan of God.

We have all been "bitten by sin." If not treated, the bite is fatal. We have only two choices: Ignore God's command to look to Jesus and be saved or obey God's command to look toward the sin-bearer, Jesus Christ, as an act of obedience and live. When we obey this command we are embracing what Jesus accomplished for us—**His death in our place to give us deliverance from death and hell.** The sin-bearer, Jesus, takes the venom of sin to Himself (II Corinthians 5:21) and we receive new life by believing in (looking to) Him. This is the greatest offer ever made to mankind. Only a fool would reject it.

Again, I must state the obvious. Any true revival sent from God will place Jesus Christ as the central object of faith. All revival preaching will be aflame with this message: **Look to Jesus and be saved!** If the "revival" does not lift Jesus up as the one and only object of faith then that revival is not from God.

It is that simple.

2. True revivals elevate the Word of God to its rightful place.

Have you ever heard a sermon that was so anointed that it caused your hair to stand up on the back of your head? How about a sermon that unmasked your sinful heart and compelled you to submit your stubborn will to the will of God? My Christian friend, these are the kinds of sermons that are commonplace when true revival spreads across the land.

When true revival comes God's Word will burn into your heart magnifying His voice a thousand times. What power! What love! What earth-shaking emotions flood your soul when you hear God-filled preaching from the holy Word! When a true revival appears all other books are laid aside and the Bible takes its rightful place.

It is a mystery to me how many in the modern church do not recognize the power of God's Word. Consider the following thoughts:
- The Word of God is living and active and sharper than a two-edged sword...it judges the thoughts and attitudes of the heart (Hebrews 4:12-13). So why is it dismissed?
- The Word of God is the eternal seed that brings spiritual birth, turning human beings from mere hell-fuel to heaven's heroes (I Peter 1:23-25). So why is it ignored?
- The Word of God is so powerful that it brought forth the created universe. So why is it not spoken? (Hebrews 11:3).
- The Word of God contains all we need to live godly and successful lives (Psalm 119:9-11). So why is the Word not observed?

The war waged against God's Word

The truth is that there is a war being raged against God's Word. It is an all out struggle of God vs. Satan; good vs. evil, lies vs. truth. The first recorded battle in this war occurred in the Garden of Eden when Satan questioned God's Word by saying, *"Did God really say?"* Since that fateful day, the Word of God has been the target of the enemies of God. There is no escaping this conflict waged daily on our televisions, our radios, in the movie theaters, in the workplace, in the public square, in the schools, in our own homes and even in some churches.

Did I really say that the war against God's Word is occurring in some churches? Yes. The beginning of the twentieth century saw the appearance of a new wave of modern liberal thought that questioned the Bible's veracity. Many in the established mainline churches, long removed from the genuine movements of God that first birthed their denominations, were captured by the deception. Enticed by liberal speculations they dismissed the Bible as an antiquated book to be consigned to a dusty shelf, entire denominations caved in to the pressure and the age of the liberal, apostate church was birthed. Today many of these churches have gone so far that they deny the "historical Jesus" and believe that He was only a myth devised by the early church.[20]

Saddled with such a crushing load of liberal baggage, the sermons from these apostate pulpits are bereft of any power and authority. On any Sunday you can hear one of their "pastors" spend two minutes reading a verse, and then spend twenty-eight minutes watering it down and/or

---

[20] **The Jesus Seminar:** A group of 150 liberal biblical scholars founded in 1985 to debunk the historical record of Jesus Christ. The members were all from liberal, apostate churches, seminaries and denominations that had long since jettisoned genuine belief in the Word of God. They had one goal---the denial of the Bible as a viable source of information concerning Christ and His historical reality.

redefining it to make it fit into the labyrinth of political correctness. Other pastors in these churches go a step further and dispense with the Scripture altogether, and give a short message from the latest self-help book or a comedy routine direct from *Saturday Night Live.*

I was recently told by a sister in Christ that her pastor at a local mainline liberal denomination was doing a series of teachings on the sayings of Buddha! She said that before this he used the funny papers as his sermon illustrations. It is my opinion that a sermon based on the funny papers is not funny at all and a sermon using Buddha's saying as a text is an act of blasphemy. If you attend a church where the pastor routinely does these things my advice is to get out as fast as you can.[21] A church like that is really no church at all. Your family is in danger just by sitting under such spiritually bankrupt leadership. It would be better if the property was sold and turned into condos.

In a true revival the participants will discover that their worldly opinions of God evaporate and are replaced with a biblical foundation based on the revealed Word. Even if questionable ideas concerning Christ were present within the mind of the revival participant before conversion, the input of anointed teaching and the ministry of the Holy Spirit will put the new believer's theology in line with revealed, historic Christianity. In essence, they will readily accept the biblical Christ and not the "Christ of speculation." Exposed to the fire of biblical, revival preaching they will believe the following:

- That Jesus and only Jesus is Lord. This profound truth puts to rest any claim that other religions are on an equal plain with Christianity. Simply put, they're not.
- That Jesus is the divine God in human flesh and one of a kind. There is no other Savior.
- That Jesus died for mankind's sins. This is the one and only payment available. There is no other way to heaven.
- That Jesus was raised from the dead on the third day. No other "religious" leader can claim this.
- That Jesus is the living Savior Who indwells the hearts of His people. The very fact that Jesus can indwell millions of people at once proves His supernatural, unlimited power.
- That Jesus will return to earth to judge mankind. The world will be divided into two groups—those who believe the truth and those who do not.
- That there is an eternal heaven and an eternal hell.

---

[21] A famous story concerning the Apostle John in Ephesus: There are those who heard from Polycarp (a leader in the early church) that John, the disciple of the Lord, going to bathe at Ephesus, and perceiving Cerinthus (a false prophet) within, rushed out of the bath-house without bathing, exclaiming, "Let us fly, lest even the bath-house fall down, because Cerinthus, the enemy of the truth, is within."

- That Jesus is the only way to God. It is Jesus + nothing.
- Quite simply, a revival not based on the Word of God is a sham. *How can a young man keep his way pure? By keeping it according to Your word. With all my heart I have sought You; Do not let me wander from Your commandments. Your word I have treasured in my heart, that I might not sin against You. Blessed are You, O Lord; teach me Your statutes. With my lips I have told of all the ordinances of Your mouth. I have rejoiced in the way of Your testimonies, as much as in all riches. I will meditate on Your precepts and regard Your ways. I shall delight in Your statutes. I shall not forget Your word* (Psalm 119:9-16).

No opinions of finite man can bring and sustain a true revival. The Bible alone is the supernatural Word of the living God. It was authored by God and is illuminated by the Holy Spirit to be the one and only guidebook given by the Creator of the universe for the advancement of His kingdom. Within its pages you will find the answers to life's questions: *Who is God? What is He like? Who is Jesus? What did He do for me? How should I respond to Him? How can I be saved from death and hell? How then should I live? Where will I spend eternity?*

All true revivals will experience a return to the **"ancient path"** (Jeremiah 6:16).[22] The ancient path is simply a return to the simple message given to mankind by God Himself. This is the gospel message devoid of any "spiritual" pretense and not adulterated by modern thinking and its accompanying fog of speculation and denial. The ancient path is clearly marked by the many signposts found within the Word of God. When a true revival is upon us you will know it. The supernatural Word will come alive and quicken your soul and you will never be the same again.

3. True revivals magnify the repentance of sin:

This begs the question—what is sin? Sin is described in the Bible as transgression of the law of God (I John 3:4) and rebellion (disobedience) against God (Deuteronomy 9:7; Joshua 1:18).

The word "sin" is an Anglo-Saxon word used in archery to state that an arrow had missed its mark. The archer, missing the target, had committed a "sin." In our Biblical context we could say—human beings, missing God's mark in morals, actions, thoughts, etc. have committed sin.

Anything that contradicts God's character of holiness is sin. Sin may be against God's Person and thus be defilement or godlessness; or it may be against God's laws and thus be lawlessness or rebellion. No matter how we define sin, when not repented of, it still brings death.

---

[22] The ancient path is discussed in more detail in chapter 9.

Therefore, just as through one man sin entered into the world, and death through sin, and so death spread to all men, because all sinned— (Romans 5:12).

In a true revival the fact of sin becomes a burning issue that compels the revival participant to seek the remedy—Jesus Christ. All other human remedies evaporate and fall by the wayside. It is at this time that repentance becomes the indispensable act of obedience.

What is repentance?

The root meaning of the word "repentance" (Greek: *metanoia*) is a change of mind or heart. This change should be viewed as an "about face"—a 180 degree turn around from the destructive direction the sinner has been following. Every part of man is involved—thoughts, actions, feelings, purpose, emotions, etc. With true repentance comes a change within the human being. He/she is no longer the same.

"I have been crucified with Christ; and it is no longer I who live, but Christ lives in me; and the life which I now live in the flesh I live by faith in the Son of God, who loved me and gave Himself up for me" (Galatians 2:20).

There is a putting off of the "old self" and a putting on of the "new self."

Therefore consider the members of your earthly body as dead to immorality, impurity, passion, evil desire, and greed, which amounts to idolatry. For it is because of these things that the wrath of God will come upon the sons of disobedience, and in them you also once walked, when you were living in them. But now you also, put them all aside: anger, wrath, malice, slander, and abusive speech from your mouth. Do not lie to one another, since you laid aside the old self with its evil practices, and have put on the new self who is being renewed to a true knowledge according to the image of the One who created him— (Colossians 3:5-10).

The converted person is literally a new person, transported out of the kingdom of darkness into the kingdom of the Son He loves.

For He rescued us from the domain of darkness, and transferred us to the kingdom of His beloved Son, in whom we have redemption, the forgiveness of sins (Colossians 1:13, 14).

A person experiencing a revival will seek the repentance that cleanses the human heart. They soon discover that the power of the enemy to manipulate their sin and use it to undermine themselves and the Lord's kingdom agenda is mortally crippled. In the words of the Apostle Paul the forgiven will not repent of their repentance (forget their deliverance from sin) when faced with temptation:

For the sorrow that is according to the will of God produces a repentance without regret, leading to salvation, but the sorrow of the world produces death. (II Corinthians 7:10).

Repentance is required for God to move in the lives of human beings. Without repentance there will be no blessing. This is an unalterable fact. In a revival **repentance** is the foundational message that will echo throughout the land.

How blessed is he whose transgression is forgiven, whose sin is covered! How blessed is the man to whom the Lord does not impute iniquity, and in whose spirit there is no deceit! When I kept silent about my sin, my body wasted away through my groaning all day long. For day and night Your hand was heavy upon me; My vitality was drained away as with the fever heat of summer. I acknowledged my sin to You, and my iniquity I did not hide; I said, "I will confess my transgressions to the Lord", and You forgave the guilt of my sin. (Psalm 32:1-5).

NOTE: *People on earth hate to hear the word repent! Those in hell would love to hear it just once more.* –Anonymous

A true story

On January 23, 1996 Rev. Joe Wright, the pastor of the 2,500 member Central Christian Church in Wichita, Kansas was invited to give the opening prayer at a session of the Kansas House of Representatives. Expecting the typical syrupy prayer given at such venues, the politicians present were unprepared for what they heard. Rev. Wright gave the following prayer for repentance:

Heavenly Father, we come before you today to ask Your forgiveness and seek your direction and guidance. We know Your Word says, "Woe to those who call evil good," but that's exactly what we've done. We have lost our spiritual equilibrium and inverted our values.

We confess that:
- *We have ridiculed the absolute truth of Your Word and called it moral pluralism.*
- *We have worshipped other gods and called it multiculturalism.*
- *We have endorsed perversion and called it alternative lifestyles.*
- *We have exploited the poor and called it the lottery.*
- *We have neglected the needy and called it self preservation.*
- *We have rewarded laziness and called it welfare.*
- *We have killed our unborn and called it choice.*
- *We have neglected to discipline our children and called it building esteem.*
- *We have abused power and called it political savvy.*
- *We have coveted our neighbor's possessions and called it ambition.*
- *We have polluted the air with profanity and pornography and called it freedom of expression.*
- *We have ridiculed the time honored values of our forefathers and called it enlightenment.*

- *Search us O God and know our hearts today; try us and see if there be some wicked way in us; cleanse us from every sin and set us free.*
- *Guide and bless these men and women who have been sent here by the people of Kansas, and who have been ordained by You, to govern this great state.*
- *Grant them Your wisdom to rule and may their decisions direct us to the center of Your will. I ask it in the name of Your Son, the living Savior, Jesus Christ.*
  Amen.

Some irate Democratic congressman walked out in the middle of the prayer. Others gave angry speeches that condemned Rev. Wright's "message of intolerance." The Democratic House Minority Leader called it a Republican plot.

Ignoring such blatant attacks, Rev. Joe Wright issued no apology for his prayer. He instead claimed that it was the truth. Wright later explained: *"I thought I might get a call from an angry congressman or two, but I was talking to God and not them. The whole point was to say that we all have sins and that we need to repent—-all of us. The problem, I guess, is that you're not supposed to get too specific when you're talking about sin."*

The angry Kansas congressmen were right in one aspect. Rev. Wright's prayer was a "message of intolerance." It was a message of God's "intolerance" toward sin. Simply stated, a holy God cannot tolerate the malignant sin that is destroying mankind. He will judge all who embrace their rebellion against their righteous Creator. Sin is sin and those who reject the truth will discover themselves standing at the Judgment Seat of Christ with no defense. I extend kudos to Reverend Joe Wright who literally walked into the lion's den to bring the message from God. It would be exciting to see Christians like Reverend Joe Wright standing up in every legislature in America proclaiming the truth.

True revivals are based on deep repentance of sin. Without this repentance nothing of any spiritual significance will occur and the people will stand around as if waiting for a bus…that never comes. The message is clear: **No repentance = no revival.**

We will instead miss the mark.

Confession of sin is a biblical foundation

The importance of repentance of sin is clearly seen by the prominent place it is afforded in both the Old and New Testaments.

In the Old Testament:
- God's command to repent (Ezekiel 14:16).
- The central place that repentance should occupy in the hearts of those who desire relationship with God (Deuteronomy 30:20).

- God's utter dismay at the lack of repentance in his people (Jer. 8:6).
- God's promise to heal the land (send revival) if the people repent (II Chronicles 7:14).
- God's warning that without repentance the people will be judged (Ezekiel 18:30).

In the New Testament:
- Repentance was the central focus of John the Baptist's and Jesus' preaching (Matthew 3:1, 2, 4:17).
- Jesus, in His first recorded sermon, demanded repentance (Matthew 4:17).
- Jesus said that He had not come to call the righteous but the sinners to repentance (Matthew 9:13).
- Jesus soundly criticized the cities that had seen His power but had not repented (Matthew 11:20).
- The Disciples all preached repentance (Mark 6:12).
  Repentance of sin was the main focus in the Great Commission (Luke 24:47).
- Peter's call for repentance in his sermon on Pentecost (Acts 2:38).
- Repentance is God's will for all men (II Peter 3:9).
- God commands all men to repent (Acts 17:30).
- Failure to repent will result in death (Luke 13:3).

The fact is inescapable. In true revivals, the participants will be confronted by their sin. There will be no wiggle room for the revival participant and he/she will be offered only one option—confess their personal sin and receive Christ's remedy or remain in their sins which will result in death. Those that resist this message are literally playing with fire. They will discover that God does not negotiate on this point. It is His way or the highway. Any revival message will contain this truth or the message is false.

It is that simple.

4. True revivals are exceedingly fruitful.

In any genuine move of God an important evaluative measure for success must be the fruit produced and the fruit that remains. Jesus gave this standard to us when He said,

"I have appointed you that you should go and bear fruit and that your fruit should remain." (John 15:16).

The words Jesus spoke bear witness to the following facts:
- The call (appointing) of believers to any involvement in revival comes from God. He is the sum total of what a revival is and what it will accomplish. We do not make revivals. God makes them, empowers them, leads them and is completely in charge.

Like Paul, we are the bond servants of God (Romans 1:1). Servants are expected to…serve.
- In a revival we **"go."** We get up off our backsides and go out after the "fish." Fishermen do not catch fish by sitting on the sofa watching the Fishing Channel. Fish do not swim into your bathtub and jump into your net. You go where the fish are and do the work of fishing.
  *"All authority has been given to Me in heaven and on earth. **Go** therefore and make disciples of all the nations, baptizing them in the name of the Father and the Son and the Holy Spirit, teaching them to observe all that I commanded you; and lo, I am with you always, even to the end of the age."* (Matthew 28:18-20).
- The fruit we bear is the souls of men who are caught by the "Great Fisherman." We, as the children of God, get to assist Him in this holy work. What a privilege to share in these supernatural endeavors that produce fruit for eternity.
- Our job is to get the fish into the boat. It is God's job to clean the fish. Human beings cannot see into another human being's heart and our attempts to clean the fish will result in great damage to the fish, rendering it as being useless. We must resist our natural inclination to do God's job and focus on ours.
- God will keep what He has caught. There is no "catch and release" in the plans of God.

To say that a true revival will bear much fruit is an understatement, especially when we have the examples of the revivals throughout history that brought thousands to Christ.

On the day before Pentecost Peter was hiding from the soldiers patrolling the streets looking for the bewildered and scattered disciples. On the Day of Pentecost, Peter's sermon ignited a fire in three thousand souls (Acts 2:41). On that eventful day he was thrust out into those same streets as a burning torch lighting the way into eternity. The difference in Peter after Pentecost is attributed to his incredible spiritual transformation resulting from the outpouring of God's supernatural power. The anointing continued and a few days later another five thousand souls were added (Acts 4:4). The harvest had arrived and the church was gathering in the fruit.

When a true revival occurs, the people of God become evangelism machines. They seem to be tireless in their efforts to bring Christ to those who are lost and held captive by the corrupt culture. I have seen people that are experiencing revival seek the lost in ways that would have been unheard of in their lives before the revival fires descended upon them. They embraced the Apostle Paul's admonition to Timothy, making it a very personal word from God to their hearts:

But you, be sober in all things, endure hardship, **do the work of an evangelist***, fulfill your ministry* (II Timothy 4:5).

I want to make this point again, with great emphasis: When the Lord reveals Himself to a new convert in a revival the impact is very deep and profound. Those who are confronted by His presence for the first time are completely changed by the experience. Almost invariably, the very first thing I have seen them do is to go and find someone else to bring the message—**JESUS CHRIST IS LORD!** When we find Jesus, it will result in our intense desire to include others. This is a common reaction that is fueled by the Holy Spirit:

The next day He (Jesus) purposed to go into Galilee, and He found Philip. And Jesus said to him, "Follow Me." Now Philip was from Bethsaida, of the city of Andrew and Peter. Philip found Nathanial and said to him, "We have found Him of whom Moses in the Law and also the Prophets wrote[23]*—Jesus of Nazareth, the son of Joseph." Nathaniel said to him, "Can any good thing come out of Nazareth": Philip said to him, "Come and see."* (John 1:43-46).

5. True revivals open the participant's hearts to embrace the love of God:

The Beatles sang that all we needed was love. The world joined in with the chorus and everyone experienced human love on steroids. But human love is only an injection of human feelings coupled with human opportunity and desire. As purveyors of love, we humans have not posted a sterling track record to prove that we are genuinely plugged into the love of God. Human love is nothing but the warm fuzzies directed in such a way to guarantee a beneficial outcome for us…only us. We love in order to be loved back.

This is unadulterated fact.

God's love is different. It is a genuine love expressed toward the unlovely by the lover (God) that is never driven by self-aggrandizement or opportunity. God's love is beyond the two other forms of love mentioned in the Scripture: The love of brothers (phileo) which is the root word for Philadelphia (the city of brotherly love) and the love of sexual desire called (eros) from which we get "erotic love." God's love is called agape, which is a love expressed toward the unlovable and completely centered on the love of the greater toward the lessor. God loves the unlovable and those that follow Him are also required to extend this kind of love toward others.

We love, because He first loved us (I John 4:19).

The Christian that experiences the power of a revival will receive a love from God that is a literal "act of the supernatural." This love is

---

[23] God mentioned to Moses in Deuteronomy 18:17-19 that He was sending another prophet (like Moses) to bring the message to the earth. This prophet was to be the Messiah—Jesus Christ.

extended out to all who hear the message and respond to the gospel. This love is infectious and is beyond anything they have ever experienced:

"A new commandment I give to you, that you love one another, even as I have loved you, that you also love one another. By this all men will know that you are My disciples, if you have love for one another." (John 13:34, 35).

This power of love is not earthly. It is so powerful that it cannot be explained away. Many have written songs and books to describe this love, but only the real experience can reveal the staggering truth behind it. Revival brings an outpouring of God's love that changes everything.

Hatred stirs up strife, but love covers all transgressions. (Proverbs 10:12; see also I Peter 4:8).

In a revival, Christians are led by the Spirit of God to cross over every known boundary. I have seen lifelong racists, of all races and colors, melt under the outpouring of God's love during a revival and jettison their fanatical hatred toward those of a different race. Black and white become brothers and sisters in Christ, individuals born in different lands become one nation in Christ, human beings born and raised in different traditions and cultures become members of the one kingdom of God that is universal. There are no differences that can shake the foundation of those that have joined the kingdom of God. We are joined by the love of God. It is a non-dissolvable bond.

When revival comes upon a church or group the agape love of God floods their hearts and they are changed. This love is discerned through the proofs of Scripture. It is defined as follows:

- **God's love is a weapon used in spiritual warfare:**
  *Above all, keep fervent in your love for one another, because **love covers a multitude of sins.** Be hospitable to one another without complaint. As each one has received a special gift, employ it in serving one another as good stewards of the manifold grace of God* (I Peter 4:8-10).
- **God's love conquers all powers and forces arrayed against God and His purposes:**
  Hate evil, you who love the LORD, Who preserves the souls of His godly ones; He delivers them from the hand of the wicked (Psalm 97:10).
- **God's love is sacrificial:**
  I have been crucified with Christ; and it is no longer I who live, but Christ lives in me; and the life which I now live in the flesh I live by faith in the Son of God, who loved me and gave Himself up for me (Galatians 2:20).
- **God is love:**

The one who does not love does not know God, for God is love (I John 4:8).
- **God's love prompts us to love:**
We love, because He first loved us (I John 4:19).
- **God's love is eternal:**
The LORD appeared to him from afar, saying, "I have loved you with an everlasting love; Therefore I have drawn you with lovingkindness" (Jeremiah 31:3).
- **God's love never fails:**
Love is patient, love is kind and is not jealous; love does not brag and is not arrogant, does not act unbecomingly; it does not seek its own, is not provoked, does not take into account a wrong suffered, does not rejoice in unrighteousness, but rejoices with the truth; bears all things, believes all things, hopes all things, endures all things. **Love never fails** (I Corinthians 13:4-8).

When I first experienced the outpouring of the Holy Spirit in 1970s California, many new and different sights and sounds flooded my soul. It seemed that every day was special as I was thrust onto a learning curve that was steeper than a Rocky Mountain road. With all the different experiences hitting me daily I was most impressed with the expressions of love that seemed to be present in every revival meeting in the state.

Forty years later, long after the revival fires had dissipated, I have searched far and wide attempting to recapture those exciting days when God's Spirit moved across the land. I have had a lot of time to think about what once was and what we no longer have—the power of God in every meeting, souls coming to Christ each and every day, and the Word of God exploding in our hearts. It seems that the one thing that I miss the most is the intensive love of God that was universally present during those times. After much thought I have come to the conclusion that only a revival will transport us into a new outpouring of the love of God.

In true revivals, the participants will have a deep, abiding love for Jesus that appears to be boundless. The presence of the Spirit of God will be obvious in their lives and their desire to be nearer to their Lord cannot be quenched. A young believer in my church many years ago expressed it best:

"Pastor Bob, I have a burning desire to crawl up on the Lord's lap, throw my arms around and tell Him that I love Him. I just want to be with Jesus all the time."

The love of Jesus will intensify and spread out to include all people, even the most difficult to love. The revival participants will immerse themselves in the love of God in such a profound depth that it fills their thoughts completely. A true revival lights the fire of love in all that are touched by it. Love is the sign of God's presence.

"A new commandment I give to you, that you love one another, even as I have loved you, that you love one another. By this all men will know that you are My disciples, if you have love for one another." (John 13:34, 35).

6. True revivals are led by the Holy Spirit.

This is more important than many may imagine. A "revival" led by man is an act of the flesh and at best will not bear fruit, and at worst will be massively destructive. The Holy Spirit must have complete control in any true revival. It must be said with absolute clarity: *If human beings attempt to lead the revival without the Holy Spirit's guidance and input the Holy Spirit will pull back and the human beings will be left to their own devices. This is a fearful prospect. Remember, a person wrapped up in himself is in a small package.*

How the Holy Spirit leads revivals

- The Holy Spirit calls for the revival by speaking to the hearts of those who are seeking a move of God. Oftentimes, these saints have no clear understanding where their inspiration comes from. They just feel a deep call within their hearts and they respond.
- The Holy Spirit draws His people into **prayer for revival**. This can mean many prayer warriors or even just one person that He has anointed for this task. The blueprint is clear: All revivals are preceded by prayer…intense, spirit-wracking, bone-shaking prayer that detonates the mountain of sin, unbelief and despair that has smothered the earth. Most importantly, this prayer is directed by the Holy Spirit.

In the same way the Spirit also helps our weakness; for we do not know how to pray as we should, but the Spirit Himself intercedes for us with groanings too deep for words; and He who searches the hearts knows what the mind of the Spirit is, because He intercedes for the saints according to the will of God (Romans 8:26, 27).

- The Holy Spirit gives the anointing and unction to the persons who will preach and teach within the revival. The messages are revealed in the hearts and minds of these preachers and teachers in an ordered sequence that is a roadmap for the direction of the revival. This fact is often overlooked until long after the revival is spent and the people recount the events. What seemed random and spontaneous had the hand of God's perfect structure on it.

*Then **Peter, filled with the Holy Spirit, said** to them, "Rulers and elders of the people, if we are on trial today for a benefit done to a sick man, as to how this man has been made well, let it be known to all of you and to all the people of Israel, that by the name of Jesus Christ the Nazarene, whom you crucified, whom God raised from the dead—by this name this man stands here* *before you in good health. He is the STONE WHICH WAS REJECTED by you, THE BUILDERS, but WHICH BECAME THE CHIEF CORNER stone. And there is salvation in no one else; for there is no other name under heaven that has been given among men by which we must be saved."* (Acts 4:8-12).

- The Holy Spirit speaks to the people and will give clear direction—**if they are listening.**
  "He who has an ear, let him hear what the Spirit says to the churches." (Revelation 3:6; see also Luke 12:11, 12).
- The Holy Spirit manifests the presence of Jesus Christ and extends His ministry of the miraculous through the people. Signs and wonders accompany true revivals for the purpose of advancing the Person and presence of Jesus. Important fact: **The miracles will all point toward Jesus and not toward the preacher.**
  And Stephen, full of grace and power, was performing great wonders and signs among the people. (Acts 6:8).
- Like a watchful and caring father, the Holy Spirit warns of any harmful input within the revival, whether generated by humans or by demonic spirits. This is extremely important in light of the spiritual warfare that will be waged against the move of God.
  They passed through the Phrygian and Galatian region, having been forbidden by the Holy Spirit to speak the word in Asia; and after they came to Mysia, they were trying to go into Bithynia, and the Spirit of Jesus did not permit them; and passing by Mysia, they came down to Troas. (Acts 16:6-8).
- Again, I must say that the Holy Spirit must have full command of the revival for it to remain true to God's plans and purposes. Revivals that fail to have the Holy Spirit's direction and leading are destined to drive into the ditch.

7. True revivals experience the miraculous:

It is a matter of historical record that when God pours out His Spirit in a revival signs and wonders become an integral part. There are just too many examples that appear throughout revival history concerning signs and wonders for the honest Christian to discount their validity.

I would be amiss, however, if I did not state clearly that "signs and wonders" are a sign that cannot be used independently to prove the genuineness of a revival. Let me explain my statement:

Since signs and wonders can be generated by the enemy and his agents (Deuteronomy 13:1-5; II Thessalonians 2: 9-12), it is imperative that they be evaluated to determine their source. My suggestion is that signs and wonders pass a rigid test before they can be wholeheartedly embraced. The Apostle John's words are clear,

"Dear friends, do not believe every spirit, but test the spirits to see whether they are from God, because many false prophets have gone out into the world." (I John 4:1).

The test is simple and consists of two parts: First, the expression of power must be firmly based on scriptural ground. Any sign or wonder that violates the integrity of God's Word should be ignored. God will not perform signs and wonders that overturn His Word, add to it, take away from it, or bring disrepute on it. The question should always be, *"What does it say in the text?"*

And secondly, any worker of signs and wonders should be questioned concerning their beliefs about Christ. In II Thessalonians 2:9-12 the Apostle Paul warns the church that false prophets preach a "false" Christ. His litmus test is the personal question asked by Christ Himself in Matthew 16: 13-20 *"But Who do you say I am?"* Peter's answer—*"You are the Christ the Son of the living God"* brought the imprimatur from Jesus' own mouth. A false prophet will proclaim a different Jesus (II Corinthians 11: 3). Some things that a false prophet might say:

- Jesus is not God.
- There are many ways to God.
- We are all Jesus…and/or God.
- I (the false prophet) am Jesus and/or God.
- There is no such thing as sin.
- The gospel is Jesus +something else.
- Follow me and I will be your Messiah.
- Christ did not die for your sins.
- Christ did not rise from the grave in His physical body.
- The gospel has changed and now includes new ideas that may have once been considered non-Christian.
- After death we are reincarnated.
- A denial of Christ altogether.
- etc.

The way to check a prophet's status is to ask him/her the pertinent questions concerning their belief in the Biblical Jesus. In this way you can evaluate their position in Christ. It is not what the prophet is "doing" that is the clue. It is what they believe…or preach. Ask them for their doctrinal statement and evaluate.[24] This is better than just blindly rejecting all signs and wonders because a well-meaning pastor suggested that you do so to protect yourself from possible error. Truth and not fear

---

[24] If a leader refuses to give his/her doctrinal statement concerning Christ or acts annoyed at your questioning they should be dismissed in your mind as a genuine leader. Any Christian leader worth their salt would be ecstatic that you were astute enough to pose the questions.

is the governing factor. I wish to direct readers to my chapter *Revival Power* on page 172 for a more in depth treatment of this question.

8. True revivals are opposed:

Before I respond to this sign I must be clear that representing the gospel does not give us an automatic "pass" if we express obnoxious behavior. *Being a jerk for Jesus* is not an attitude that receives God's support and approval. With that said I recognize that there are people who will reject you no matter how nice you are. Remember, opposition is seldom personal, (except those who are obnoxious), but is directed against the Lord.

All true revivals have been opposed. The opposition will certainly come from the apostate world, but it also can come from the professing church.

So why the intensity of opposition?

The easy answer is spiritual warfare. Satan hates revival and will do all in his power to frustrate it and minimize its effect. For those who believe that Christians cannot be duped by Satan into opposing God and His plans, a reading of Christ's words to Peter in Matthew 16:23 should clear up the confusion: *"Get behind Me, Satan! You are a stumbling block to me; you do not have in mind the things of God; but the things of men."* The astute reader will understand that Jesus' remarks to Peter occurred immediately after the Lord had complemented Peter on his spiritual insight and wisdom (Matthew 16:15-19). It appears that Satan's ability to attack even the most trusted disciple of Christ is a possibility to be guarded against.

Although spiritual warfare is the major issue, there are many other reasons for the professing church's resistance to revival:

- Established church leadership fearful of losing position will often oppose revival.
- The opposition of established church leadership to revival is extremely common. I cannot remember studying even one of history's revivals without reading about the opposition to that revival advanced by the established leadership. The reasons are many, but are all connected in some way to the fear of losing position. It is a sad fact, but many leaders of churches and denominations faced with a move of the Holy Spirit will often champion opposition to that move of God. *So the chief priests and the Pharisees called together the Sanhedrin and said, "What are we doing? For this man is performing many signs! If we allow him to go on in this way, everyone will believe in him, and the Romans will come and take away both our place and our nation."* (John 11:47, 48).
- Human sin and rebellion against the things of God. *What then? Are we better than they? Not at all; for we have already charged*

that both Jews and Greeks are all under sin; as it is written, there is none righteous, not even one; there is none who understands, there is none who seeks for God; all have turned aside, together they have become useless; there is none who does good, there is not even one. Their throat is an open grave, with their tongues they keep deceiving, the poison of asps is under their lips; whose mouth is full of cursing and bitterness; their feet are swift to shed blood, destruction and misery are in their paths, and the path of peace they have not known. There is no fear of God before their eyes (Romans 3:9-18).

- Fear of the unknown. *Thus they told him, and said, "We went in to the land where you sent us; and it certainly does flow with milk and honey, and this is its fruit. Nevertheless, the people who live in the land are strong, and the cities are fortified and very large; and moreover, we saw the descendants of Anak there. Amalek is living in the land of the Negev and the Hittites and the Jebusites and the Amorites are living in the hill country, and the Canaanites are living by the sea and by the side of the Jordan." Then Caleb quieted the people before Moses and said, "We should by all means go up and take possession of it, for we will surely overcome it." But the men who had gone up with him said, "We are not able to go up against the people, for they are too strong for us."* (Numbers 13:27-31).
- Church traditions and teachings that reject the supernatural. *And He (Jesus) answered and said to them, "Why do you yourselves transgress the commandment of God for the sake of your tradition?"* (Matthew 15:3).
- The intertwining of the world's corrupt culture with the church. *Peter said to them "Repent and each of you be baptized in the name of Jesus Christ for the forgiveness of your sins, and you will receive the gift of the Holy Spirit. For the promise is for you and your children and for all who are far off, as many as the Lord our God will call to Himself." And with many other words he solemnly testified and kept on exhorting them, saying, "Be saved from this perverse generation (culture)."* (Acts 2:38-40).
- A lack of teaching concerning revival. *My people are destroyed for lack of knowledge. Because you have rejected knowledge, I will also reject you from being My priest. Since you have forgotten the law of your God, I also will forget your children* (Hosea 4:6).
- Lack of faith (obedience).*And without faith it is impossible to please Him* (God), *for he who comes to God must believe that He is and that He is a rewarder of those that seek Him* (Hebrews 11:6).

NOTE: *I will expand on these issues later in this book.*
What about questionable revivals?

All revivals will receive criticism. It must be said that in some cases the criticism has been valid. I feel that the following points should be made concerning some of the signs that we should look for in revivals that are spurious:

- Any "revival" that promotes "new" doctrines or truths should be rejected out of hand. The Lord of the church is not hatching new doctrines or truths, but will instead highlight the simple gospel that has been *"once and for all delivered to the saints"* (Jude 3). A revival is a return to the "ancient path," and not some vehicle for the expressing of new ideas and truths that have just popped up on the radar screen (Jeremiah 6:16).

  NOTE: *Recently, I attended a prayer conference. The speaker was describing an encounter that a friend of his supposedly experienced. According to the speaker, his friend entertained the Apostle Paul in a supernatural visitation. He made it clear that the Apostle Paul was a specter sent from God to encourage and lead his friend to new truth. I sat there speechless as the people in attendance clapped in delight at the bizarre story. Immediately, a number of verses flooded my mind that detailed with great clarity God's warnings against talking to the dead:* (Isaiah 8:19; Leviticus 19:31; Luke 16:25-26 and Deuteronomy 18:10) *to name just a few. When I reflected on the scriptural fact that Jesus was the only "Mediator" between God and man* (I Timothy 2:5), *I knew for certain that I was hearing false doctrine. The simple truth: Christians are not permitted to talk with the dead. Because the Lord of the church has placed a permanent ban on that activity, it can never be part of Christian experience…ever.*

  No matter who is attempting to sell it.

- Any revival that has been generated by men and/or led by men, (without God's obvious oversight and leading), deserves intense scrutiny. The problem may be two-fold: It was a genuine revival that has been "taken over" by men—which means it will soon be history. Or it was never genuine but was contrived (worked up) by men and is an act of the flesh. We can never "work up" God and any attempt to do so is a pitiful exercise of futility.[25]

- A true revival will be all about repentance and salvation—not just signs and wonders. Signs and wonders may appear—and rightfully so—but they can never be the focus of the revival.

---

[25] Any revival worked up by human beings will become a breeding ground for cultism. This is a sobering truth.

The purpose of revival is to promote the Savior and His message of salvation. Signs and wonders are given to advance the Lord's agenda and not ours.
- Some of the modern revivals have had strange occurrences that are very questionable. This does not necessarily discount the revival, but does draw deserved criticism for the leaders who fail to bring correction.
- In some purported revivals I have seen people bark like dogs, oink like pigs and slither like snakes. To be honest, a genuine move of God will engender excitement and some things may appear strange, but to be strange just for the sake of being strange is only—***being strange.***
- Using revival as a cover for exhibitionist behaviors is an act of the flesh or maybe worse. God is not running a circus sideshow, but is engaged in a serious effort to draw lost people into the family of God. Remember that Jesus wants us to be like Him. Just imagine Jesus barking like a dog, oinking like a pig or slithering like a snake? The thought makes you stop and think. Or should.
- All true revivals are evangelistically oriented and should be taken outside of the church walls and into the streets. Be careful of the ingrown "revivals" that only create a "bless-me-club" by staying within the church walls. God never sent a revival as a method to give us the "warm fuzzies." God sends revivals to advance His kingdom by leading the lost to the Savior. Period…
- **An acceptance of the call to witness:** In true revivals, the participants will have a deep desire to testify of the acts of God. The anointing with the Holy Spirit will compel them to carry the gospel message to the nations. The "nations" may be across the oceans or in your own neighborhood, but you will go to them and reach out. Simply put, true revivals will "charge" the people that experience them with a new desire to obey the Lord's command to evangelize.
- **An answering to the call to prayer:** In a true revival, the participant will have an intense desire to pray. Prayer becomes so important that it is a common occurrence in the lives of those that are involved.

9. True revivals will accentuate God's holiness:

When referring to God the word "holiness" means that He is completely separated from evil and sin. The one and only holy God is set above all that He has created and entirely moral and pure in His mind and actions. He never wavers in His holy character and is completely trustworthy. All things that He touches are regarded to be holy—set apart for His purpose—because of their connection to His Person. We speak of the holy place, holy ground, the Holy Sabbath, the Holy of Holies, and holy people—all things we acknowledge to be set apart for His use.

When referring to God's people the word holiness indicates that true believers are set apart for God's service and are in the process of evolving into the moral agents of God. Their holiness is both divinely imputed (through the acceptance of the sacrifice of Christ) and emerging via the process of obedience to God's Word. The evolving holiness of God's people is directed by the indwelling Holy Spirit. This process is called sanctification and is influenced by time and obedience.

Although the word "holy" appears over 600 times in the Holy Scriptures, the concept of God's holiness and His demand that His people partake in that holiness is probably the least understood truth in modern Christianity. The reasons for this can be distilled down to the following two points:

Presenting God's holiness and the requirement of a believer's participation in the pursuit of that holiness may run afoul of our modern emphasis of the grace of God. Let me be clear, God's grace is a paramount truth and is scripturally based on a sure foundation, but any attempt to use "grace" as a cover for unconfessed serial sin is a serious mistake. The Scriptures must be taken as a whole and cannot be segmented and dissected in an attempt to fashion an acceptable modern theology by adding to it, removing from it or de-emphasizing or over emphasizing any portion of it. Jesus said it from His own mouth when He confronted the Pharisaical attack against His Deity.

- *The Jews picked up stones again to stone Him. Jesus answered them, "I showed you many good works from the Father; for which of them are you stoning Me?" The Jews answered Him, "For a good work we do not stone You, but for blasphemy; and because You, being a man, make Yourself out to be God." Jesus answered them, "Has it not been written in your Law, 'I SAID, YOU ARE GODS'? If he called them gods, to whom the word of God came **(and the Scripture cannot be broken)** do you say of Him, whom the Father sanctified and sent into the world, 'You are blaspheming,' because I said, 'I am the Son of God'? If I do not do the works of My Father, do not believe Me; but if I do them, though you do not believe Me, believe the works, so that you may know and understand that the Father is in Me, and I in the Father." Therefore they were seeking again to seize Him, and He eluded their grasp.* (Jn 10:31-35) [26]

---

[26] Jesus quotes from Psalm 82:6. The Psalm's purpose is to show God's will that human beings are to judge the sinful acts of mankind and exercise judgment in the Name of Yahweh. These judges are to be seen as filling the role of God on earth by passing capital punishment when necessary. It is not an attempt to indicate that human beings are somehow "gods," as many cults like to teach.

- Many of today's modern churches systematically ignore God's requirement of holiness and present a gospel where references to holiness are conspicuously absent. I feel that this omission is not because of a lack of understanding of the biblical requirement, but a conscious decision to create an acceptable atmosphere for the new believer or first-time visitor. This watering down of the gospel is consistently found within the "seeker friendly" movement that designs a church's ministry in line with the desires of the "least common denominator" (church shoppers). If a revival hits a seeker friendly church this soft-sell on holiness and other biblical truths rapidly disappears as the Holy Spirit gains control of the church and returns it to the ancient path.[27]

Modern Christianity is undergoing a crisis. This crisis is based on the loss of regard for the holiness of God. The Scriptures are full of the truth concerning God's holiness. These truths advance the concept of God's holiness and the holiness He expects in His people.

The Scriptures present God's holiness

- God is separate from any evil: *This is the message we have heard from Him and announce to you, that God is Light, and in Him there is no darkness at all.* (I John 1:5).
- God is and always will be holy: *And the four living creatures, each one of them having six wings, are full of eyes around and within; and day and night they do not cease to say, "HOLY, HOLY, HOLY is THE LORD GOD, THE ALMIGHTY, WHO WAS AND WHO IS AND WHO IS TO COME."* (Revelation 4:8).
- Because God is holy He cannot be tempted by evil: *Let no one say when he is tempted, "I am being tempted by God"; for God cannot be tempted by evil, and He Himself does not tempt anyone.* (James 1:13).
- God in His perfect holiness never changes: *"For I, the LORD, do not change"* (Malachi 3:6)

And,

Jesus Christ is the same yesterday and today and forever (Hebrews 13:8).

- God hates sin no matter where He finds it: *Also let none of you devise evil in your heart against another, and do not love perjury; for all these are what I hate,' declares the LORD."* (Zechariah 8:17).

God will punish those that sin: *For behold, the LORD is about to come out from His place to punish the inhabitants of the earth for their iniquity; and the earth will reveal her bloodshed and will no longer cover her slain.* (Isaiah 26:21).

---

[27] The seeker friendly movement is investigated in Chapter 4.

And,

But because of your stubbornness and unrepentant heart you are storing up wrath for yourself in the day of wrath and revelation of the righteous judgment of God, who WILL RENDER TO EACH PERSON ACCORDING TO HIS DEEDS: (Romans 2:5-6).

The required holiness of believers

- God's grace is given to permit our choice of holiness: *For the grace of God has appeared, bringing salvation to all men, instructing us to deny ungodliness and worldly desires and to live sensibly, righteously and godly in the present age* (Titus 2:11, 12).
- Those in Christ are expected to be holy: *For God has not called us for the purpose of impurity, but in sanctification* (I Thessalonians 4:7)
- Without holiness no human will see God: *Pursue peace with all men, and the sanctification without which no one will see the Lord* (Hebrews 12:14).
- Holiness is required to live a dedicated life: *Therefore, if anyone cleanses himself from these things, he will be a vessel for honor, sanctified, useful to the Master, prepared for every good work* (II Timothy 2:21; see also Psalm 15).
- Christ's sacrifice makes true believers holy: *By this will we have been sanctified* (made holy) *through the offering of the body of Jesus Christ once* for all (Hebrews 10:10).
- If we do not obey God He will not listen: *If I regard wickedness in my heart, the Lord will not hear* (Psalm 66:18).
- Holiness is the evidence of our salvation: A*nd everyone who has this hope fixed on Him purifies himself, just as He is pure* (I John 3:3).

When a true revival is poured out upon the church there will be a new and vibrant return to the understanding of God's personal holiness and of the requirement of holiness within the hearts and lives of God's people. The Holy Spirit will drive us to our knees to express our allegiance to the holy God and His righteous agenda for mankind. Those impacted by revival will seek God's anointing as He creates a desire for personal holiness as expressed in obedience. True revivals are the great call to the ancient path, a return to the unalterable, unwavering plan of redemption. True revivals will invariably ignite a holy fire that will burn away the chaff that is clogging revival throughout the land. True revival will elevate the holiness of God and emphasize the requirement of holiness within His people.

10. True revivals are usually initiated through an individual person

The pattern of revivals seems to highlight the fact that the Lord begins His outpouring on an individual person that "infects" others initiating a domino effect. Evan Roberts is the perfect example. Mr. Roberts was led by God to be the initiator of the Welsh Revival of 1904.[28] He was a regular person who heard the call of God and responded to it. His close friends were touched by God through him and the revival exploded and many thousands were brought to repentance. It is not a stretch to say that the 1904 Welsh Revival still has an effect in our day.

The Word of God makes it clear that God is seeking a person to stand up and call for God's intervention. In the Book of Ezekiel the Lord lays out His accusations against Israel because of its coldness toward God. He presses His case against the leadership and the people and states that one person, full of faith and power, could turn around the national sin. He also explains what will happen if that person doesn't step up:

*And the word of the Lord came to me saying, "Son of man, say to her (Israel), 'You are a land that is not cleansed or rained on in the day of indignation.' "There is a conspiracy of her **prophets** in her midst like a roaring lion tearing the prey. They have devoured lives; they have taken treasure and precious things; they have made many widows in the midst of her. Her **priests** (spiritual leaders) have done violence to My law and have profaned My holy things; they have made no distinction between the holy and the profane, and they have not taught the difference between the unclean and the clean; and they hide their eyes from the Sabbaths, and I am profaned among them. Her **princes** (governmental leaders) within her are like wolves tearing the prey, by shedding blood and destroying lives in order to get dishonest gain. Her prophets have smeared whitewash for them, seeing false visions and divining lies for them saying, 'Thus says the Lord,' when the Lord has not spoken. The **people** of the land have practiced oppression and committed robbery, and they have wronged the poor and needy and have oppressed the sojourner with injustice. I searched for **a man** among them who would build up a wall and stand in the gap before Me for the land (intercede for the people), so that I would not destroy it; but I found no one. Thus I have poured out My indignation on them; I have consumed them with the fire of My wrath; their way I have brought upon their heads," declares the Lord God.* (Ezekiel 22: 23-31).

And,

In the year of King Uzziah's death I saw the Lord sitting on a throne, lofty and exalted, with the train of His robe filling the temple.

---

[28] Evan Roberts is discussed in chapter 11.

Seraphim stood above Him, each having six wings: with two he covered his face, and with two he covered his feet, and with two he flew. And one called out to another and said, "Holy, Holy, Holy, is the LORD of hosts, the whole earth is full of His glory." And the foundations of the thresholds trembled at the voice of him who called out, while the temple was filling with smoke. Then I said, "Woe is me, for I am ruined! Because I am a man of unclean lips, and I live among a people of unclean lips; for my eyes have seen the King, the LORD of hosts." Then one of the seraphim flew to me with a burning coal in his hand, which he had taken from the altar with tongs. ⁷ He touched my mouth with it and said, "Behold, this has touched your lips; and your iniquity is taken away and your sin is forgiven." **Then I heard the voice of the Lord, saying, "Whom shall I send, and who will go for Us?" Then I said, "Here am I. Send me!" He said, "Go, and tell this people: 'Keep on listening, but do not perceive; keep on looking, but do not understand.'** (Isaiah 6:1-9).

Pray for revival.

Chapter Four

How Did We Get Here?

When the foundations are being destroyed, what can the righteous do? -Psalm 11:3

How did this nation that was birthed to advance religious freedom become such an enemy to the gospel? How can so many Americans forget that the Founding Fathers honored the name of Jesus Christ and used His Word as the foundational principle on which our country was established? How is it possible that a nation once a lighthouse to the world has become such a purveyor of darkness and rebellion? How did we get to this place?

The explosion of evil

The Bible clearly details the bloody history of humanity's rebellion against God and His Word. In the Book of Genesis the evil of mankind reached such depths of depravity that God Himself was forced to intervene to save the besieged earth:

Then the LORD saw that the wickedness of man was great on the earth, and that every intent of the thoughts of his heart was only evil continually. The LORD was sorry that He had made man on the earth, and He was grieved in His heart. The LORD said, "I will blot out man whom I have created from the face of the land, from man to animals to creeping things and to birds of the sky; for I am sorry that I have made them" (Genesis 6:5-7).

God sent the flood upon the antediluvian world and eradicated sinful man. Only righteous Noah and his family were spared to repopulate the earth in order to give the human race a new start.

Unfortunately, sin began to take root again within the heart of man and the drumbeat of spiritual anarchy has resounded unabated. Today we seem to have come full circle—with one major difference:

The staggering difference is the extraordinary proliferation of evil that has exploded in the twentieth and twenty-first centuries. It is a fact beyond dispute that the world, and especially America, has embraced evil so savage and despicable that only the most blind and ignorant would refuse to admit that we are living in the prophesied last days. The message is clear:

But realize this, that in the last days difficult times will come. For men will be lovers of self, lovers of money, boastful, arrogant, revilers, disobedient to parents, ungrateful, unholy, unloving, irreconcilable, malicious gossips, without self-control, brutal, haters of good, treacherous, reckless, conceited, lovers of pleasure rather than lovers of God, holding to a form of godliness, although they have denied its power; Avoid such men as these. For among them are those who enter into households and captivate weak women weighed down with sins, led on by various impulses, always learning and never able to come to the knowledge of the truth (II Timothy 3:1-7).

This chilling verse from the pen of the Apostle Paul was written as a clear warning of the future apostasy that would descend upon the earth in the last days. Only the most imperceptive among us would make the claim that the sins mentioned in this list are not intensifying before our very eyes. Let's examine the facts: First, the verse itself claims to be a prophecy of the end times—*in the last days difficult times will come*. Secondly, the verse infers that all these listed disturbing acts of sin, although certainly present throughout history, are different because of an intensification of their severity and overwhelming prevalence.

When the verse mentions: "brutal." It can only mean a brutality beyond anything seen in human history—which is staggering since Adolph Hitler, Josef Stalin and Mao Zedong pushed the envelope of brutality beyond any civilized limit. When it says "unholy" it can only mean an ungodliness never dreamed of. When it says "ungrateful" it can only mean a denial of God so militantly perverse that it exceeds the deepest blasphemies ever known. When it says "without self-control" it means that all controls are erased and we are left with the vilest of human behaviors. When it says always learning and never able to come to the knowledge of the truth it is accurately describing our modern society—filled with worldly "wisdom"[29] and yet devoid of any desire to know the true God and His Word.

The stunning truth is that no matter what we have seen over the last two millennia—murders, rapes, brutality, wars, ethnic cleansing, sexual perversions of all types, idolatry, thefts, blasphemies, etc.—the severity of the "new" acts of sin in these last days will be off the chart. And lastly, faced with such fearful truth, those that know the Word can only cringe when they ponder what is coming.

Wail, for the day of the LORD is near! It will come as destruction from the Almighty. Therefore all hands will fall limp, and every man's heart will melt. They will be terrified, pains and anguish will take hold of them; they will writhe like a woman in labor, they will look at one another in astonishment, their faces aflame. Behold, the day of the LORD is coming, cruel, with fury and burning anger, to make the land a desolation; and He will exterminate its sinners from it (Isaiah 13:6-9).

The river of corruption

The invasion of soul-destroying sin can be likened to the swollen Mississippi River at flood stage. Like the endangered towns along the

---

[29] In the Book of Daniel the Lord spoke these words to Daniel in Chapter 12:4: "conceal these words and seal up the book until the time of the end; many will go back and forth and knowledge will increase." These words were spoken in context with the outpouring and increase of evil in the last days. It appears that the increasing knowledge mentioned is not from God but from the fallen nature of man.

banks of that mighty river during flood season, nothing can stand against the deluge of toxic, polluted waters that have found their way from the heartland of the nation to become a deleterious hand of judgment. To take the metaphor further, the mighty river of sin in these last days is overflowing its banks and destroying all in its path. Western civilization cannot endure such a heightened attack and will cease to exist as God brings His final judgment. The streams of evil that have joined to form that mighty, pestilential river of corruption are:

The drug culture

The emergence of the drug culture of the 1960s introduced millions of Americans to soul-poisoning drugs. Moral inhibitions long respected in our culture for centuries were shattered overnight turning human beings into pathetic, licentious beasts who gave up any responsibility for their sins. Law enforcement agencies, faced with the inconceivable task of controlling illegal and aberrant behavior in our embattled society, have gone on record as pointing at illegal drug use as the main factor generating the massive increase of vicious, criminal behavior. The western civilization of today is so inundated with the drug culture through its music, films, fashions, recreational choices and media that the Bible's dark prophecies concerning the last days are coming to pass,

For when they maintain this (their disbelief), it escapes their notice that by the word of God the heavens existed long ago and the earth was formed out of water and by water, through which the world at that time was destroyed, being flooded with water. But by His word the present heavens and earth are being reserved for fire, kept for the Day of Judgment and destruction of ungodly men. But do not let this one fact escape your notice, beloved, that with the Lord one day is like a thousand years, and a thousand years like one day. The Lord is not slow about His promise, as some count slowness, but is patient toward you, not wishing for any to perish but for all to come to repentance. ***But the day of the Lord will come like a thief, in which the heavens will pass away with a roar and the elements will be destroyed with intense heat, and the earth and its works will be burned up.*** *Since all these things are to be destroyed in this way, what sort of people ought you to be in holy conduct and godliness, looking for and hastening the coming of the day of God, because of which the heavens will be destroyed by burning, and the elements will melt with intense heat! But according to His promise we are looking for new heavens and a new earth, in which righteousness dwells* (II Peter 3:5-13).

Since the beginning of time sexual predators have universally used intoxicants (drugs and alcohol) to lower the inhibitions of their prey so that they can perform their acts of sexual deviancy. The Word of God pronounces a curse upon those that serve the intoxicants used to accomplish their nefarious purposes:

Woe to you who make neighbors drink. Who mix in your venom even to make them drunk so as to look on their nakedness! You will be filled with disgrace rather than honor. Now you yourself drink and expose your own nakedness. The cup in the Lord's right hand will come around to you (God's judgment and wrath), and utter disgrace will come upon your glory." (Habakkuk 2:15).

The truth is inescapable. Drug abuse is from the pit of hell and is bringing mankind to the precipice. Without the intervention of true revival the destruction of the earth is inevitable. Mankind's only hope is revival.

True revival.

The rise and acceptance of abortion on demand

Abortion is murder and is severely judged by God. The judgment on those that commit murder was pronounced before the giving of the Law on Mt. Sinai.

"Whoever sheds man's blood, by man his blood shall be shed, for in the image of God He made man" (Genesis 9:6).

In God's mind, murder is so evil that it was mentioned in the Ten Commandments,

"You shall not murder" (Exodus 20:13).

In the New Testament murder was listed in the acts of sin that when not repented of would guarantee the judgment of eternal death upon the perpetrator.

Everyone who hates his brother is a murderer; and you know that no murderer has eternal life abiding in him (I John 3:15).

The Lord Jesus made it clear that children are special to His heart and that anyone harming them would incur a special curse. The workers of iniquity that murder God's children in the womb have obviously rejected the chilling curse from Jesus' own mouth.

"If you harm one of these little ones, better for you that a millstone be draped around your neck and you be dropped into the depths of the sea" (Luke 17:2).

The slaughter of the innocents has spread to all levels of society—rich and poor, illiterate and highly educated, and all races. In our new age "enlightened" society, there are thousands of unborn children murdered every day in the name of the freedom of choice—some estimates put it at 3300 each day. That is 1.2 million each year![30] A blood drenched America is literally steeped in the sin of the murder of the innocents and has made their father Satan proud.

Some astute sociologists believe that the failure of our governmental system to call abortion murder was a personal decision based on

---

[30] Imagine millions of innocent children butchered each year in order to spare the mother the "indignity" of incurring stretchmarks...and thus, mass murder is performed in the name of cosmetic vanity.

expediency—their reasoning: Many of the lawmakers had wives and daughters (and in some cases mistresses) who had experienced abortions. Not wanting to make their own relatives criminals, the lawmakers embraced **the lie of reinterpretation**[31]—the conscious decision to replace the word "murder" with the word "choice" removed the stigma of premeditated murder from their protected loved ones and the slaughter was on.

Like the Hebrews of the Old Testament, modern society, claiming that it is smarter than God, has jettisoned the true God and His call for holiness to worship the pagan gods and idols of our time. It does not take a Bible scholar to see that the slaughter of the innocents is nothing more than a child sacrifice to their father in hell.

"Go out to the valley of Ben-hinnom, which is by the entrance of the potsherd gate, and proclaim there the words that I tell you, and say, 'Hear the word of the LORD, O kings of Judah and inhabitants of Jerusalem: thus says the LORD of hosts, the God of Israel, "Behold I am about to bring a calamity upon this place, at which the ears of everyone that hears of it will tingle. Because they have forsaken Me and have made this an alien place and have burned sacrifices in it to other gods, that neither they nor their forefathers nor the kings of Judah had ever known, and because **they have filled this place with the blood of the innocent and have built the high places of Baal to burn their sons in the fire as burnt offerings to Baal,** *a thing which I never commanded or spoke of, nor did it ever enter My mind; therefore, behold, days are coming," declares the LORD, "when this place will no longer be called Topheth or the valley of Ben-hinnom, but rather the valley of Slaughter. I will make void the counsel of Judah and Jerusalem in this place, and I will cause them to fall by the sword before their enemies and by the hand of those who seek their life; and I will give over their carcasses as food for the birds of the sky and the beasts of the earth. I will also make this city a desolation and an object of hissing; everyone who passes by it will be astonished and hiss because of all its disasters"* (Jeremiah 19:2-8).

The final judgment is coming…

The acceptance of perversion as an alternative lifestyle

Sexual perversions have become so commonplace in our time that they have become the "new norm." Just turn on a TV and you will see some supporter of deviant behaviors proclaiming their "sexual perversion rights" on a talk show. The studio audience, eerily reminiscent of the debauched rabble at the ancient Roman Coliseum, cheer them on as they describe the wonders of homosexuality, adultery, pornography,

---

[31] The government has practiced the lie of reinterpretation in many specific cases in our military history. Examples: calling a war a "police action" and calling dead civilian victims of bombing "collateral damage."

voyeurism, pedophilia, transgenderism, and even bestiality as if they were celebrating some glorious "spiritual" encounter.

The incessant exposure to sexual filth has literally worn down American society to such a low level that everyone—the young, the old, the rich, the poor, all races and even supposed Christians—are parroting the big lie. The big lie: **Anyone who dares question the foul displays of public depravity is a "hater."** The acceptance of this big lie is, in my opinion, Satan's most "glorious" achievement amongst carnal men. Imagine! Those who attempt to honor God and practice morality are the immoral ones! Those who know that sexual perversions are foul and blatant crimes against God are now the outcasts! This is like inviting a pig to the Passover feast.

Like Jeremiah, true Christians are forced to live in a perverse and decadent society that demands acquiescence to its pervasive sin. And like Jeremiah, true Christians see the warnings from God's Word coming to pass right before our eyes while a wicked world sees nothing.

You can expect the "remnant" of true believers who refuse to stamp sin with the imprimatur of acceptance to become the target of the evil system that attacks any and all who refuse to accommodate society's wickedness. The Antichrist's war against the saints will be supported by billions of corrupted sinners and apostate former believers who will attempt to destroy all opposition to their perversions. Only the coming of Christ will stave off a complete and utter destruction of the human race as it experiences the total corruption birthed through unrestrained immorality.

They worshiped the dragon (Satan) because he gave his authority to the beast (Antichrist); and they worshiped the beast, saying, "Who is like the beast, and who is able to wage war with him?" There was given to him a mouth speaking arrogant words and blasphemies, and authority to act for forty-two months was given to him. And he opened his mouth in blasphemies against God, to blaspheme His name and His tabernacle, that is, those who dwell in heaven. ***It was also given to him to make war with the saints and to overcome them,*** *and authority over every tribe and people and tongue and nation was given to him* (Revelation 13:4-7).

The use of the media to spread evil

People who were once shielded from the cesspool of human defilements by society's agreement to practice restraint are now exposed to the lowest levels of human depravity every night during prime time. The constant barrage of increasingly graphic news, sexual exploitation programs, sexually explicit advertising, godless sitcoms and reality TV has scarred us all and affected our moral reasoning. Even good Christians, indoctrinated by the 24 hour a day tsunami of filth, struggle with drawing the line between right and wrong. The immoral attack on our minds lends proof to an inescapable fact: You cannot live in a sewer and not pick up the stench.

If you need any proof of the widespread collapse of morality consider the attack on our children waged by our machines (computers, I-Phones, etc.). Just peer over a teenager's shoulder and see what they are watching on their viewing screens. Every pathetic creep in the world is displaying their degeneracy on the screen and calling out to our children to join in the universal parade to hell. Prostitutes, pimps, pornographers, drug dealers, thieves, cultists, perverts, pedophiles and worse are blowing the trumpet 24/7. Our children, glued to their machines, are answering the call and are walking like lemmings over the cliff into the darkness below.[32]

This is appalling.

The corrupt influence of Hollywood

The history of Hollywood is an unconventional but accurate yardstick to measure society's shift from a belief in the traditional Christian God and its subsequent slide into utter liberal depravity. In its early years, Hollywood mirrored the traditional faith of America by making films that highlighted the victory of faith over doubt, good over evil and God over Satan. Slowly, as the Christian tradition evaporated in America the Hollywood themes changed. The crucial changes began in the mid-1950s.

I remember going to the theater to watch the original 1953 film "The War of the Worlds." I sat in the blackness of the theater and gazed transfixed at the silver screen. The Martians were landing their invading capsules all over the countryside while the earthlings were caught unawares.

I wanted to warn everyone.

The opening salvo of the Martian attack was initiated by the actions of a Christian clergyman who slipped out from the military's defensive perimeter and felt that he could make peace with the alien invaders. He approached their war machines with nothing but his faith and a Bible. The clergyman's reasoning—the Martians were God's creatures and should be offered the gospel. The Martians displayed their "spiritual sensitivity" to the truth of the gospel by blasting him with their death ray. The Christian minister was reduced to a pile of ashes. I was speechless. I could not believe that someone would blast a preacher, especially when he was holding up a Bible.

The War of the Worlds was one of the first films to reveal how secular America was starting to view biblical Christianity. Even I got the filmmaker's point when those Martians opened up with their death ray:

---

[32] Many Christian parents are realizing that the power of the corrupt media is so extreme that their abilities to protect their own children from its blatant attack is severely impaired.

The minister, although devout, was no match for the alien intruders who had no respect for our traditions of faith in God. The cryptic, subconscious message was sent to my young and impressionable mind: An evolved civilization with the scientific knowhow to send spaceships to earth was not influenced by our "earthbound" Christian spiritual traditions. Disturbing questions were implanted in my mind: Maybe our Christian faith was just confined to the earth and not throughout the universe as the church had always taught? Maybe our views were too restrictive? Maybe we should make room in our spiritual understanding for other, more unconventional ideas?[33] I wasn't aware that my reservations were fertile ground for the eventual implantation of secular propaganda through the efforts of the atheist social engineers that control America's educational systems. I was nothing but a pathetic target—stripped bare and open to any new age re-interpretation.

At the end of the film the narrator appeared to do an about face and make a stand for God by saying that the Martians were defeated by God's lowest creatures—the microbes. I sat in the back row and did a silent "Go God!"

It was not until years later that I realized that the narrator was not supporting the traditional, biblical God, but was instead presenting support for some strange and impersonal New Age force. His subtle point was burned into my consciousness: The weakness of the Christian faith, first illustrated by the death of the naive clergyman, was overturned by the microbes that were created by nature's impersonal god. And God, although defined "inaccurately" (in their opinion) by Christian religious traditions, could rise to the occasion and triumph as nature's god. I was being unconsciously prepped for the acceptance of the "brave new world" of secular rationalism.

In today's films there is no attempt to send subtle messages. Decadent Hollywood's present mantra is that the biblical God is weak and/or non-existent and definitely not associated with the Christian religious tradition. The "impotent" Christian God's only recourse is to be rescued by the wise and resourceful pagan—as evidenced by the 2005 remake of "The War of the Worlds." In that film, Tom Cruise, the representative typical unchristian American, fights the alien invasion with his human wits and tenacity. He overcomes the aliens, with some help from nature's microbes, and saves the world, allowing that world to exercise its "right" to continue its ongoing pilgrimage to annihilation via the immoral sewer of secular humanism. In their opinion, the Christian God was trumped and no longer a viable reality. The message was loud

---

[33] This is precisely the message that modern college students are force-fed by their atheistic, liberal progressive professors. These corrupt persons usurped God's message of sin and redemption and interjected the message of godless rationalism that trumpeted the antichrist message that has poisoned all political discourse.

and clear: The Christian God was nothing but a historical aberration that was now being redefined by the great minds of secular humanism.

Hollywood's previously veiled insinuations of the impotence of the Christian God has mushroomed into a full-blown rejection of all things even remotely traditional as evidenced by Clint Eastwood's "Pale Rider." Eastwood's mysterious character rides into a gold mining camp as a man of peace who wears the traditional collar of a preacher. He befriends the tin pan prospectors who are locked in a struggle with an evil rich man who is trying to steal their claims for his larger commercial mining company. Eastwood attempts to implement his way of peace to derail the coming crisis, but discovers it is too weak and not up to the task. He "wisely" reverts to his gun slinging past and straps on his guns. The message is clear: The gunslinger turned preacher has now returned to "his senses." He heads into town to face his destiny. In a classic shootout he triumphs by killing all the bad guys one by one. In essence it is the triumph of evil over a bigger evil. Eastwood rides off into the sunset with no clergyman's collar in sight. The "man of peace" has now reverted to reality and will now live his life free of Christianity's restraining morality. To the non-Christian mind he is the ultimate American hero and the lockstep march to destruction is now forever established.

Hollywood has reached the bottom of the sewer. Any pretense of respectability has long been discarded. Going to a Hollywood film today is no different than buying a ticket for the Roman Coliseum to watch the depths of corruption. Murder, perversion, rape, incest, homosexuality and evil of the most decadent forms imaginable play across the silver screen driving society to newer depths of depravity.

The race to hell is forever immortalized on film for all to see. The opportunist Hollywood purveyors of cinema immorality, safe behind their studio desks, smile as their celluloid filth fills their wallets with the "almighty" dollar. And their customers, now immune from God's conviction, slide silently and without resistance into the darkness of hell.

The rise and acceptance of the thug culture

Thugs of all types are the latest heroes in society's repudiation of commonsense and rationality. Instead of a well-deserved invitation to take up residence in a prison cell, gangs of criminals are issued a pass by the liberal politicians and courtroom judges of our time that now preside over the dissolution of American sanity.

The truth is that gangs of all colors and persuasions are threatening everyone in sight. Every inner-city neighborhood has thousands of thugs hanging out in every doorway and alley trying to exercise the crudest brutalities imaginable as a civil right. It seems that every act of criminality is excused by the cry of "civil rights" and enthusiastically protected by the liberal social engineers that are the new apologists of evil. The true facts are that no one in their right mind would attempt to drive through the embattled hood when the sun goes down—unless they are in an Abrams battle tank. But because of the new rules of political correctness the liberal pawns of the new age denial of reality have become the willing fools in this act of "abandonment of societal judgments" masquerading as an exercise of enlightened tolerance.

NOTE: Every malcontent with a cause vies for exposure on the nightly news. Protest rallies conducted to draw attention to the "civil rights" of sociopathic thugs receive credibility from the media parasites in search of a story. Just how a lynch mob can serve as serious representatives of social activism is a stretch beyond the wildest imagination of even the shallowest protestor with a sign and a bullhorn. It seems that America has lost its collective mind as the idiots are given access to the public megaphone so they can make their absurd demands. Ordinary Americans sit on their sofas at night and watch the parade of goons and creeps that rape, rob, murder, commit acts of abuse, blaspheme, lie, and then smile at the TV camera while making an obscene gesture. All we really need to complete the pathetic scenario is a televised show patterned after The Hunger Games where law enforcement officers become the human targets of marauding gangs of thugs.

It would probably win an Emmy.

The explosion of cults and false religions

Cults are spreading their wretched doctrines like a plague in twenty-first century America. Every street corner has a cultist selling their perverse doctrines and every college campus is a hotbed for phony gurus hawking their wares. Witchcraft is one of the fastest growing religions in America. Ordinary housewives pick up The National Inquirer at the local market to read the latest stories about celebrities that are attending New Age meetings,[34] or communicating with demons. School children are organizing covens that meet during lunch to cast spells on their rivals. Every week we hear of another Hollywood film hitting the theaters that glorifies the stories of witches, warlocks, werewolves, zombies, vampires and other things that go bump in the night. One of the fastest growing sections in the local bookstores is the section dedicated to the occult and New Age mysticism. Ordinary Americans crowd around the shelves and buy their books.

Satan's purpose for cults is quite simple: to provide an alternative "truth" that will dilute the Christian message, create a diversion from the gospel and destroy the ability of human beings to see the uniqueness of God's plan. America, once an avid supporter for the Christian message, has sold its soul for a bowl of rancid soup. Anything goes in this

---

[34] The term "New Age" is another name for witchcraft and/or the occult. The association with the occult is not a stretch since the philosophy of the New Age is almost an exact representation of the philosophy of witchcraft. There is no discernable difference.

spiritual smorgasbord and only biblical Christianity is demonized and excluded.[35]

It doesn't take a Bible scholar to realize that there is an unholy "revival" sweeping through our Western culture like a plague. People, rejecting the historic doctrines of the Christian church, are pursuing the "doctrines of demons" and are being corrupted within their souls by demonic spirits eager to instruct the demented Americans seeking a false spiritual reality. The biblical warnings have come to pass,

Come, house of Jacob, and let us walk in the light of the Lord (a call for national revival). For You (the Lord) have abandoned Your people, the house of Jacob, because they are filled with influences from the east (Eastern mysticism), and they are soothsayers (occultists) like the Philistines, and they strike bargains (treaties) with the children of foreigners (people that are not part of God's people). (Isaiah 2:5, 6).

And,

The Spirit clearly says that in later times some will abandon the faith and follow deceiving spirits and things taught by demons. Such teachings come through hypocritical liars, whose consciences have been seared as with a hot iron. (I Timothy 4:1, 2).

Deluded Americans, untouched by God's input of truth, are becoming an army of satanic fools and are gleefully advancing his perverted message.

And they love it so...

The perverted union of law and psychology

Liberal/progressive defense attorneys and judges, using every loophole they can find, dismiss the most heinous of crimes with a psychological defense. This turned the judicial system, once based on God's Law, into a sham. The criminals are now viewed as victims and are set free on technicalities by liberal judges to go back to their besieged neighborhoods and terrorize the real victims. Protected by these progressive fools, the criminals have gone wild and our nation is going up in smoke. Isaiah's warning has come to pass,

"Woe to those who call evil good and good evil; who put darkness for light and light for darkness; who put bitter for sweet and sweet for bitter. Woe to those who are wise in their own eyes, and clever in their own sight. Woe to those who are heroes at drinking wine and champions at mixing drinks; who acquit the guilty for a bribe, but deny justice to the innocent." (Isaiah 5:20-23).

---

[35] To prove this assertion take a trip to a college campus and go to the student union. There you will find hundreds of posters and information for cults, atheist groups, communist lectures, Islamic indoctrination lectures, homosexual encounter groups, and other godless endeavors. Christianity, when mentioned, is attacked openly while all other false religions and anti-Christ groups are praised and tolerated. Francis Schaeffer once said that there is "open season" on Christians in the twentieth century. The world has learned that anyone can kick a Christian...and do. My suggestion to non-believers that reject my observations: Try to kick a Muslim and watch the heads roll...literally..

NOTE: The progressive defense attorneys and the liberal judges all live behind their protective gates and escape the criminal deluge. Protected from the violence that chokes everyone else, they are free to practice their social engineering on the American public without any effect on themselves.[36] It is an absolute fact that if their children (who are protected by armed guards and gates) were murdered by marauding criminals, those criminals would be quickly controlled.

That is an indisputable fact.

The devastating effect of corrupt politics

Politics has always been rife with corruption, theft, and avarice. History is filled with the stories of corrupt politicians, kings, premiers, ruling classes, political movements, etc. The Bible contains verses of warning concerning the sins of politicians and those who lead:

Your rulers are rebels, and companions of thieves; everyone loves a bribe and chases after rewards. They do not defend the orphan, nor does the widow's plea come before them (justice is dispensed to the highest bidder). (Isaiah 1:23).

And,

If a ruler listens to falsehoods, all his officials will be wicked. (Proverbs 29:12).

And,

The princes of Judah have become like those who move a boundary (they lie, cheat and steal). On them I will pour out My wrath like water. (Hosea 5:10).

Although corrupt politics has always been a plague, it must be said that the politics of our time has descended to exceptional levels of debasement. At no time in recorded history have we seen more lies told, more outright deceptions promoted than in our day. The reason is simple: Politicians can count. They know that there are more Americans that are dead in their sins and live lives of extreme immorality and decadence and still vote. It doesn't take a rocket scientist to figure out that these profane voting Americans are the majority and that godly Americans are losers when it comes to the numbers game. Politicians, supported by the immoral rabble, now can stand in front of a television camera and lie unashamedly. Like the seared conscience of a psychopath they speak untruths solely for the purpose of advancement of their cause or themselves. Almost to a person, male or female, politicians are bought and paid for by heathen interest groups and power brokers. They sell their political power to the highest bidder and have little concern for a greater good. Finding an honest politician is a fool's errand and our culture has been destroyed from within by the very politicians who

---

[36] Liberal attorneys and judges all have been trained by liberal professors at their liberal colleges. This is the perfect example of the blind leading the blind. It is pathetic that these individuals that live in their ivory towers are the leaders in our society.

superciliously swear oaths to protect the nation. It is sad, but it looks like the era of Boss Tweed and his corrupt political machine is still with us, but now running on a turbocharger.[37]

Although the sins of politicians today are no different than the sins committed by the politicians of the past, there is one addition that marks the difference. In the old days politicians sinned like their constituents—adulteries, lying, cheating, stealing, selling their influence to the highest bidder, etc. Today the modern politicians have expanded their sins, choosing, for political reasons, to support gross immorality in all of its forms—legalized drugs, sexual promiscuity, homosexual perversion, the legalization of pornography, sex-change operations, abortion, blasphemy, the transgender idiocy, rebellion against God, support for entitlement scammers, etc. Their sole reason for this support is to gain the endorsement of the sinful masses that will only vote for the most corrupt politicians they can dredge up that will assist them in their quest to exercise their immoral degeneracies. It is truly a partnership birthed in hell.

NOTE: It now can be said that the road to hell passes through Washington D.C.

The all-out assault on God's Word

TV sitcoms, comedians, public figures, politicians and educators wage a twenty-four hour a day war on the Word of God. The similarities in their verbal attacks reveal the evil, supernatural source. The constant litany has brainwashed America driving this once Christian nation into the ditch of apostasy.

The liberal, apostate churches, eager to receive the support of the sin-soaked rabble, have embraced a criticism of God's Word that denies every doctrine of historic Christianity and replaces them with rationalism, support of godless causes—abortion, sexual perversion, new age witchcraft, etc. –and outright denial. Sharing the Word of God with a populace that has been exposed to such intense mockery and criticism of God and His Word has made Christian ministry more difficult.

And millions slide into the gaping mouth of hell.

The only defense against such blatant attacks against God's Word is more in-depth biblical teaching coupled with believing prayer. Any church that wastes time by replacing bible study with "busy" stuff is fulfilling a death wish. With only fifty-two Sundays a year the church has no time for silly stuff and needs to promote serious bible study and prayer.

---

[37] William M. Tweed (April 3, 1823—April 12, 1878) He was called "Boss Tweed," the leader of the Tammany Hall New York City Democratic Party political machine that ruled New York during the 1800s. Tweed and his minions stole millions of dollars (some estimate it at a billion) by playing ethnic groups in New York off each other to support his acts to control the entire city and state. He is the model of all ruthless political machines that have appeared in history.

Suggestion: Christian youth leaders should cut back on the trips to the pizza parlor, laser tag, and other time wasters and try teaching the Bible. Enhancing a young person's biblical study skills is probably much better than helping them perfect their pool game.

Just a thought…

The marriage of eastern mysticism and perverse western atheism:

Eastern mysticism became a major player in the culture of the West during the twentieth century. The major premise of this imported alien philosophy is that human beings can manipulate reality through the power of their own minds. In eastern mysticism truth is relative and becomes what the adherent decides that it is. To the followers of these absurd philosophies rocks and trees can become "conscious" and take on the attributes of humanity and even "god." Persons can change their birth genders by their own perverted will. The marriage of eastern mysticism and western atheism has become an imposing force that has changed the entire culture of America and the western nations. Lying and deception has always existed but a liar fueled by the foundational premise of eastern mysticism becomes a powerful force that can shred reality. When coupled with western atheism those advocates for the New Age rebellion project false realities with a complete lack of morality. This is guaranteed to sink all rational discourse, turning the culture into a deadly, corrupt, diseased system of destruction. America is filled with the corrosive effects of this evil system and we will all suffer the consequences.

And again, the Antichrist cometh.

The leftwing educational system:

God has been thrown out of our schools by the liberal progressives that consider themselves to be smarter than God. The activists of the 1960s, who marched in our streets against everything, grew up and took over the educational system.[38] Steeped in new age philosophy and leftist propaganda, these education czars run the public educational system with all the atheistic control of the former Soviet Ministry of Education. Because of their anti-God stance coupled with their worship at the altar of political correctness they, like the Soviets of old, will even change history through the act of historical revisionism to meet their heinous ends.[39]

---

[38] Liberal progressives, because of their academic titles, are considered the only worthy evaluators of America's spiritual and educational condition. They are the new gurus that pronounce the acceptable blueprint for our nation's advancement into a brave new world. The glaring fallacy: *If you have a PhD attached to your name you are infallible…when in fact oftentimes a PhD might indicate that your human wisdom is nothing but the degenerate wisdom of man…only piled higher and deeper.*

[39] **Historical Revisionism:** Is the reinterpretation or eradication of historical data in order to alter an orthodox view of history. The revisionist attempts to slant the view of evidence and motivation

History books are being re-written through the lenses of historical revisionism in order to ignore the importance of religion and faith in the formation of our country. The example of the expulsion of George Washington's Farewell Address from the public schools is a valid illustration:

When George Washington wrote his farewell address in 1796, he added the following paragraph concerning America's indispensable faith: "Of all the dispositions and habits which lead to political prosperity, religion and morality are indispensable supports.[40] In vain would that man claim the tribute of patriotism, who should labor to subvert these great pillars of human happiness, these firmest props of the duties of men and citizens. The mere politician, equally with the pious man, ought to cherish them. A volume could not trace all their connections with private and public felicity. Let it simply be asked: Where is the security for property, for reputation, for life, if the sense of religious obligation deserts the oaths which are the instruments of investigation in courts of justice? And let us with caution indulge the supposition that morality can be maintained without religion. Whatever may be conceded to the influence of refined education on minds of peculiar structure, reason and experience both forbid us to expect that national morality can prevail in exclusion of religious principles."

In Washington's opinion, national morality based on revealed Christian truth was mandatory for the success of America's great experiment of national freedom. Our first President inferred that any attempt to restrict the faith in the Christian God would spell doom to the nation because freedom without the restraining influence of true Christian faith would produce chaos.

Washington's Farewell Address used to be required reading in America's schools. Imagine there was an existing document from the pen of the Father of our country concerning his dire warnings of the heinous coming attacks against the fledgling nation that was suppressed by the leftwing educational czars. Who in their right mind would attempt to ban such a gift from the first President to our beloved country?

---

surrounding an historical event to promote liberal ideology, advance political purposes and to foment outright denial of accurate history. This is done to support a subversive agenda, advance a political or social cause or to undermine the contributions and importance of rival groups. This battle is being currently fought within the public school curriculum committees meeting to rewrite textbooks. These committees are almost invariably controlled by left-wing ideologues who are dedicated to the support of liberal causes and goals. Examples: Removal of all credible evidence of any positive Christian influence in the founding of the country coupled with the inclusion of the contrived lie of a supposed negative Christian influence in American history to minimize the positive contributions of Christianity; also the redefining of the Founding Fathers as egocentric white men with dark motives; and the attributing of guilt to America for all of its wars and diplomatic problems; and over-inflating the importance of certain fringe individuals and groups. It has been defined as "the theft of true history by the professional ideological liars."

[40] It must be crystal clear that Washington was referring to biblical Christianity and not to any list of non-Christian religions known to man.

In the 1970s the "great leftist secular minds" that control our educational system were fearful of any message of national sanity and colluded in their efforts to exclude this and any other document of reason from the public school's curriculum. Their reasons were fourfold: First, George Washington's comments concerning the importance of true biblical Christianity as a foundational requirement for the successful establishment of freedom was a fatal blow to the iniquitous social engineers that deeply desire a godless, immoral nation. Flushed with their late nineteenth century victories in the clash of cultures—unrestrained immorality vs historic Christian morality—the champions of unfettered degeneracy demanded the removal of any and all historical supports of conservatism. Washington's Farewell Address was one of many historic documents that had to be removed from the public discourse to insure the victory of liberalism.[41] With cold and focused resolve the liberal education czars, with the stroke of a pen, banned Washington's Farewell Address to the ash heap of history. With that action, the rush to apostasy became a headlong sprint.

Secondly, George Washington's strong admonitions against overspending by the government had to be minimized.[42] The reason—the adherence to any reasoned approach to a national budget was a death blow to the liberals that need the stolen billions of taxpayer dollars to support their entitlement industry. The liberals, realizing that restrictions on spending would severely limit their ability to secure votes from the new entitlement class, fought to the death for their right to commit the treasonous act of deficit spending. In a short while the national debt, inundated with demands to feed the coffers of liberalism, grew to monstrous proportions, ensuring a day of reckoning when the nation eventually goes bankrupt.

Thirdly, Washington's warnings against foreign treaties and entanglements that invariably lead to foreign wars. These warnings if circulated would deal a death blow to the American military-Industrial complex that needs those foreign wars to fill their coffers. And lastly, the great strides toward communism that have been advanced by the American left could be hindered by an examination of our founding documents that directly oppose such political re-structuring. The secular liberal progressive education czars, fearful that Washington's comments

---

[41] The attacks against the restraining founding documents have followed two paths: First, an attempt to foster ignorance of their existence by ignoring their validity and refusing to teach about them to the young American students and, in the case of the U.S. Constitution, the act of re-interpretation and dismissal. An act of historical revisionism that is massive in scale.

[42] George Washington accurately diagnosed deficit spending as a destructive force that will eventually destroy the United States. At this time in our history we have allowed the greedy politicians to amass a national debt beyond comprehension. The impact of those trillions of borrowed dollars is many fold: The control of our republic exercised by the powers that hold that debt is just one of the detrimental results.

might cause a disturbance if read by young, impressionable and malleable students, decided to expunge his farewell address from the public record in order to create an acceptable atmosphere for the imposition of their brand of socialism, secularism, immorality and atheism. This erasing of history was to them a self-defense action. They knew that to allow our first President's message to be read in the public square might put a crimp in their plan to fashion America into a European secular liberal progressive state steeped in atheistic socialism—a result that is repugnant to the godless liberal progressive social engineers.

Again, I want to emphasize that Washington's main point was that freedom without the restraining morality that comes from a relationship with the true Christian God will produce chaos. This is precisely what has happened to America. Our freedoms have become a camouflage for utter depravity and sin. Beginning at the start of the twentieth century, the secular liberal progressive social engineers, smelling the blood in the water, promoted this "freedom from God" that poisoned America's soul. With no guilt, no sin consciousness, no internal moral restraints, and without God reprobate modern America exercised its "freedom from God," causing it to become a sewer of sin and despair. The facts are undeniable—because of pagan America's demand to live in a nation that rejects the Christian God and His restraining influence, chaos reigns.[43]

And sin and destruction fill the void.

Nothing is left to chance as the unrepentant czars of the leftwing educational junta rule their prayer-free, Bible-free educational zones like the atheistic schools of the former Soviet Union. With God erased from the system and patriotism demeaned and ridiculed, the students of modern America are free to investigate the deep sewers of sin and depravity. With no moral restraints the guttural cry is—"**Sex, drugs and rock and roll!**" Like the children in the well-known fairy tale, the youth of America are being led away to destruction by the pied pipers of apostasy.

And Satan rejoices at the death of Christian culture.

The spiritual destruction of America's youth

The 1950's parents who drew the lines of discipline in the sand are dead and gone. Trapped by the rising cost of living, today's parents must leave their children at home alone to raise themselves while they work multiple jobs to survive. Unsupervised and free from discipline and restraints, an entire generation wanders the streets searching for the happiness they will never find. They hang out at shopping malls wearing

---

[43] Any person who glibly states that America is not drowning in an immoral sewer is drinking Kool-Aid. A peripheral reading of a daily newspaper and/or a turning in to the evening news will derail those attempts to alter reality in a heartbeat. The only truth that seems to be present in our daily experience is that every new day is getting worse. The only hope is a return to God…a revival.

hundreds of dollars of designer clothes, expensive athletic shoes, nose and lip rings and turned around baseball caps. It seems that getting a tattoo or a body piercing is the highest goal in a teenager's life. Occult and witchcraft is the latest fad and the children embrace it with passion. Our children, regardless of our misplaced redefinitions of reality, are becoming nothing but hell-fuel for the Antichrist when he shows up and becomes the new Pied Piper leading them to the abyss.

Christian parents, restrained from using Christian schools because of financial realities, send their children to public schools where they are indoctrinated into the corrupt world system. Those who go to the most prestigious colleges and universities are taught by godless professors who spread the pitiful disease of Marxism and atheism. The last remnants of faith once implanted in their hearts at a church retreat are stamped out by blasphemous peers who lead them into the darkness of a Christless eternity. Our children, embracing the myth that rebellion against authority is a civil right will die in the ashes of mankind's funeral pyre. There will be no survivors of God's judgment.

Unless they repent and return to the ancient path.

The weakness of the established church

It is true that the satanic revival of our time is a large part of the reason that non-believers are encouraged to live their lives without God. Their demands to live in a dark environment of evil in order to hide their gross immorality have certainly stoked Satan's fires that are indeed consuming us all. But with all that said, I must be honest and say that the truth is that America's descent into full-scale rebellion against God, although certainly fueled by the above mentioned streams of corruption, is largely the result of the collapse of the Christian church.

Yes, I know that many of my readers may balk at this statement. They would prefer to believe that pagan mankind is totally responsible for the deplorable condition of the earth. They may argue that the Christian church is so minimized, discounted and demeaned by the heathen mob that it has no ability to change the spiritual temperature of the nation. They may argue this, but they are wrong. God has continuously stated the fact—from the Old Testament era to the New Testament and on into our modern day—that He holds the church responsible for the state of the earth. In God's opinion, only the people of God can bring change to the earth's spiritual condition and that this lack of change is the result of its failure to fulfill that mission. Let me explain:

The greatest call to revival in the Bible is in the Book of Second Chronicles. This verse has appeared on more bumper stickers than any other, but with such exposure it is certainly puzzling why it is one of the most misunderstood verses in existence. The verse:

If my people, which are called by my name, shall humble themselves, and pray, and seek my face, and turn from their wicked ways; ***then*** *will I hear from heaven, and will forgive their sin, and will heal their land* (II Chronicles 7:14).

The two most important words within the context of the verse are the words **"IF"** and **"THEN."** It is not a stretch to understand that these two small words are probably the most important theological words in the holy text. There are hundreds of other verses in the Old and New Testament that contain these two small words as found in this famous verse. What they reveal is so important that mankind's very survival is at stake. Let's take a closer look at this revealing scripture:

- The verse opens with the word **"IF."** There is no doubt that the reality of the verse, its expected successful completion, is contingent on a proper response. Nothing can happen without the proper response. Only **"IF"** something is done will the remaining promise be fulfilled.
- The Lord makes it clear that He is dealing with His people and only His people. This is true because only people indwelt and led by God's Holy Spirit have the capacity to submit their stubborn wills to the sovereign Lord. Unbelievers, dead in their sins and completely helpless, cannot obey God at any level. It is useless for God to order a human being, saturated with rebellion and only good for Hell fuel, to perform a spiritual task. Only the church has the ability to perform the required obedience.
- The Lord makes clear His requirements: His people must humble themselves, pray without ceasing, seek God's face (His divine presence) and repent of their wicked sins. It is clear from the context that the lack of these requirements in God's people are the cause of the terrible condition of the nation and the earth. In essence, the lack of humility, the lack of prayer, the decision to live their lives without God's holy presence, and the giving over to our corrupt sinful nature has brought the world to the precipice. There is no mention of the responsibility of unbelieving mankind because they are completely and thoroughly dead to God and unable to obey His Word.
- It is now the interjection of the word **"THEN"** that completes the verse that is so often misunderstood. God states unequivocally that the giving of His blessings are only in response to the church's obedience in humbling themselves, praying, seeking God's presence and repentance. Without the church's active obedience there will be no blessing. This is the forgotten truth that has put the modern church at odds with the Lord and has brought such destroying judgment upon the land. The separation of obedience from the blessings of God is the

direct cause of the outpouring of hellish power in the satanic revival we are experiencing. As long as Christians leaders refuse to tell the truth that Christians must obey God and be His servant in order to receive His blessings the deadly shroud of sin and judgment will remain upon the land.
- The final portion of the verse nails the door shut on any possible re-interpretation. God's mercy, His hearing of our desperate prayers for revival, will only take place when we **"DO"** His bidding. God's forgiving our sin and the subsequent healing of our land will only become fact when we obey the entire context of the verse.

The brutal but naked truth is that the church as we know it has ceased to be the salt of the earth. We have jettisoned our mandate from God and joined the rebellion. The Lord Himself issued us a dire warning:

"You are the salt of the earth; but if the salt has become tasteless, how can it be made salty again? It is no longer good for anything, except to be thrown out and trampled under foot by men" (Matthew 5:13).

And,

"Why do you contend with Me? You have all transgressed against Me," declares the LORD. "In vain I have struck your sons; they accepted no chastening. Your sword has devoured your prophets like a destroying lion." "O generation, heed the word of the LORD. Have I been a wilderness to Israel, or a land of thick darkness? Why do My people say, 'We are free to roam; We will no longer come to You'? "Can a virgin forget her ornaments, or a bride her attire? Yet My people have forgotten Me days without number (Jeremiah 2:29-32).

The streams of moral and doctrinal pollution running through the established church are well documented. I will mention only two to illustrate the appalling truth:

The accommodation with the world

Leonard Ravenhill spoke against the stunning error of accommodation that has gripped the modern American church. He was tireless in his attempt to make churches and denominations, once birthed by great historic revivals, realize that they have embraced the poison of false doctrine carried like a virus in the tide of modern liberalism. The writer of Psalms focused the light of scrutiny upon those that lead the rebellion within the very house of God:

Remember Your congregation, which You have purchased of old, which You have redeemed to be the tribe of Your inheritance; and this Mount Zion, where You have dwelt. Turn Your footsteps toward the perpetual ruins; the enemy has damaged everything within the sanctuary. Your adversaries (those that have sold their souls to the agents of apostasy) *have roared in the midst of Your meeting place; they have set up their own standards for signs* (Psalm 74:2-4).

Leonard Ravenhill's message was clear and to the point. Any church or denomination that toys with the accommodations that must be embraced in order to "fellowship" with the world is on the road to apostasy. This problem is becoming more prevalent with the "peace at all costs" mentality that has made its appearance at the end of the twentieth century. Christians, convinced that they are to accommodate the world system in order to have a right to speak, have embraced the lie that they are to avoid any and all controversy in order to receive that "right." This is not only foolish but is completely unscriptural:

And this is love that we walk according to His commandments. This is the commandment, just as you have heard from the beginning that you should walk in it. For many deceivers have gone out into the world, those who do not acknowledge Jesus Christ as coming in the flesh. This is the deceiver and the antichrist. Watch yourselves that you do not lose what we have accomplished, but that you may receive a full reward. Anyone who goes too far and does not abide in the teaching of Christ, does not have God; the one who abides in the teaching, he has both the Father and the Son. If anyone comes to you and does not bring this teaching, do not receive him into your house, and do not give him a greeting; for the one who gives him a greeting participates in his evil deeds (II John 6-11).

And,

Do not love the world nor the things in the world. If anyone loves the world, the love of the Father is not in him. For all that is in the world, the lust of the flesh and the lust of the eyes and the boastful pride of life, is not from the Father, but is from the world. The world is passing away, and also its lusts; but the one who does the will of God lives forever (I John 2:15-17; see also James 4:4-5).

The attempt by the professing Christian church to seek common ground with the world has occurred because of the following factors:

- The failure to understand the uniqueness of the Christian church:
- The true Christian church is a supernatural body and not some human club organized to support some social program. It is to be led by and filled with the Holy Spirit so that it can be the spearhead of God's divine interventions in the world. The church must learn the sobering truth: It is the conduit of God's power on earth and is never to sell, barter, or give away its unique position. The Christian church must allow God's Spirit to burn the words of God into its very soul:

    The LORD will make you the head and not the tail, and you only will be above, and you will not be underneath, *if you listen to the commandments of the LORD your God, which I charge you* *today, to observe them carefully, and do not turn aside from any of the words which I command you today, to the right or to the left, to go after other gods to serve them* (Deuteronomy 28:13-14).

The failure of the Christian church to recognize that it has no right to redefine itself: The Christian church is what God says it is and must operate according to His plan. No holy conferences, church conclaves, no denominational meetings, no human traditions, no church council meetings, no reasoned machinations, no historic councils, nothing at all can alter one jot or tittle uttered by God concerning His church. We do it His way or the highway. It is that simple.

For My thoughts are not your thoughts, nor are your ways My ways," declares the LORD. "For as the heavens are higher than the earth, so are My ways higher than your ways and My thoughts than your thoughts (Isaiah 55:8-9).

- The Christian church must understand that it was never meant to be a group of "peaceniks" expected to remain quiet while Satan and his minions rule public discourse.
- Quite literally, the Christian church is an army and its members are warriors. Warriors are expected to fight. Losing is not an option.

Blessed be the LORD, my rock, Who trains my hands for war, And my fingers for battle; my lovingkindness and my fortress, my stronghold and my deliverer, my shield and He in whom I take refuge, Who subdues my people under me (Psalm 144:1-2).

- Too often we hear from our modern pulpits that Christians are to roll over and accept whatever comes in order to accommodate the opinions and/or agendas of the world. This is a complete lie birthed by the father of lies who is desperately attempting to control any and all encounters with God's people to insure his victory. God spoke to Jeremiah and made it clear what was expected of His warriors:

"See, I have appointed you this day over the nations and over the kingdoms, To pluck up and to break down, To destroy and to overthrow, To build and to plant" (Jeremiah 1:10).

- Christians, although rightly expected to express the love of God, are also commanded to make war against the purposes and plans of Satan. Christians are never supposed to let Satan and his minions rule public discourse but to stand against the attacks and confront them through the power of God. Since Christians are expected to judge angels and nations and rule with God upon His throne, it is high time for us to begin our training in the present world we live in (1 Corinthians 6:2,3; Revelation 3:21-22).

- **The Christian church needs to acknowledge that believers are commanded to not be bound together with unbelievers.**
  The Word of God is plain. Christians are not to be led by the erroneous ideas, mores, philosophies, imaginations and any other concept universally embraced by the unbelieving world. Christians cannot avoid God's command to refuse partnership with non-believers:
  Do not be bound together with unbelievers; for what partnership have righteousness and lawlessness, or what fellowship has light with darkness? Or what harmony has Christ with Belial, or what has a believer in common with an unbeliever? Or what agreement has the temple of God with idols? For we are the temple of the living God; just as God said, "I WILL DWELL IN THEM AND WALK AMONG THEM; AND I WILL BE THEIR GOD, AND THEY SHALL BE MY PEOPLE. "Therefore, COME OUT FROM THEIR MIDST AND BE SEPARATE," says the Lord. "AND DO NOT TOUCH WHAT IS UNCLEAN; And I will welcome you. "And I will be a father to you, and you shall be sons and daughters to Me," Says the Lord Almighty (II Corinthians 6:14-18).

  What this verse does not mean:

- It does not mean that we withhold God's love. Christians are to exhibit God's love at all times, but they are also commanded to reject the impulse to use God's love as a cover for uninhibited sin—whether theirs or the persons they are ministering to.
- It does not mean that we are to be mean and hateful.[44] It is certainly true that non-believers will always view any opposition to their full expression of sin as mean and hateful. This is nothing but a ruse and cannot be entertained as a valid argument against expressing truth. True believers, in my opinion, should be smart enough to understand the difference.
- It does not mean that we cannot listen to the world's arguments when respectfully presented.[45] It must be said, however, that listening to an argument does not mean that we must accept a false premise. We are commanded to exercise the intelligence to sort it all out:
  *Therefore, thus says the LORD, "If you return, then I will restore you—Before Me you will stand; and **if you extract the precious from the worthless, you will become My spokesman.** They for their part may turn to you, But as for you, you must not turn to them* (Jeremiah 15:19).

---

[44] Q: "What does it usually mean when a non-Christian calls you hateful?"
A: "It probably means you are telling the truth about their sins…"

[45] It must be said that many non-believers will not "respectfully" offer their contrary opinions. The combative nature of non-believers is widely known. It is, however, something to be hoped for.

- It does not mean that we resist society's laws and rules when they do not conflict with God's eternal laws of morality. Christians are to be law-abiding, but not be supporters of godless laws that ignore God and His Word.

Peter's defense:
When they had brought them, they stood them before the Council. The high priest questioned them, saying, "We gave you strict orders not to continue teaching in this name, and yet, you have filled Jerusalem with your teaching and intend to bring this man's blood upon us." But Peter and the apostles answered, **"We must obey God rather than men"** (Acts 5:27-29).

What this verse means:
- It means that we do not marry or become yoked (equal business partnership) to a non-believer.
- It means that we must obey God rather than man (when man's law conflicts with God).
- It means that we never accommodate the world's false opinions of God and use those opinions as meaningful interpretations of God's Word.
- It means that we seek peace whenever we can, but we never relinquish the warrior spirit when the world demands that we do so in order to clear the path for their evil and rebellion.

NOTE: Remember that Christians are really the only people in the room that truly have the answer. Non-believers, no matter how brilliant they claim to be, have no clue concerning God and His ways. Asking a non-believer to give you insight on the biblical God is like asking a goat to perform brain surgery. Simply put, non-believers have nothing to add to God's divine Word on how to conduct true ministry. With that in mind, let's take a penetrating look at one of the most disturbing trends in this modern re-interpretation of the church's role in society.

The advent of the Seeker Friendly Movement

The heathen of the first century were afraid of the church. The church was awake then and full of the Pentecost power of the Holy Spirit. God-filled Christians spoke against sin and sinners fell to their knees begging for mercy. The sick and the lame were healed with a word. The church was armed and ready to stand against Satan's schemes and the order of the day was "forward!"

Nothing could stand against the church in the first century because the days and nights were filled with intercessory prayer. The church prayed and God acted. It was a simple blueprint, but it lifted the gospel from its small beginnings and borne it throughout the world.

Today, pagan America laughs at the powerless church, and dismisses it with disdain. This embarrassing turn of events was birthed in one generation. We must ask the question: What fueled the weakening of the impact of the American church?

The embarrassing truth is that the prayer warriors that led the thrust of the American church for two hundred years have gone the way of the Dodo bird. The few that remain are hidden away in church backrooms like a crazy uncle. There are many reasons for this—the rise of the liberal unbelieving church, the spread of apostasy, the godless media explosion, the aforementioned streams of corruption, and the passing of the "Greatest Generation" are a few—but there is one reason that is a recent phenomenon—the "Seeker Friendly" or "Seeker Sensitive" movement.

This modern movement, birthed in church growth meetings and not in prayer closets, is universally accepted in our time. Any Christian bookstore will carry scores of books written to present a human blueprint on how the church should be planted, grown and directed through human strength and planning. Those who are the strongest advocates of this church growth philosophy present a polished argument to support their position. Their argument:

- They believe that the church must shed its unsophisticated past and join the modern era:
- They argue that the "old ways" to advance the gospel no longer work in our new, more sophisticated age. They use as a foundational text in the teaching manuals they "sell" at their church growth conferences—after a payment of a steep fee for entrance—from the words of the prophet Isaiah:

"Do not call to mind the former things, or ponder things of the past. "Behold, I will do something new, now it will spring forth; will you not be aware of it? I will even make a roadway in the wilderness, rivers in the desert. (Isaiah 43:18, 19).

They fail to complete the verse, tearing it torn and bleeding from its context, to obfuscate the true meaning of God's words. Instead of prophesying of a modern new approach to ministry (the church growth movement) it is a clear revelation of the blessings that God has promised His people when they repent and confess their sins and seek His face. The Isaiah verse in its entirety:

"Do not call to mind the former things, or ponder things of the past. "Behold, I will do something new, now it will spring forth; will you not be aware of it? I will even make a roadway in the wilderness, rivers in the desert. "The beasts of the field will glorify Me, The jackals and the ostriches, because I have given waters in the wilderness and rivers in the desert, to give drink to My chosen people. "The people whom I formed for Myself will declare My praise. Yet you have not called on Me, O Jacob

(have not repented of your sins); *But you have become weary of Me, O Israel* (gone your own stubborn way). (Isaiah 43:18-22).

Further continuation of the Isaiah passage explains in more depth that God is referring to their "sins" that have been committed against God by their lack of repentance and renewal. God promises that "the new thing" that He is referring to is a cleansing of the people and the land that will result when they pray for and experience a revival. In essence, the old time religion confronts the "old time sins" and God wins.

If we let it happen.

- **They attempt to replace the old ways to share the gospel with a marketing scheme:**
The leadership within the church growth movement, tirelessly labor to present their main thesis: In their opinion, they believe that directly confronting the world with its sin and desperate need for Christ may be construed as an offensive act by the non-believers being "confronted" and must be replaced with a more reasoned "civilized" approach. Rejecting the old "unsophisticated" methods, their main goal is to make Christianity acceptable to non-believers by removing any and all hindrances to the public's perception so that a successful "sale" can be made. The intensive intercessory prayer of the past has given way to the modern promotional methods utilized by secular advertising corporations. In essence, it is a "packaging campaign" that follows corporate America's promotional schemes.

- Although the advocates of the Seeker Friendly Movement claim that seeking the lost is a primary goal, I must challenge their premise by stating that evangelism is lost in the machinations of this marketing system and becomes only a hoped for by-product. In all honesty, the primary accomplishment of the Seeker Friendly movement is the lowering of the bar of Christianity to make it simple for "customers/non-believers" to come and "taste" the church to see if it is compatible with their opinions and lifestyle.

  NOTE: *It is not a stretch to say that intercessory prayer meetings have been replaced in the modern church with— potlucks, movie night, Super Bowl parties, laser tag for the youth, music concerts, square dances, and anything else that can be cooked up to draw a crowd.*

- **They elevate the non-believer as the chief evaluator of spiritual endeavors:**

The Bible makes it clear that non-believers cannot and will not be a reliable source of spiritual understanding. This fact is set in concrete and will never be superseded:

For to us God revealed them (spiritual truths) *through the Spirit; for the Spirit searches all things, even the depths of God. For who among men knows the thoughts of a man except the spirit of the man which is in him? Even so **the thoughts of God no one knows except the Spirit of God.** Now we have received, not the spirit of the world, but the Spirit who is from God, so that we may know the things freely given to us by God, which things we also speak, not in words taught by human wisdom, but in those taught by the Spirit, combining spiritual thoughts with spiritual words. But **a natural man** (unsaved person) **does not accept the things of the Spirit of God, for they are foolishness to him; and he cannot understand them, because they are spiritually appraised.**[46] But he who is spiritual appraises all things, yet he himself is appraised by no one. For WHO HAS KNOWN THE MIND OF THE LORD, THAT HE WILL INSTRUCT HIM? But we have the mind of Christ.* (I Corinthians 2:10-16).

- The church growth movement has effectively made the customer/non-believer the judge of the Lord's gospel and elevates their complete lack of spiritual understanding as the yardstick of evaluation. The plans for ministry in this movement are based on the negative or positive feedback of the casual church visitor. All that is needed to scrap a method, a sermon or a ministry plan is a negative reaction from a visitor (potential buyer).[47] Can you imagine how successful Moses and the other prophets would have been under those circumstances? Moses would have been stoned before he took one step out of Egypt and the prophets would have been skinned alive before they could say, "Thus saith the Lord." The complete ridiculousness of this concept deserves the criticism it receives from those who have seen a real church and know the difference.

Unfortunately, the leaders of this movement have discovered that they can grow their churches (in numbers and not in faith) through the slick techniques they have learned at Church Growth Seminars without any real effort at engaging in intense intercessory prayer. Just a bit of

---

[46] This is a "Catch-22." Being a natural man, a person unsaved and without the Holy Spirit, you cannot understand God. In other words you have to accept God to understand God. This is an unchanging, unalterable fact.

[47] A common technique in these seeker friendly churches is to hand out information cards with boxes that are checked by a visitor. In essence the visitor evaluates the service and gives their input. The church staff reads these cards and utilizes the information gathered for designing the weekly services. This is like asking men about their experiences in giving childbirth. I'm sure there would be some interesting responses but nothing of value.

tinsel, some sparkle and a little gold paint can make a church look spiffy and ready to compete in the local church competition in our cities and neighborhoods. But is this what God wants?

On the contrary, I believe that God is losing patience with prayerlessness and the resulting weakening of our churches. The lack of serious intercessory prayer and obedience to God borders on full-scale rebellion. The sounds of the drumbeat of debilitating sin echoes throughout the land and we continue our march toward the abyss.

So what is the fruit of the seeker friendly movement? What can they point to in order to validate the truth of their message?

- **They have big churches (in numbers).** This doesn't fulfill the requirement for evaluation since Jesus Himself claimed that very few will accept His message. *"Enter through the narrow gate; for the gate is wide and the way is broad that leads to destruction, and there are many who enter through it. For the gate is small and the way is narrow that leads to life, and there are few who find it"* (Matthew 7:13-14).
- **They avoid what they consider confrontational evangelism.** Seeker friendly churches, committed to the comfort level of their potential customers, hesitate to promote evangelism, seeing it as too confrontational to the public. It must be said that any member of one of these congregations that is enthusiastic about true evangelism will discover that they may be labeled a mean-spirited, judgmental malcontent. In other words they may be labeled "a hater."
- **They have "nifty" books that describe their agenda and purpose.** These books and CDs are found in their bookstores right next to the latte and coffee shop. A reader of these slick books will soon learn that the outreach efforts utilized with great success over two thousand years by anointed Christians have become passé. Of course, there will be no discussion in those "enlightened" pages concerning the possibility that the modern church's failure to evangelize is possibly linked to the modern church's failure to seek God with the same intensity as our forefathers.
- **They have very little spiritual power.** Since spiritual power is directly generated through intense intercessory prayer and obedience to God's Word it is not common in many of the modern seeker friendly churches. So this evaluation would be ignored by most seeker friendly leadership that have made it a policy to run their church through human planning and effort without reliance on the Holy Spirit. The spiritual truth is etched in stone: *If you deny the Holy Spirit's power you will not experience His power in your church.*

- **They have very few real prayer warriors.** Most of their prayer warriors have moved on to more prayer friendly churches to escape the inquisitions or have been reprogrammed to take a submissive role in what the seeker friendly leadership would proudly present as a "fanatic free environment." No matter what form the opposition takes in order to control intercessory prayer, the spiritual environment, without intense prayer, will suffer.

  NOTE: *I turned on the TV on a recent Sunday and watched a pastor of a laid-back seeker friendly church focus his sermon on the famous 1743 Jonathon Edwards sermon "Sinners in the hands of an angry God." The pastor mocked Edwards' attempt to convict his listeners of their sin and need for repentance and said, "All my life I've wanted to preach a sermon that presented the exact opposite message to rescue Christians from the deluded histrionics of Jonathon Edwards." His sleepy congregation took a break from their nap and clapped. Of course the pastor made no reference to the fact that thousands of Edwards' hearers turned to Christ and escaped the judgment of an eternal Hell. He didn't make any reference to the fact that many of his own parishioners wouldn't know Jesus if He walked into the room. He just belittled Edwards for another 20 minutes and then closed the service so that he could rush home to watch the golf channel.*

- **They don't emphasize holiness and repentance, etc.** These topics usually fall under the heading of confrontational and embarrassing to visitors and are either reinterpreted or discounted entirely. In their place you will hear "feel good" sermons that are designed to support the personal interests of the church shoppers.[48]

- **But again, they do grow in numbers...** This is not a fair evaluative tool since even the JWs and the Mormons grow when they follow their own blueprints.

  NOTE: Unfortunately, it seems that Americans are only impressed with numbers when they consider success or failure. This is especially true when evaluating the fruit of a ministry. I remember talking with a friend that was questioning my observations concerning the seeker friendly movement in general and a specific television ministry of a popular seeker friendly preacher in particular. His final comment to my concerns was, *"Well, he's got a lot of people attending his church and buying*

---

[48] Take a look at the sermons being preached in the typical seeker friendly church. You will discover lectures with names like: "Six ways to discover success." "How to invest in your individual goals," "God's desire to re-invigorate your relationships," "Sex and the Bible," "God wants you fulfilled," and other inane subjects that have zero bearing on biblical truth.

his books. He must be doing something right…" On the surface this sounds like the coup-de-grace to my analysis of the questionable ministry. I must admit that his statement caught me off guard for a minute until I answered: *"Well, I'm a student of history and I can tell you that the Nuremberg Rallies in the 1930s in Nazi Germany had more people in attendance from 1933-1938 than all the seeker friendly ministries in America combined over the last six years. Do you really want to make a large crowd your evaluative tool of measuring the truth or falsehood of any movement?"*

He thought a moment and then said, *"Ah…no…."*

I said, *"I didn't think so…"*

A prayer for the church

Oh God, please send men and women filled with the Holy Spirit who will clean out the temples of our day! Help your righteous people to rediscover their heritage! Let us know that what we see in the modern church is not what you intended, but only an aberration that has been transformed to cripple a vibrant and life-filled church! Have mercy on us and consider that we have been captive to Satan's plot to remove the remembrance of your divine blueprint! Please send a move of your Spirit that will re-ignite the fires in our cold churches and erupt into the revival that will cleanse our land! Forgive us our individual and corporate sins and look upon your repentant children with favor! And bring salvation and restoration to our sin-soaked nation! In Jesus' name…Amen.

Pray for revival.

Chapter Five
Prayer: The Fire that Ignites Revival

"After they prayed, the place where they were meeting was shaken. And they were all filled with the Holy Spirit and spoke the words of God boldly." -Acts 4:31

History's great revivalists have gone on record stating that prayer is the key to any revival. No matter the historical era—from the Old Testament, to the birth of the church in the first century, and on to our time today—their comments are uniquely similar as they proclaim the truth: *revivals are birthed in prayer, directed by prayer, carried by prayer and brought to an end whenever prayer ceases.* The steady drumbeat is: Prayer is the fire that ignites revival.

Their words:

"The man who mobilizes the Christian church to pray will make the greatest contribution to world evangelism in history." -Andrew Murray

"Prayer can never be in excess." -Charles H. Spurgeon

"Prayer does not fit us for the greater work, prayer is the greater work." -Oswald Chambers

"God does nothing except in response to believing prayer." -John Wesley

"The same church members who yell like Comanche Indians at a ball game on Saturday sit like wooden Indians in church on Sunday." -Vance Havner

"Is prayer your steering wheel or your spare tire?" -Corrie ten Boom

"No one is a firmer believer in the power of prayer than the devil; not that he practices it, but he suffers from it." -Guy H. King.

Prayerlessness—our corporate guilt

I attended an Easter pageant at a mega-church in California many years ago. The church was one of those slick California churches—Jesus T-shirts, lots of unattached singles looking for relationships, cool staff pastors wearing nifty Hawaiian shirts, beige slacks and open-toed sandals, creased designer jeans, color coordinated halls with trendy wicker furniture, a water fountain that expelled scented water that danced and shimmied to the music of the latest Christian singer or rock group, a refreshment bar with delicious lattes and exotically flavored coffees with heavily inflated prices, and professionally designed posters and church bulletins. I asked a volunteer usher with an official-looking nametag and a plastic walkie-talkie about the intercessory prayer meeting. He stared at me like I had six noses, paused a moment to ponder my question, shrugged his shoulders and finally directed me to the ministry board.

The ministry board took up an entire wall in the hallway leading into the main sanctuary. It was made of imported Philippine cork and was trimmed with pictures of flowers, sunsets, smiley faces, puppies and leaping dolphins. All the recognized ministries of the church were on that board. I started looking through the dozens of fliers and 3x5 cards stapled to the board searching for the intercessory prayer meeting and saw the following: *God's surfers, Christian Bikers for Christ, Singles Explosion, Jogging for Jesus, the Sewing Ministry, Christians and Pets Together, Hikers for Jesus, Christian Gourmet Cooking, God's Golfers, The Camping Ministry, Algebra for Believers, Christian Coffee Time, The Christian Chess Club, Softball Practice Schedule, Christian Soccer Moms, Christian Pool Players, Dog Walking for Spiritual Growth, The Computer Club, Beauticians for Jesus and a multitude of ads for Christian businesses like---Christian Body Hair Removal, Christian Crabgrass Control, Buster's Hair Restoration and Christian Sleep Apnea Therapy.*

I stood in front of the board realizing that there was nothing on it that was even remotely associated with intercessory prayer, or even Bible study, missions or evangelism. The official looking usher with the nametag noticed my confusion and spoke:

"Can I help you sir?"

I looked at him for a second and asked, "I can't find the prayer meeting. Can you help me find one? Maybe on a Thursday or Friday?"

He looked up and down at the ministry board, stroked his chin and then said, "Hmmm...I don't see anything on the board for any day of the week......ah...what about God's Golfers? They meet on Thursdays..."

God's Golfers? I gave up and just watched the pageant.

I loved the live camels.

The above story illustrates the lamentable truth—*the least attended meeting of the church is the prayer meeting.* Instead of mounting a defense when confronted with this righteous criticism the church should repent of its prayerlessness and cease sitting on our sofas, immovable, attempting to find ways to avoid God's command to pray. The fact is that prayerlessness is only conquered by prayer. I know it sounds too simple, but I believe that that is what it is. Prayerlessness is only defeated by prayer—not reading about prayer, not by going to conferences about prayer and not by listening to sermons about prayer. Prayer occurs when we pray. And here is the exciting perspective. If you start praying you will notice the obvious connection between your prayers and God's answers. When that occurs you will want to pray more. And then the vision and power for prayer will grow in you and you will become a genuine prayer warrior.

Why we do not pray

The simplest answer is that Satan attacks prayer and those who engage in it as if it was a life and death issue with him...and it is. Any perceptive Christian knows that when he/she begins to pray the telephone will ring, the neighbors will knock at the door, the dog will get sick on the carpet, or something else will just come up. A few of these occurrences strung together should tip Satan's hand. Prayer is the last thing that Satan wants you to do and he will oppose it with everything at his disposal. My suggestion: *Find out the things that Satan doesn't want you to do and then do them.*

The following are some of the reasons why we don't pray:

We have been trained not to:

The world system is arrayed against prayer and considers it a medieval practice that brands the participants as imbeciles...or worse. Television sitcoms, late night comedians, our own peer groups and non-Christian educators all engage in our "training." The world hates prayer and wants to eradicate it from the public square. They will use any and all methods to do so, including mockery and disregard. The simple fact is that modern pagan American culture trains us to not pray, and many of us have bought in to it.

My suggestion: Permit the Holy Spirit to be your teacher and ignore the "training" from the corrupt world and its pagan toadies. I can guarantee that when you pray and see the powerful results you will realize how empty the world's reasons for not praying are. A million insults shoveled out upon God's kingdom principles cannot offset the blessings of a prayer-filled life.

NOTE: *Any mature Christian should know that the world and its attractions cannot hold a candle to the blessings that come from the living God. It should not take much thought for us to ignore the world's input and press into a deep prayer relationship with the true God Who has saved us from death and hell.*

The specter of time:

It seems like we never have time for prayer. The tyranny of the urgent presses in on all of us. We have to do the mundane things of life just to survive—work, pay the bills, cultivate business relationships, be soccer parents, love our families, etc. These things scream at us for attention and can drown out the Holy Spirit's still small voice beckoning us into the prayer closet. The only answer is to just make the time and do it. Remember the prayer in Psalm 5 dealing with the fact of continual prayer being offered to God,

Give ear to my words, O LORD, Consider my groaning. Heed the sound of my cry for help, my King and my God, For to You I pray. In the morning, O LORD, You will hear my voice; in the morning I will order my prayer to You and eagerly watch (Psalm 5:1-3).

My suggestion: *Start your schedule with Christ at the center. Then add the other things that need to be included. Like the psalmist in Psalm 5 meet with your Lord early in the morning and ask Him for your daily marching orders. He will answer you and guide your steps. Redeem the time and pray!*

We have so few models:

When I first became a Christian, many years ago, I read a book called ***Praying Hyde.***[49] John Hyde was a Christian who was famous for being a prayer warrior. The man prayed so intensely and for such lengthy periods of time, that he became a model for prayer consistency and dogged determination. Many people around the world contacted John Hyde whenever they were faced with an impossible prayer. He would pray and ask the Lord if He wanted him to undertake the task and if given permission from the Lord would take on the burden and pray it through—no matter how long it took. The testimonies concerning John Hyde's prayer victories are prodigious. He was the epitome of a prayer warrior. Unfortunately, I haven't heard of any prayer warrior that seems to be on the same level as John Hyde in our day.

I do remember that during my early years as a Christian I did meet many serious and powerful prayer warriors. It seemed at that time that every church had at least one or more of those special people. Unfortunately, in our modern day of slick churches and fast-food ministries the supply of prayer warriors seems to have dried up. Any that do survive are considered dinosaurs by the new wave of trendy twenty-first century Christians.

This is a sad situation.

We are lazy:

There is no nice way to put it. Like many people in our modern society, we are lazy and universally seek the easy way out of everything. American culture is predicated on fast foods and time saving shortcuts. Christians are not exempt from society's mad dash to the sofa. Simply put, prayer is hard work. There is no fast way to pray and get it out of the way. Faced with the "work" of prayer it is easy for us to ignore it.

---

[49] Praying Hyde: The Life of John Praying Hyde edited by: E. G. Carre Bridge-Logos Publishing/ 1983

My suggestion: *See prayer as a form of exercise—spiritual exercise. Get up off the sofa and exercise your spiritual muscles. Just get it done, before you start getting flabby and out-of-shape and ready to join the march toward oblivion. One prayer warrior told me that her way to counter her tendency to fall asleep during prayer is to take a "prayer walk." She described how she will get up and take a walk around the neighborhood or go to a high school track and pray while putting in the laps. She lost weight and built up her prayer muscles at the same time.*

We are selfish:

Revival prayer by its very nature is never self-centered. The persons that cry out for revival are going to be concerned about other people's needs and the condition of the church—personal desires will always be secondary. For thousands of years the prayer warriors in God's kingdom have followed this path. It is only recently that a new theology has appeared in the American church. It is labeled "the name and claim it movement" or "the health and wealth gospel" and is based on personal self-interests. The leaders in this movement are easily recognized by their focus on their main goal of pushing a personal aggrandizement doctrine that centers on getting stuff from God. The "faith teachers" all speak a mantra that claims that personal human faith is the key factor in getting our perceived needs met.[50] In their theology, the central proof of successful faith is the reception of the things that you ask God for. If you don't get what you want you don't have enough faith and if you do get what you want you get to write a book, sell some CDs, buy a plane and three houses and get booked on TBN. The movement from top to bottom is a typical American phenomenon that doesn't fit well with the unselfish foundation of revival prayer.

The Book of Joel and Prayer

The Book of Joel (approximately 835 B.C.) is one of those Old Testament books that are read for one set of verses and seldom read in its entirety. The standout verses are in chapter 2 verses 28-32. They are the verses that promise the outpouring of the Holy Spirit in the last days:

It will come about after this (the last days) that I will pour out My Spirit on all mankind; and your sons and daughters will prophesy, your old men will dream dreams, your young men will see visions. Even on the male and female servants I will pour out My Spirit in those days. I will display wonders in the sky and on the earth, blood, fire and columns of smoke. The sun will be turned into darkness and the moon into blood before the great and awesome day of the Lord comes. And it will come about that whoever calls on the name of the Lord will be delivered... (Joel 2:28-32).[50]

---

[50] The Apostle Peter in the Book of Acts answered the question concerning whose faith is responsible for the miraculous. It was on the occasion of the miracle performed on the lame beggar in Acts 3:11-16. Peter made two major points when faced with the crowd's adulation for the

The importance of the Book of Joel, however, isn't just because of those prophetic verses. It is a blueprint concerning how God's people are to respond to great threats and tragedies that are befalling the nation (any nation and at any time in history). In it we are introduced to a major threat to the land of Israel and the possibility of the non-survival of its population. The threat was the disaster brought about by an invasion of locusts that had destroyed the crops and all vegetation leaving a barren and utterly destroyed land that was devoid of any food or water. This locust invasion was so devastating and thorough that the Lord blurs the distinctions between an army made of insects, driven by instinct, to comparisons with future human armies, driven by greed, violence, and satanic purposes.

The word of the Lord that came to Joel, the son of Pethuel: Hear this, O elders, and listen all inhabitants of the land. Has anything like this happened in your days or in your father's days? Tell your sons about it, and let your sons tell their sons, and their sons the next generation. What the gnawing locust has left, the swarming locust has eaten; and what the swarming locust has left, the creeping locust has left, the stripping locust has eaten; awake, drunkards, and weep and wail all you wine drinkers, on account of the sweet wine that is cut off from your mouth. For a nation has invaded my land, mighty and without number, its teeth are the teeth of a lion, and it has the fangs of a lioness. It has made my vine a waste and my fig tree splinters. It has stripped them bare and cast them away; their branches have become white. (Joel 1:1-7).

The Lord spends the next verses (8-13) describing the utter devastation that has fallen upon the land. He lists: The grain offering and the drink offering are cut off (v. 9); the fields are ruined (v.10-12); all the fruit trees are destroyed (v. 12); and the very offerings used in the temple worship are missing (v. 13). The Lord speaks to the devastated people and informs them that they are responsible for the outpouring of wrath because of their act of ignoring God and despising His rule:

Be ashamed, O farmers, wail O vinedressers, for the wheat and the barley; because the harvest of the field is destroyed. (v. 11).

The Lord's point cannot be missed. The people must realize that they have caused the destruction because of their lack of intercession and repentance. The truth is crystal clear—God will not be mocked. His

---

performance of the miracle: First he said: "Why do you gaze at us, as if by our own power or piety (faith) we had made him walk." Peter then said, "And on the basis of faith in His name, it is the name of Jesus which has strengthened this man whom you see and know; and the faith which comes through Him has given this perfect health in the presence of you all." NOTE: It is the faith that comes from Jesus that is the key. Not some personal human faith that we pump up like a bicycle tire.

people must seek Him and His holiness or experience judgment. There is no escape. There is no vacation we can take away from God.

The Lord, true to His heart of mercy, explains the pathway to forgiveness and healing. He tells them plainly that their only option is to seek His face and cry out for forgiveness.

Gird yourselves with **sackcloth**[51] *and lament, O priests; wail, O ministers of the altar! Come, spend the night in sackcloth O ministers of my God, for the grain offering and the drink offering are withheld from the house of your God.* **Consecrate a fast, proclaim a solemn assembly;** *gather the elders and all the inhabitants of the land to the house of the Lord your God, and cry out to the Lord (seek God's forgiveness and repent). Alas for the day! For the day of the Lord is near, and it will come as destruction from the Almighty (the coming of the Lord for judgment).* (1:13-15).

Threatened with starvation, **God calls on His people to seek revival through prayer and fasting.** He makes it clear that these spiritual exercises and the revival they will create are the only cure for the attack. To make His point the Lord mentions His call to repentance two more times with the addition of the command to "Blow a trumpet in Zion!"

Blow a trumpet in Zion, and sound an alarm on My holy mountain! Let all the inhabitants of the land tremble; for the day of the Lord is coming; surely it is near, a day of darkness and gloom, a day of clouds and thick darkness as the dawn is spreading over the mountains... (Joel 2:1, 2).

And,

Blow a trumpet in Zion, consecrate a fast, proclaim a solemn assembly, gather the people, sanctify the congregation, assemble the leaders, gather the children and the nursing infants. Let the bridegroom come out of his room and the bride out of the bridal chamber. Let the priests, the Lord's ministers, weep between the porch and the altar, and let them say, "Spare Your people, O Lord, and do not make Your inheritance a reproach, a byword among the nations. Why should they among the peoples say 'Where is their God?'" (Joel 2:15-17).

The important points in these commands to pray for revival:
- **Blow a trumpet:** The trumpet was blown to warn "all" the people. It was the call to gather to "do" the Lord's command.
- **Let all the inhabitants of the land tremble:** This is serious business—life and death. No one is given a pass. The

---

[51] **Sackcloth:** A very course, rough fabric woven from flax or hemp. Sackcloth was used in the Old Testament times as a symbol of debasement, mourning, and/or repentance. Someone, a prophet or intercessor, wanting to express a repentant heart would wear the sackcloth covering, sit in ashes, and put the ashes on top of their head. The course material was so rough that it caused a severe itching on the skin of the intercessor/repentant to keep them from relaxing and falling asleep. The ashes signified destruction and ruin and served as a reminder of the seriousness of the situation.

arguments against fasting and holding a solemn assembly are scrapped. Holding a fast and a solemn assembly is just done...period.
Unless we have a suicidal death wish.

NOTE: *It is not a time to hold a potluck or sell CDs. Intercessory prayer, confession of sin, and the receiving and extending forgiveness is the order for the day. Nothing else. Let the performers perform...but do it elsewhere.*

- **Consecrate a fast, proclaim a solemn assembly:** The command to consecrate a fast and proclaim a solemn assembly is the bedrock point of the Lord's argument in the Book of Joel. God's desire is to prompt the nation to intercede so that He may extend the option of grace to offset the fruits of their refusal to obey. It must be said that the intensity of God's commands are not to be minimized. In fact, I feel that in today's climate of apostasy and rebellion the call is even more profound. America's Christians should thank God for the chance to intercede instead of looking for ways to avoid prayer.
- **Sanctify the congregation:** Prepare the people for spiritual intercession (warfare against darkness). The sanctification process is exercised through prayer, confession of sin and repentance. The Word of God makes it clear that without repentance there is no forgiveness of sin (Matthew 4:17).
- **Assemble everyone**: Children, infants, priests, and even a wedding is not enough to keep you away from this serious activity. I think that the take away from this is that there is no valid excuse for non-participation.

NOTE: I make this point for the pastors and leaders. If you are a leader (staff pastor or deacon) within the church and cannot make time to join the congregation in prayer you need to retire. Any senior pastor reading this must understand how important this is. Leaders that are taking the vacation cruise with Jesus instead of joining the battle to save the church and the country need to consider submitting their resignation. We need men and women that understand the importance of intercession and not tourists.

- **Intercessory prayer is unleashed**: Cry out for deliverance with no restraint. There is no stopwatch attached to this action. It is to be exercised until completed.

NOTE: After many years of preaching I have only one pet peeve. It is the fact that every church I have ever preached in has a person chosen to watch their watch and let me know when to wrap up my sermon so the people can escape the church and go off to do the important stuff—like watch NASCAR on TV or a football game. The person with the watch is always the ultimate "bean counter" that has for years guarded the halls of the church to make sure that no real ministry ever takes place. My personal observation—these persons are tenacious.

Suggestion: Put away your watches and remove the clock from the sanctuary. God's people have His work to do. And God isn't on the clock. Oh, and find something for the bean counter to do, like count the beans.

- **When God answers the prayers of His people the world will know that He exists:** The carrying out of God's purposes are so clear and tangible that unbelievers will see the Lord's actions and make the connection. It is a spiritual eye opener and no one will be able to say "Where is their God?"

The connection between prayer and revival

The connection of prayer and revival is indisputable. Every move of God recounted in church history was preceded by and driven by intense, Holy Spirit led prayer. The testimony of the Apostles bear witness along with the testimonies of those great names that roll off the tongue when discussing revival: Edwards, Whitefield, Wesley, Finney, Murray, Booth, Taylor, Brainerd, Campbell, Roberts, Seymour and many more bore witness to the power of prayer to ignite true revival. A revival without prayer is like a plane without an engine.

It will not fly.

Let us look at the prayer that occurred the days before Pentecost:

*They all joined together **constantly in prayer,** along with the women and Mary the mother of Jesus, and with His brothers.* (Acts 1:14).

On the Day of Pentecost the disciples were meeting in prayer,

When the day of Pentecost came, they were all together in one place. Suddenly a sound like the blowing of a violent wind came from heaven and filled the whole house where they were sitting. They saw what seemed to be tongues of fire that separated and came to rest on each of them. All of them were filled with the Holy Spirit and began to speak in other tongues as the Spirit enabled them. (Acts 2:1-4).

After Pentecost the disciples continued to pray,

*They devoted themselves to...**prayer.*** (Acts 2:42).

So what should we do?

First and foremost we must come to the conclusion that revival is needed and is mandated by the Lord. Once we are clear on that we should pray and ask the Holy Spirit how we should proceed.[52] If others do not share your concern and interest you should pray alone. But if you do find like-minded brothers and sisters you can do the following:

---

[52] This truth is key. Christians should always ask God how they should pray. To come to a prayer meeting and pull out some "old manna"—prayers performed according to a pattern we have learned or pray in a ritualistic way--- is not the way to start off a prayer meeting. Remember, God wants to communicate with us and lead the acts of His church: *upon this rock I will build My church; and the gates of Hades will not overpower it.* (Matthew 16:8).

Gather at various times to pray specifically for revival:

On their release, Peter and John went back to their own people and reported all that the chief priests and elders had said to them. When they heard this they raised their voices together in prayer to God. "Sovereign Lord," they said, "You made the heaven and the earth and the sea, and everything in them. You spoke by the Holy Spirit through the mouth of your servant, our father David: Why do the nations rage and the peoples plot in vain? The kings of the earth take their stand and the rulers gather together against the Lord and against His Anointed One. Indeed Herod and Pontius Pilate met together with the Gentiles and the people of Israel in this city to conspire against your holy servant Jesus, whom you anointed. They did what your power and will had decided beforehand should happen. Now Lord, consider their threats and enable your servants to speak your word with great boldness. Stretch out your hand to heal and perform miraculous signs and wonders through the name of your holy servant Jesus." After they prayed, the place where they were meeting was shaken. And they were all filled with the Holy Spirit and spoke the word of God boldly. (Acts 4:23-31).

A specific time for prayer is a great idea. Fixing a schedule not only helps you to keep yourself focused, but will also allow others to rearrange their schedules to coincide with the important task of calling for revival. Revival prayer warriors will look forward to that special time to seek the Lord.

Declare a fast:

It seems that serious fasting has all but disappeared in many churches. Fasting is hard and has a cost, but it is an indispensable action that is cemented within the revealed Word of God. The important point to remember is that God calls for a fast when He so chooses,

Is not this the kind of fasting I have chosen: to loosen the chains of injustice and untie the cords of the yoke, to set the oppressed free and break every yoke! (Isaiah 58:6).

And,

Put on sackcloth, O priests, and mourn: wail, you who minister before the altar. Come, spend the night in sackcloth, you who minister before my God; for the grain offerings and drink offerings are withheld from the house of your God, Declare a holy fast; call a sacred assembly. Summon the elders and all who live in the land to the house of the Lord your God, and cry out to the Lord. (Joel 1:1 14).

Jesus explained that spiritual warfare was to be accompanied by prayer and *fasting*. His point was clear—some demonic powers can only be dislodged from their control of persons and events when believers engage in prayer and fasting. Instead of arguing with the Lord and attempting to empty the word of its meaning we should heed the call,

"...this kind (demon) *goeth out only by prayer and fasting."* (Matthew 17:21).

Declare a fast and pray for revival. Remember the Book of Joel.

Pray without ceasing:

Revival prayer is hard. If it was easy then many more would be doing it. When a person or persons decide to seek the Lord for an outpouring of revival they should understand that it will take time. There is no surefire way to figure out how long it will take until the Lord pours forth His power and presence. The truth is that we are His body and He is the head. We should roll up our sleeves and start praying, because "the head" has ordained it,

Be joyful always' pray continually (without ceasing); give thanks in all circumstances, for this is God's will for you in Christ Jesus. (I Thessalonians 5:16).

Never give up…keep praying.

Pray in faith:

Praying for something that you do not believe in will quickly become an exercise in futility. Faith is required by all who seek the Lord.[53] "Knowing" that God will answer will encourage any prayer team that is seeking the Lord's best and carry them into the experience of the glorious answer. God will honor the prayer uttered from the faithful heart,

Are any of you in trouble? He should pray. Is anyone happy? Let him sing songs of praise. Is any of you sick? He should call the elders of the church to pray over him and anoint him with oil in the name of the Lord. And the prayer offered in faith will make the person well; the Lord will raise him up. If he has sinned, he will be forgiven. Therefore confess your sins to each other and pray for each other so that you may be healed. The prayer of a righteous man is powerful and effective. (James 5:13-16).

Engage in Spiritual Warfare:

Powerful forces are arrayed against revival. It is the last thing that Satan wants. With this understanding, it should be the first thing that we want. Be led by the Holy Spirit and come against the powers that resist the outpouring of the Lord's revival:

Finally, be strong in the Lord and in His mighty power. Put on the full armor of God so that you can take your stand against the devil's schemes. For our struggle is not against flesh and blood, but against the rulers, against the authorities, against the powers of this dark world and

---

[53] Faith is clearly defined in John 3:36 as **obedience** (NASB and KJV see also Hebrews 3:18; 4:6, 11; 5:9). This proves that faith is not a mental assent, an acceptance of a learned doctrine, or a knowledge of religious facts. It is simply—**obedience** to the commands of God (the story of Abraham's offering up of Isaac in Genesis 22:1-18 is a prime example). The truth is paramount to Christians, but is often re-interpreted by modern faith theologies.

against the spiritual forces of evil in the heavenly realms. (Ephesians 6:10-12).

And,

Opening his mouth, Peter said: "I most certainly understand now that God is not one to show partiality, but in every nation the man who fears Him and does what is right is welcome to Him. The word which He sent to the sons of Israel, preaching peace through Jesus Christ (He is Lord of all)— you yourselves know the thing which took place throughout all Judea, starting from Galilee, after the baptism which John proclaimed. You know of Jesus of Nazareth, how God anointed Him with the Holy Spirit and with power, and how He went about doing good and healing all who were oppressed by the devil, for God was with Him. (Acts 10:34-38).[54]

Be led by the Holy Spirit:

It is a fact that human beings are innately powerless. God, however, is all-powerful. Any human being that follows his/her own way will end up in a place they never wanted to go. Always be led by the Holy Spirit and you will find rest,

In the same way, the Spirit helps us in our weakness. We do not know what we ought to pray for, but the Spirit Himself intercedes for us with groans that words cannot express. And He Who searches our hearts knows the mind of the Spirit, because the Spirit intercedes for the saints in accordance with God's will. (Romans 8:26, 27).

Pray in the name of Jesus:

Nowhere are the effects of liberal political correctness felt more than in the United States military's chaplaincy. Recent stories have surfaced concerning complaints arising against Christian chaplains offering prayers in the name of Jesus.[55] The general argument against the use of Jesus' name is usually presented in this form: *Since there are other faiths represented in the military chaplaincy the use of Jesus' name is an affront to those other chaplains and their constituency.* The advocates of the "no prayers in Jesus' name" position make the following invalid points:

- Christian chaplains demanding the right to pray in the name of Jesus are just following "outdated" Christian traditions and really have no theological need to do so.[56]

---

[54] To understand that Jesus Christ Himself relied upon the Holy Spirit to lead and empower His ministry of the supernatural is a sobering fact…or should be.

[55] It must be said that chaplains of other faiths like Judaism, Buddhism, Islam and Hinduism are not censored by the DOD. The arguments are only directed toward Christian chaplains. Simply put, other religions wouldn't stand for any meddling in their activities while it is common knowledge that anyone can kick a Christian…

[56] This is a strange argument in light that the non-Christians using it really have no right to use it against any faith in God that is defined by creed. This fact is embedded in the U.S. Constitution. Imagine a Christian telling a Muslim that the use of Allah is not important to their practice of faith?

- God has many names and is defined in many ways. All of these names are equally valid.[57]
- Political correctness trumps all religious dogma, cultural rules and traditions.[58] Making someone uncomfortable is to be avoided at all costs.

NOTE: The modern twenty-first century church has been battered by the forces of political correctness and has not only been shaken but has been bent and even broken. The Christian church is in fact the only religious institution that must deal with the inhibitions placed on it by an unbelieving society. Jewish Rabbis, Muslim Imams, Buddhist and Hindu priests and all others in the military chaplaincy are never instructed on how to pray in a public service by the powers that be. It is only the Christian chaplains that must "readjust" in order to be allowed to speak. In my opinion, this is a direct interdiction imposed upon Christianity by the new priests of political correctness. And some "Christian" pastors have acquiesced.

So what does the Scripture say about praying in the name of Jesus? Let me present a few of the pertinent verses:

What was the disciples' answer to the Pharisees that demanded to know by what name was the miracle on the lame beggar performed?

When they (the ruling authorities) *had placed them* (the disciples) *in the center, they began to inquire, "By what power, or **in what name**, have you done this?" Then Peter, filled with the Holy Spirit, said to them, "Rulers and elders of the people, if we are on trial today for a benefit done to a sick man, as to how this man has been made well, let it be known to all of you and to all the people of Israel, that by **the name of Jesus Christ the Nazarene**, whom you crucified, whom God raised from the dead—by this name this man stands here before you in good health. He is the* STONE WHICH WAS REJECTED *by you,* THE BUILDERS, *but* WHICH BECAME THE CHIEF CORNER *stone. And there is salvation in no one else; for there is **no other name** under heaven that has been given among men by which we must be saved."* (Acts 4:7-12).

What did Jesus say about praying in His name?

*Whatever you ask in **My name**, that will I do, so that the Father may be glorified in the Son. If you ask Me anything in **My name**, I will do it.* (John 14:13-14).

And,

I would guess that there are a couple of thousand civil rights attorneys that would fight for the right to take the case.

[57] This is a theological opinion and is universally rejected by the chaplains of other faiths. Again the arguments are only directed against Christianity.

[58] Again I must make it clear that this position only effects Christianity. No one can get away with imposing this standard on Islam. To do so would incur the wrath of those very liberals that have no problem with imposing standards on Christianity.

*In that day you will not question Me about anything. Truly, truly, I say to you, if you ask the Father for anything in **My name**, He will give it to you. Until now you have asked for nothing in **My name**; ask and you will receive, so that your joy may be made full. "These things I have spoken to you in figurative language; an hour is coming when I will no longer speak to you in figurative language, but will tell you plainly of the Father. In that day you will ask in **My name**, and I do not say to you that I will request of the Father on your behalf; for the Father Himself loves you, because you have loved Me and have believed that I came forth from the Father.* (John 16:23-27).

In what name are prayers for healing heard?

*Is anyone among you sick? Then he must call for the elders of the church and they are to pray over him, ¹anointing him with oil **in the name of the Lord**;* (James 5:14).

NOTE: I want to make a valid point. If the Word of God states plainly that the prayers for supernatural healing are to be said in the name of Jesus Christ the contrary must also be true - without praying in the name of Jesus the intercessor shouldn't expect healing to occur.

In what name are Christians commanded to pray?

*Always giving thanks for all things in **the name** of **our** Lord Jesus Christ to God, even the Father;* (Ephesians 5:20).

And,

*To the church of God which is at Corinth, to those who have been sanctified in Christ Jesus, saints by calling, with all who in every place call on **the name** of our Lord Jesus Christ, **their Lord and ours**:* (I Corinthians 1:2).

How did the disciples handle a command from the government to cease using the name of Jesus?

*When they had brought them, they stood them before the Council. The high priest questioned them, saying, **"We gave you strict orders not to continue teaching in this name,** and yet, you have filled Jerusalem with your teaching and intend to bring this man's blood upon us." **But Peter and the apostles answered, "We must obey God rather than men.** The God of our fathers raised up Jesus, whom you had put to death by hanging Him on a cross. He is the one whom God exalted to His right hand as a Prince and a Savior, to grant repentance to Israel, and forgiveness of sins. And we are witnesses of these things; and so is the Holy Spirit, whom God has given to those who obey Him."* (Acts 5:27-32).

What was Jesus' warning to those that refuse to mention His name before men?

"Therefore everyone who confesses Me before men, I will also confess him before My Father who is in heaven. But whoever denies Me

before men, I will also deny him before My Father who is in heaven. (Matthew 10:32-33).

It doesn't take a Bible scholar to realize that praying in the name of Jesus Christ is a big deal. No power on earth, government bureaucracy, military top brass, politician, or frightened, cowering Christian has the authority to change the will of God on any subject. We have been given severe warnings in several places in the Bible concerning any changes that we may try to make to God's Word.

I am amazed that you are so quickly deserting Him who called you by the grace of Christ, for a different gospel; which is really not another; only there are some who are disturbing you and want to distort the gospel of Christ. But even if we, or an angel from heaven, should preach to you a gospel contrary to what we have preached to you, he is to be accursed! As we have said before, so I say again now, if any man is preaching to you a gospel contrary to what you received, he is to be accursed! (Galatians 1:6-9).

And,

"For I testify unto everyone who hears the words of the prophecy of this book, if anyone adds to these things, God will add to him the plagues that are written in this book; And if anyone takes away from the words of this book of this prophecy, God shall take away his part from the Book of Life, and from the holy city, and from the things which are written in this book." (Revelation 22:18-19).

And,

"Now, O Israel, listen to the statutes and the judgments which I am teaching you to perform, so that you may live and go in and take possession of the land which the LORD, *the God of your fathers, is giving you. You shall not add to the word which I am commanding you, nor take away from it, that you may keep the commandments of the* LORD *your God which I command you.*(Deuteronomy 4:1-2).

In my opinion, any chaplain in the military that claims to be representing Jesus Christ should stand his ground and not budge in the matters of the faith. Like Peter, they should disobey any satanic orders (no matter who issues them) that demand them to deny the living Christ. There is no argument that can be mounted to prove otherwise.

NOTE TO THE MILITARY CHAPLAINS: *Instead of being afraid of losing your pension you should be more afraid of the judgment of God. Don't preach a watered down gospel to the soldiers, sailors, air men and marines that may die in combat to protect our families. They are depending on you for the undiluted message of Christ that will save their souls and prepare them for their possible death. Do not take part in the satanic liberal plan to empty the gospel of its power in order to partake in the opportunity to eternally damn the souls of these extremely important members of our society. Remember, you are a Christian first* *and a soldier second. Obey God or remove your chaplaincy cross from your uniform and get out.*

Just a thought.

A final point: *Prayer warriors are worth their weight in gold. If you are fortunate enough to have some in your church treat them with deep respect. If the truth be known they are literally dragging you and the rest of your church into the blessings of God. Don't force them to do this while you are "kicking and screaming" over your perceived right to sit on the sofa like a beached whale and forego prayer. Get a clue: Prayer warriors are worth more than a dump truck load of robotic church council members. They are far and away the most important people you know in God's kingdom.*

Pray to God that they do not get tired of your neglect and go elsewhere…

In closing

Prayer is the most indispensable part of our relationship with God. Without it we become like ships in the night passing by our safe harbor and never making landfall. Prayer opens up the doors of God's possibilities, drawing our human spirits into an alignment with His Spirit. One praying Christian could alter the path of history and touch a million souls. One praying Christian could light the fire of revival. One praying Christian could literally save an entire nation.

Pray for revival.

Chapter Six
Whatever Happened to Sin?
"Who can say, 'I have kept my heart pure; I am clean and without sin?'" - Proverbs 20:9

In the 1970s comedian Flip Wilson was all the rage.[59] The man was a comic genius. One of his most famous characters was "Geraldine," a street wise black woman who always excused her indiscretions by saying, *"The Devil made me do it."* Geraldine's declaration was such a hit that it was emblazoned on T-shirts and circled the globe.

Mr. Wilson's comic routine was just for fun, but he hit upon a change that was taking place in our society—the shifting of all personal responsibility for any bad personal choices to outside factors. Overnight, people all over the world were saying *"the Devil made me do it"* whenever faced with any indiscretions or personal problems. On the surface it was all for comic relief, but when considered soberly and honestly, the truth cannot be ignored: Sin is a personal problem that exists because of personal choices.[60] The Geraldine defense, *"the Devil made me do it,"* might be partly true, Satan can interject temptation into the situation, but it simply isn't the full truth.

In order for any clear understanding of the reality of sin we need to make an investigation of its origin. The only sure way of doing this is to go to the only trustworthy source—the Holy Bible.

The origin of sin

With respect to the origin of sin in the universe, we are faced with two choices: First, we can accept the thousands of theories and opinions presented by mankind, or secondly, accept the biblical account. Some of the theories and opinions of unbelieving mankind are:

- There is no such thing as sin. Sin is just variances within human behavior that are considered "evil" according to human standards, myths and cultural traditions.
- Sin against God is impossible since there is no God.
- Sin may have some resemblance to fact, but God is changeable and can see things differently when he reflects on how human behavior is altered by the events and circumstances that confront

---

[59] **Flip Wilson** (December 8, 1933-November 25, 1998) was an African American comedian and actor. In the early 1970s, Wilson hosted his own weekly variety series, the Flip Wilson Show. The series earned Wilson a Golden Globe and two Emmy Awards. He died of liver cancer in 1998.
[60] In Chapter three I presented a definition of sin. In this Chapter I will again define the word. **SIN:** Is the Old English archery term for "missing the mark." In theological terms sin is anything contrary to Law of God. For example: If you lie you have sinned (Exodus 20:16). If you commit murder you have sinned (Romans 20:13). Sin is lawlessness (I John 1:3) It is unrighteousness (I John 5:17). Sin leads to separation from God, bondage and eternal death (Romans 6:14-23).

human beings. In other words, God is adaptable to our needs—the evolving God theory.
- Sin is just another name for "wrong thinking." Wrong thinking is the definition used by secular psychiatry and therapy.
- And ad infinitum...

The major problem with all of these theories and opinions is that those developing them weren't present at the creation of the universe and don't have a clue what happened. The Bible addresses this problem:

Then the Lord answered Job out of the whirlwind and said, "Who is this that darkens counsel by words without knowledge? Now gird your loins like a man, and I will ask you, and you instruct Me! Where were you when I laid the foundation of the earth? Tell Me, if you have understanding. Who set its measurements? Since you know. Or who stretched a line on it?" (Job 38:1-5).

The answer, of course, is that the only valid source of information regarding these questions is God. He alone is the only Person present at the beginning and thus the only source of truth concerning the questions of the origin of sin.

According to the Scriptures sin was birthed at the time of the angelic creation—when God spoke the angels into existence and gave them positions within His creation. For some reason a third of them rebelled against God's decisions and attempted a mutiny.[61] The Scriptures describe it:

And there was a war in heaven, Michael and his angels waging war with the dragon (Satan). The dragon and his angels waged war (rebellion against God), and they were not strong enough, and there was no longer a place for them in heaven (judgment). And the great dragon was thrown down, the serpent (snake in the Garden of Eden) who is called the devil and Satan, who deceives the whole world; he was thrown down to the earth, and his angels were thrown down with him. (Revelation 12:7-9 see also Jude 6 and II Peter 2:5).

It seems obvious that the fallen angels were dissatisfied with God's rulership and decided to rebel against His authority. The leader of the rebellion was Lucifer, one of the archangels, who was renamed Satan or the Devil (Isaiah 14:12-15).

---

[61] Many theologians believe that one-third of the angels rebelled with Lucifer. They state two reasons for their position. First, the verse in Revelation 12:1-9 that describes the war in heaven where it is mentioned that the Devil (Serpent) was cast down to earth with his angels and that his tail swept away a third of the stars of heaven and threw them to the earth. The stars, according to many theologians, were the angels that followed Satan in his rebellion. Secondly, they state the fact that three archangels are mentioned in the Bible—Michael, Gabriel and Lucifer. In their opinion, this is an indication that Lucifer (Satan) had command of one-third of the angels and the other two archangels had their two-thirds.

The impartation of sin to the human race

The events concerning mankind's fall in the Garden of Eden chronicled in Genesis is the scriptural explanation of sin's pathway into the human race. The non-believing world attempts to dismiss the story through mockery—by pointing toward its supposed unsophistication. This attempt to minimize the biblical account is quite laughable, especially since the "experts" weren't there and have no plausible justification for judging the biblical account. The biblical story is simple and yet profound.

We begin in Genesis 3 after the Lord made the heavens and the earth and after the fall of Satan and his angels. God had created Adam and Eve and told them that the only thing in the Garden that was withheld from them was the tree of knowledge of good and evil.[62] The Lord made it clear that if they would disobey His commands to not eat of the fruit, they would suffer death. It seemed like a simple request, but Satan, smarting from the judgment that short-circuited his rebellion against God, decided to carry his revolution into the hearts of mankind.

Now the serpent (Satan) was more crafty than any beast of the field which the Lord God had made. And he (Satan) said to the woman, "Indeed, has God said, 'You shall not eat from any tree of the garden'?" The woman said to the serpent, "From the fruit of the trees in the garden we may eat; but from the fruit of the tree which is in the middle of the garden, God has said, "You shall not eat from it or touch it, or you will die."" The serpent said to the woman, "You surely will not die! For God knows that in the day you eat from it your eyes will be opened, and you will be like God, knowing good and evil." When the woman saw that the tree was good for food, and that it was a delight to the eyes, and that the tree was desirable to make one wise, she took from the fruit and ate; and she gave some to her husband with her, and he ate. Then the eyes of both of them were opened, and they knew that they were naked; and they sewed fig leaves together and made themselves loin coverings. They heard the sound of the Lord God walking in the garden in the cool of the day, and the man and his wife hid themselves from the presence of the Lord God among the trees of the garden. Then the Lord God called to the man, and said to him, "Where are you?" He said, "I heard the sound of You in the garden, and I was afraid because I was naked; so I hid myself." And He (God) said, "Who told you that you were naked? Have you eaten from the tree of which I commanded you not to eat?" The man said, "The woman whom You gave to be with me, she gave me from the tree and I ate." Then the Lord God said to the woman, "What is this you have done?" And the woman said, "The serpent deceived me and I ate."

---

[62] The test was **obedience**. Would mankind obey God or would they endorse Satan's rebellion and make themselves adversaries of God?

The Lord God said to the serpent, "Because you have done this, cursed are you more than all cattle, and more than every beast of the field; on your belly you will go, and dust you will eat all the days of your life; and I will put enmity between you and the woman, and between your seed and her seed; he shall bruise you on the head, and you shall bruise him on the heel." To the woman He said, "I will greatly multiply your pain in childbirth, in pain you will bring forth children; yet your desire will be for your husband, and he will rule over you." Then to Adam He said, "Because you have listened to the voice of your wife, and have eaten from the tree about which I commanded you, saying, 'You shall not eat from it'; cursed is the ground because of you; in toil you will eat of it all the days of your life. Both thorns and thistles it shall grow for you; and you will eat the plants of the field; by the sweat of your face you will eat bread, till you return to the ground, because from it you were taken; for you are dust, and to dust you shall return." (Genesis 3:1-19).

The major points in the satanic attack:
- Satan (the serpent) contradicted God's words by saying: **"You surely will not die!"**
- Satan interjected his second lie: The accusation that God had an ulterior motive—to keep the "truth" of mankind's divine nature hidden from man: *"For God knows that in the day you eat from it* (the tree) *your eyes will be opened and **you will be like God** knowing good and evil."*

  FACT: *The human desire to be like God is the root of all human sin and extends throughout human history.*
- Eve saw that sin was pleasurable and enticing.[63] She ate the fruit.
- Eve, like all sinners, had a desire to include others in her sin. This is a universal desire—**sinners love company**. She gave the fruit to her husband and he ate. Adam's act sealed the fate of mankind.
- Adam and Eve immediately were conscious of their sin. This touched off a chain reaction of desperate evasive maneuvers. First, they tried to hide from God by covering their sin. Secondly, out of desperation they made their own coverings out of fig leaves (a type of human works) to assuage their guilt.
- God, ever the fount of grace, made an attempt to draw them out of their lies in order to extend mercy and grace.[64] Adam and

---

[63] If sin was not, in a fleshly sense, a pleasurable experience mankind would find it easier to resist. It is a universal truth that most sinful acts feel good when first experienced. It is only after the sin has been completed that negative effects associated with the sinful act surface and cause any soul-searching and regret.

[64] Many theologians believe that this was God's extension of grace. No one knows for sure what would have happened if Adam would have taken God's offer and confessed his sin.

Eve, rebellious to the core, defended themselves against God (a universal act of sinners).
- Exhibiting typical sinful behavior, both Adam and Eve blamed others: Adam blamed God and the woman by saying: *"The woman whom **You** gave to be with me, **she** gave me from the tree, and I ate."* Eve pulled "the Flip Wilson Geraldine excuse" and blamed the Devil by saying, *"The serpent deceived me, and I ate."*
- God, unmoved by their excuses, held them all responsible, Adam, Eve and the Devil (serpent), for their individual actions and judged them all—one by one.
- God taught them two universal truths: First, sin brings death. The death of the animals that God used to make the skins that covered their nakedness was exhibit A, and secondly, God's act of sacrifice showed that only a death (the shedding of blood) can cover their sins. He made this clearer as history proceeded from that moment on until the full disclosure in Christ.

The Lord then made it clear that sin brings a separation from God by driving Adam and Eve out of the Garden of Eden and stationing angelic cherubim as guards to the entrance of the garden.[65] Mankind was cursed and began the cycle of life and death that the entire race has undergone. The Scriptures make it clear that this first sin against God was the start of sin's appearance on earth. The consequence of sin is death. Without any apparent remedy death continued, unabated, until the sacrifice of Jesus occurred on Mt. Calvary. The Apostle Paul in his letter to the Romans presented a clear and concise explanation of how sin was present in mankind from the very beginning:

Therefore, just as through one man sin entered into the world, and death through sin, and so death spread to all men, because all sinned---for until the Law sin was in the world, but sin is not imputed when there is no law. Nevertheless death reigned from Adam to Moses, even over those who had not sinned in the likeness of the offense of Adam, who is a type of Him who was to come. But the free gift is not like the transgression. For if by the transgression of the one (Adam's sin) the many died, much more did the grace of God and the gift by the grace of the one Man, Jesus Christ (His sacrifice), abound to the many. The gift is not like that which came through the one who sinned; for on the one hand the judgment arose from one transgression resulting in condemnation, but on the other hand the free gift arose from many transgressions resulting in justification. For if by the transgression of the one (Adam), death reigned through the one, much more those who receive the abundance of grace and of the gift of righteousness will reign

---

[65] This is the revelation that sin—on any level—creates a separation between man and God.

in life through the One, Jesus Christ. So then as through one transgression there resulted condemnation to all men (a fallen sin nature and death), even so through one act of righteousness (the sacrifice on the cross) there resulted justification of life to all men. For as through the one man's disobedience the many were made sinners, even so through the obedience of the One the many will be made righteous...(Romans 5:12-19).

Original sin (the sin nature) is born in each human being, but the individual acts of sin enter the human experience in many ways. The acts of sin come through the modeling of others (the sinful example of friends and peers), through the lust of the eyes, the shallow promises of greed, the desire for power and control, and many other various ways. Throughout history, sin, although shaped by human culture into different adaptive forms, has been very consistent in its attacks. Only a blind and deaf man could say that he doesn't have a clue concerning the reality of sin.

Modern American culture denies the existence of sin

Although human history has always exhibited the presence of sin and evil, it has only been within the last two hundred years that outright rejection of God and His Word has become universally and officially accepted as a cultural norm. This new reality has become the standard because of the following factors:

- The elevation of humanism and its subsequent reliance on human wisdom coupled with new age knowledge (man is divine) is now the only message that is promoted in the nation's universities. Academia is closed to any biblical input and guards against it with a ferocity bordering on mania. To be a Christian at an American university is to be a modern leper.
- The majority of human beings, desiring to continue their sinful lives without the inconvenience of guilt, have jumped on the bandwagon and embraced the humanistic and new age delusion. Their acceptance of the new reality is not based on ideology like the leaders of academia but is nothing more than an act of convenience.
- The media explosion has united mankind with instantaneous support for human rebellion. Instead of sinners left to their own devices which was the reality of the past two millennia, millions of sinners can encourage each other on to new lows of apostasy at the push of a button on a cell phone. This has created instant support for universal depravity that drowns out any biblical message. The carnal rabble has finally discovered Shangri-La: *Their acts of sin are not evil because everyone is doing it.*

The modern liberal thinkers that have gained control of the American political and educational system over the last hundred years have practiced their technique of re-definition on the subject of sin with a vengeance. They have done this for one simple reason: In order to advance their "new age" agenda of the deification of humankind, God and His Word had to be eradicated from the public consciousness. Realizing that a full removal of God consciousness was impossible—there will always be genuine Christians that will resist the attack against God and His Word—the purveyors of the new age immorality and debauchery developed the concept of re-definition. Their modus operandi is simple:

Redefine sin and empty it of any divine connections.
- Undermine the Bible and make it an object of mockery.[66]
- Promote the two key lies of new age America: The lie of the innate goodness of man and the lie of human deity.
- Substitute alternative "spiritual" disciplines (false religions) devoid of any reference to the true, biblical God.[67]
- Create the atmosphere where the Apostle Paul's warning in II Timothy 3:1-5 will be emptied of any fear of impending judgment and instead embraced in the name of freedom.[68]
- Generate and fuel a war on Christianity that fulfills Isaiah's prophecy: *Woe to those who call evil good and good evil; who substitute darkness for light and light for darkness; who substitute bitter for sweet and sweet for bitter...*(Isaiah 5:20).
- A denial of any and all Christian roots concerning the founding of America. This full scale attack is present at the earliest stages of public education—beginning in grade school, continuing on through secondary school and on into college and graduate school.[69]

Make no mistake, the vast numbers of individuals engaged in this re-interpretation of history are working 24/7 to bring their "brave new

---

[66] The entirety of Western civilization has been mobilized to destroy God's word: the entertainment industry, politics, the educational system, science, etc. have all been drafted by Satan into this endeavor.

[67] The proliferation of new age and Eastern cults that deny Christianity and replace it with a false, soul-destroying gospel.

[68] There can be no serious argument raised against the fact that evil is increasing with rapidity throughout the earth.

[69] The argument of pagan America is that the United States has never been a "Christian nation." The supporters of these arguments point to the enigma of the founding fathers. Many of them were not true Christians, but only influenced by the eighteenth century Christian culture that was once a restraining influence. The Christian influence within the founding documents, according to the argument, did not reflect on the framer's personal convictions, but was only the result of the habits and traditions of the time. This is arguably true, but the argument fails to eradicate the obvious Christian contributions to the founding of America. Although the Christian influence in the founding documents is a source of embarrassment to the modern intelligentsia that would re-write these documents in order to reflect their new age principles, the facts are plain. Revealed Christianity played a major part in our history and cannot be ignored.

WARNING: *Expect a future "new Constitutional Convention" to be proposed in order to "update" the Constitution and make it more palatable to the new age mentality.*

world" into existence. They will not rest until they have accomplished their task to promote the new hedonistic concepts of sin accommodation so revered by liberal progressives. Their point of attack will be God's church and His Word. They will never cease to make the church nothing but a "cosmic killjoy" bent on undermining the new and popular "freedoms" (sins) that are enjoyed by a debauched society. Classifying the biblical church as enemies of the state was necessary to put forth abortion, adultery, homosexual perversion, greed, rebellion, governmental lying and thievery and other acts of evil as normal, acceptable human behaviors. The humanist therapists became the new priests of the liberal, humanist, new age movement, and confidently explained away sin and evil by emptying the Word of any biblical meaning and re-defining it as psychological aberrations, alternative lifestyles, and expressions of personal freedom.[70] Those that can read a Bible call it sin.

Enter the medical model

Although sin is all but forgotten in American culture and has become only the punch line of some godless comedian, the problem of sin still exists. Modern America, feeding its delusions about the goodness of human nature, still has the problem of evil. Only a blind man could say that evil does not exist and that something that looks like sin is running amok in our land. What could modern America do and still keep its fantasies intact?

The problem was solved with the emergence of the medical model. The medical model is secular psychology's attempt to explain why people do "bad" things…without the input of God and the Bible.

The secular psychologist, unwilling to accept the fact of God's existence and the concept of personal sin, reinterprets the bad actions of their clients in a different light. Their clients are victims…not sinners in need of repentance. The system excuses personal responsibility and lays blame on outside events, experiences and the reprehensible choices of other people that are not their clients. Yes, I know that sinful people, circumstances and events do have a major impact on human beings and these "actions" do play a major role in the destruction of humanity. I know this, but I also know that our sin nature is the breeding ground within our hearts that allows these seeds of depravity to germinate.

The secular psychologists and therapists ignore the sin nature of humanity and advance their goal to help the victim rebuild their self-esteem—without God's forgiveness. The lack of self-esteem, in the therapist's opinion, is the worst situation that any human being can experience.

---

[70] The Bible condemns any attempt by humankind to elevate their intellect to the level of being the yardstick of reality. God sits in the heavens and laughs at this nonsense (Psalms 2:4-6).

NOTE: *Self-esteem, when placed in context, is a good thing and definitely is biblical.*

The Apostle Paul saw healthy self-esteem as an outflow from the acknowledgement of personal sin, the acceptance of Christ's forgiveness and the elevation of Jesus Christ as Lord within the human heart. Paul's "self-esteem" was always viewed as coming from Christ and a barrier to all boasting,

May I never boast except in the cross of our Lord Jesus Christ, through which the world has been crucified to me and I to the world. (Galatians 6:14).

Secular therapists have no true understanding of sin and guilt. In their opinion, guilt is bad… and since the Bible speaks of man's guilt the Bible is bad. With this reasoning firmly in place the secular therapists reach their ultimate conclusion that preachers that sermonize against sin are bad.[71] This is why there is such a war against any preacher who publically reads the verses within the Bible concerning sin. Admitting that you are a sinner in this culture is the worst thing you can do. Recognizing that you are a sinner is a fatal blow to the inflated human self-esteem.

Billions of dollars have been funneled into the therapy industry to insure that sinners learn that anything they have done wrong is someone else's fault. It is never them. The therapy gurus teach that the human struggle is not against our propensity to sin, but our need for self-esteem.

The following is my opinion of the foundational "facts" that propel the billion dollar therapy industry:

- No one is guilty of sin because sin, in a Biblical sense, does not exist.
- People who do wrong things are sick and not sinners. Their sickness has been caused by external factors making them victims. They are victims of—society, church, false concepts of morality, actions of others, etc. It is everyone else's fault. All they need to be healed is to engage in "right thinking"— promoted by the secular therapists (the new "priests" of the psychotherapy cult).
- Secular therapy's goal is to remove all guilt because guilt is bad and hinders the self-esteem of the victim. Imagine the freedom from guilt when I discovered that the reason I hit Billy with the baseball bat was that my mom refused to give me ice cream with my apple pie at my fifth birthday party! Mom became the rat

---

[71] Food for thought: If a preacher is dismissed by the secular psychologists and therapists, it might be that the preacher is truly Christian and preaching the truth. The leaders of the new-age cult of liberalism will always find fault with a true man or woman of God.

and I became the victim...and poor Billy just got a large bump on his head.
- And the best "fact" of all. The golden goose of all secular pop therapies: Victims are never healed but are constantly "recovering." This is the perfect set up, the great holy grail of therapy. The victim can never discover that the therapy is useless because there never is an end to it. The client, trapped on the "merry-go-round" of never-ending therapy, will never understand that their only purpose is to fatten the purses of the therapist. Just imagine the land investments that have been made by the slick therapists who feed off the victims like vultures? Their final word at every session: *"I'll see you again next week."* And, oh yes, "bring the money…"

A humorous evaluation of the victim theory

The utter nonsense surrounding the victimization theory is highlighted when we take a penetrating and humorous look at a mythical secular therapy session. The client is Adolf Hitler and like millions of therapy clients he is learning to reinterpret and dismiss his guilt:

Therapist: "Mr. Hitler, does it cause you pain when you hear people accuse you of mass atrocities against humanity?"

Hitler: "Yah, it hurts mein feelings."

Therapist: "Well, your feelings will change when you discover the real reason why you gassed six million Jews and launched the world into a total war that cost 50 million lives."

Hitler: "Und how ist dat?"

Therapist: "You really had no choice, my fuhrer, you're a victim."

Hitler: "Please liebchin, tell me vhat you mean."

Therapist: "Do you remember how you felt when little Reinhardt didn't invite you to his Bar Mitzvah?"

Hitler: Oh yah, the pain vas terrible. I cried for days."

Therapist: Reinhardt's social slight damaged your self-esteem, causing you to harbor your pain deep within your psyche. When you saw those Jews you saw little Reinhardt making fun of you. You gassed them to allow your wounds to be healed."

Hitler: "So you're saying it's all Reinhardt's fault?"

Therapist: "Well, Reinhardt's one of my clients so I can't blame him. We're working on shifting the responsibility to his mother, which is easy since she's Jewish and thusly the perfect scapegoat."

Hitler: "But I liked Reinhardt's mama, she baked some vunderful strudel. Ah, can ve find someone else to blame…maybe the Russians?"

Therapist: "Only if she becomes one of my clients. Then we would have to find someone else to blame."

Hitler: "Vhat?"

Therapist: "I can't blame one of my clients...after all, they are giving me money..."
Hitler: "Oh...I see..."

Satan's devious plan to destroy sin consciousness

The eradication of sin consciousness is by far the most devious and yet ingenious plan Satan ever devised. By erasing the fact of sin and the repentance that would cleanse the sinner, he has deflected the saving gospel of Jesus Christ and insured the final destruction of billions of souls. The coming of Jesus was the full disclosure of God's plan to deal with the sin question. The eradication of the concept of sin takes away the purpose of God and insulates mankind from its only hope. Satan has polished his plan and made it the bedrock of all rebellion against God.

Let me explain:

- Without the reality of sin there is no need for a Savior. A person who believes he/she is a victim and not a sinner will not reach out for a Savior, but instead will seek the psychological answer...which is no answer at all.
- Without the reality of sin there would be no need for repentance. Without repentance there is no forgiveness. Without forgiveness there is nothing but certain death and judgment. This is the coup-de-grace for unsaved sinners.
- Without the reality of sin there is no need for Jesus to come. The coming of Christ without association with the true reason—sin—makes it a non-event.
- Without the reality of sin there is no reason for Christ to die on the cross. It becomes just a drama with no purpose. The crucifix is emptied of meaning and ends being draped around the neck of some rock star lying drunk on the floor.
- Without the reality of sin there is no need for the resurrection to prove that the sin debt has been paid.
- Without the reality of sin, the entire gospel would be gutted of its main truths and we would be left with nothing.

Satan's deception is powerful. With the eradication of sin and repentance he has literally guaranteed an army of morally bankrupt human beings who will support the Antichrist and wage war on believers. Left unimpeded, Satan will usher in his dark kingdom and crush any and all opposition to his diabolical schemes. Only a revival can thwart this.

God's plan for healing of sin

The Word of God makes it clear that God sees sin in a different way than human beings. Instead of avoiding the issue, like humans do, God presents His opinion in a forthright and completely truthful way. To

God, sin is sin, we all must deal with it, and we can only do this by following His pattern. The pattern is simple.

First, we must admit that we have a sin problem:

"If we claim to be without sin, we deceive ourselves and the truth is not in us. If we confess our sins, he is faithful and just and will forgive our sins and purify us from all unrighteousness. If we claim we have not sinned, we make him out to be a liar and his word has no place in our lives." (I John 1:8-10; see also Romans 3:10-18, 23).

And secondly, we all must acknowledge that repentance and forgiveness are God's way of dealing with our sin problem:

God sets this truth in stone when He ties our forgiveness of sins with our personal repentance. No repentance, no forgiveness.

For if you forgive men who sin against you, your heavenly Father will also forgive you. But if you do not forgive men their sins, your Father will not forgive your sins. (Matthew 6:14, 15).

And lastly, we must practice forgiveness:

After exercising our God-ordained responsibility to acknowledge our guilt, we are directed to forgive those who have sinned against us. People who have learned the power of forgiveness will receive the release from the effects of sin that has corrupted their inner being.

Without the act of forgiveness we remain bound by the acts of sin we have committed and the acts of sin committed against us. Only forgiveness can set the captives free. Only forgiveness can heal the damaged hearts of those who have been Satan's targets. If we forgive we are cleansed. If we refuse to forgive we are inextricably bound to our sin and its destructive results. God has given us no other choice.

FACT: The only cure for sin is the shed blood of Jesus Christ. No therapist, secular psychiatrist, counselor or guru can offer anything that can replace God's plan to heal the human heart. The fact is: The Savior's shed blood is the sum total of God's plan to deliver human beings from the guilt and destructiveness of sin. Revivals are the power thrust of God that sends this message like a rocket carrying a nuclear warhead. The revival targets the sin of mankind and brings the explosion of God's intervention to eradicate the debilitating power of that sin. Because of this fact, revivals are to be sought for the healing that they can only provide.

Pray for revival.

Chapter Seven
Revival Leadership
Then I heard the voice of the Lord, saying, "Whom shall I send, and who will go for us?" Then I said, "Here am I. Send me!" -Isaiah 6: 8

There is nothing more important in a revival than godly leadership. Without it, a revival will flounder and will quickly careen off the rails making negative impact. As the God of order, the Lord has set the essentials for successful revival leadership in His Word. There can be no serious pursuit of revival without an understanding of the basic requirements set forth by God regarding revival leadership. With that fact in mind I present a "top ten" list of the more important prerequisites of those that have been chosen to lead in a revival:

1. Those who lead revivals must be able to "see" the coming darkness and sound the warning:

Revival leaders are designated as "watchmen on the walls."[72] This description is found in many parts of the Bible (examples: Ezekiel 3:16, 17; 33:1-33; Isaiah 62:6; Jeremiah 6:16, 17; 31:6; II Samuel 18:24-27). When reading these passages we learn that the watchmen on the wall have been given the responsibility for warning the people of coming judgments and the need for revival. The commands to these special leaders are sobering, for the very survival of their people, their nation and themselves depends on the diligent performance of their task. A watchman for God is in reality a leader chosen to blow the trumpet (sound a warning) when danger appears on the horizon. His cries of warning are designed to call the people to the repentance that will bring the restoration promised for those who heed the call. The grim reality is that without God's watchmen the people will perish.

In Isaiah it is obvious that the Lord is always ready to reason with His wayward people and forgive their sin.

"Come now, and let us reason together," says the Lord, "Though your sins are as scarlet, they will be as white as snow; though they are red like crimson, they will be like wool. If you consent and obey, you will eat the best of the land; But if you refuse and rebel. You will be devoured by the sword." Truly, the mouth of the Lord has spoken. (Isaiah 1:18-20).

And,

Incline Your ear, O LORD, and answer me; for I am afflicted and needy. Preserve my soul, for I am a godly man; O You my God, save Your servant who trusts in You. Be gracious to me, O Lord, for to You I cry all day long. Make glad the soul of Your servant, for to You, O Lord,

---

[72] The concept of the "watchmen on the walls" is addressed in more depth in Chapter 12.

I lift up my soul. For You, Lord, are good, and ready to forgive, and abundant in lovingkindness to all who call upon You (Psalm 86:1-5).

NOTE: God's revival leaders must be spiritually attuned to the warnings of God. Sounding the alarm without accurately seeing the coming destruction will create a "Chicken Little effect."[73]

2. Those who lead revivals must have the ability to hear God:

The command to obey God rests on the foundational ability to hear what He is saying. It is only logical to believe that God requires obedience in the matters that He reveals. The story of Samuel is an example of my premise:

The boy Samuel ministered before the Lord under Eli. In those days the word of the Lord was rare; there were not many visions.

One night Eli, whose eyes were becoming so weak that he could barely see, was lying down in his usual place. The lamp of God had not yet gone out, and Samuel was lying down in the temple of the Lord, where the ark of God was. Then the Lord called Samuel.

Samuel answered, "Here I am." And he ran to Eli and said, "Here I am; you called me." But Eli said, "I did not call; go back and lie down." So he went and lay down. Again the Lord called, "Samuel!" And Samuel got up and went to Eli and said, "Here I am; you called me." "My son," Eli said, "I did not call; go back and lie down."

Now Samuel did not yet know the Lord. The word of the Lord had not yet been revealed to him. The Lord called Samuel a third time and Samuel got up and went to Eli and said, "Here I am; you called me."

Then Eli realized that the Lord was calling the boy. So Eli told Samuel, "Go and lie down, and if he calls you, say, "Speak Lord, for your servant is listening." So Samuel went and lay down in his place.

The Lord came and stood there, calling as at the other times, "Samuel! Samuel!" Then Samuel said, "Speak, for your servant is listening." (I Samuel 3: 1-10).

The Lord then gave Samuel the revelation of His coming judgment against the rebellious house of Eli. The Lord's proclamation was very detailed and was an example of the Lord's desire to tell His prophets and leaders of His plans,

Surely the Sovereign Lord does nothing without revealing his plan to his servants the prophets. (Amos 3:7).

---

[73] Chicken Little is a folk tale sometimes called "Henny Penny" that tells the story of a chicken that experiences an acorn falling on its head while sleeping under a tree (in the many different versions the chicken is either male or female). He/she immediately jumps to conclusions and expects the worst. Chicken Little hysterically runs around to his/her neighbors shouting that "the sky is falling." The message is so obviously false that he/she is humiliated. When a real crisis occurs the previous mistake is remembered and no one believes it.

Spiritual Fact: Being able to hear the voice of the Holy Spirit is an indispensable requirement for leading God's people. The Word of God explains in great detail the fact that God speaks and we are to hear,

"He who has an ear, let him hear what the Spirit says to the churches." Revelation 3:13; see also Acts 13:1-3).

The ability to hear God becomes more crucial when the Lord is calling His people to revival. A godly leader will hear the call and lead the flock into the position to receive all that God has—including revival and the accompanying presence of the Holy Spirit's power. It must be said that a leader who does not hear from God and/or does not willingly obey will oppose revival—seeing it as a usurping of their power and position. This becomes tragic and removes a powerful weapon of God from the church's arsenal.

3. Those who lead revivals must obey God's leading:

Hearing God must be accompanied by obedience to what He says for any viable revival to take place. Knowing God's will without obeying it is self-defeating, and will bring to an end any viable ministry. The plain truth: **Those who serve God must assume the role of a servant and must "do" the Lord's bidding.** The Apostle Paul knew this well and makes the point:

*Paul, a **bond-servant**[74] of God and an apostle of Jesus Christ, for the faith of those chosen of God and the knowledge of the truth which is according to godliness.* (Titus 1: 1; see also Colossians 4:12).

And,

God speaking to King Saul through Samuel:

"Has the Lord as much delight in burnt offerings and sacrifices as in obeying the voice of the Lord? Behold, to obey is better than sacrifice, and to heed than the fat of rams. For rebellion is as the sin of divination (witchcraft), and insubordination is as iniquity and idolatry. Because you have rejected the word of the Lord, He has also rejected you (King Saul) from being king." (I Samuel 15:22, 23).

Obedience to God is made easier when we keep in mind the fact that He is God and we are not. He, as the head, is the only One qualified to make decisions concerning us, the body. As the Creator of all things, the Lord has a perfect understanding of the reality of the spiritual realm. We must remember, the creativity in spiritual matters is always His and not ours. Usurping God's plans to allow the implementing of ours is always a losing strategy.

Simply stated: God speaks and we obey.

4. Those who lead revivals must be repentant:

If we think that we have no need to be "up to date" in the area of repentance after first receiving the Lord than we are truly in a sorry

---

[74] **Bond servant** is the Gr. word *doulos* which means a slave of a master.

state.[75] I want to make it clear that I am not saying that Christians need to be saved over and over. What I am saying is that salvation from sin and death is different than a daily cleansing that we all need to keep our hearts open to His leading. Just try not taking a bath for a month and explain away why everyone is staying fifty feet away from you. All Christians must be "up to date" with the Lord concerning their hearts and minds. We are to be cleansed by His Holy Spirit daily.

"Pray, then, in this way: 'Our Father who is in heaven, hallowed be Your name. Your kingdom come, Your will be done, on earth as it is in heaven. Give us this day our daily bread. And forgive us our debts, as we have forgiven our debtors. And do not lead us into temptation, but deliver us from evil. For Yours is the kingdom and the power and the glory forever. Amen." (Matthew 6:9-13; see also I John 1:5-10).

There are many excellent quotes from notable individuals concerning sin and repentance. I have included a few to assist in our study:

People who cover their faults and excuse themselves do not have a repentant spirit. –Watchman Nee

If you notice in the New Testament, the invitation comes in the form of an authoritative command. Repent and believe! –Paul Washer

Repentance, as we know, is basically not moaning and remorse, but turning and change. –J. Packer

Repentance needs to be as loud as the sin was.—John MacArthur

Lust is the craving for salt of a man who is dying of thirst.
–Frederick Buechner

Repentance is a school from which we should never graduate.
–Pete Scazzero

*So remember what you have received and heard; and keep it, and **repent**. Therefore if you do not wake up, I will come like a thief, and you will not know at what hour I will come to you.* **–Jesus Christ** (to the church at Sardis in Revelation 3:3).

---

[75] There is a movement within the modern church led by teachers that have rejected any repentance after salvation. This movement is especially popular in the American church and is gaining traction because of its appearance on Christian television and media. Any Christian leader that downplays continual repentance is looking for financial support from the biblically ignorant mob and not serving the Master Who desires repentance in His people. Simply put it is a business decision. My suggestion: reject these teachers and seek a truly biblical leader. Before it is too late.

5. Those who lead revivals must forsake all questionable habits and activities:

All that believe in Jesus Christ have been ordered by God to forsake all questionable habits and activities. This truth is even more etched in stone when evaluating leadership. This is non-negotiable.

Beloved, now we are children of God, and it has not appeared as yet what we will be. We know that when He appears, we will be like Him, because we will see Him just as He is. ***And everyone who has this hope fixed on Him purifies himself, just as He is pure.*** *Everyone who practices sin also practices lawlessness; and sin is lawlessness. You know that He appeared in order to take away sins; and in Him there is no sin.* ***No one who abides in Him sins; no one who sins has seen Him or knows Him.*** *Little children, make sure no one deceives you; the one who practices righteousness is righteous, just as He is righteous; the one who practices sin is of the devil; for the devil has sinned from the beginning. The Son of God appeared for this purpose, to destroy the works of the devil. No one who is born of God* ***practices*** *sin, because His seed abides in him; and he cannot sin, because he is born of God.*[76] *By this the children of God and the children of the devil are obvious: anyone who does not practice righteousness is not of God, nor the one who does not love his brother.* (I John 3:2-10).

NOTE: The Lord has either made us new creatures or He has not (II Corinthians 5:17). Like Joshua we all need to make that public announcement concerning our submission to the living God:

"Now, therefore, fear the Lord and serve Him in sincerity and truth; and put away the gods which your fathers served beyond the River and in Egypt, and serve the Lord. If it is disagreeable in your sight to serve the Lord, choose for yourselves today whom you will serve; whether the gods which your fathers served which were beyond the River, or the gods of the Amorites in whose land you are living; but as for me and my house, we will serve the Lord!" (Joshua 24:14, 15).

Every day that I live for the Lord I marvel at His decision to reach out and take me into His kingdom. I am just a man—a man who struggles with my carnal nature. I must confess that when I consider God's great love, I am compelled to serve Him. When He tells me that I need to allow Him to change my life so that I can be free of the sins that hold me in bondage, I must, in good conscience, make the attempt.

Therefore, prepare your minds for action, keep sober in spirit, fix your hope completely on the grace to be brought to you at the revelation

---

[76] The key is to understand the word "practice." All human beings, including Christians will sin. This is part of our "sin nature." Christians attempting to serve the Lord will sin at times, but will repent of their sinful practices and be forgiven by God. A person who claims to be a Christian and yet "practices" serial sin, is nothing but an interloper seeking a cover for their sinful practices by continuing to sin while pretending to seek redemption. In reality they are hypocrites.

of Jesus Christ. As obedient children, do not be conformed to the former lusts which were yours in your ignorance, but like the Holy One who called you, be holy yourselves also in all your behavior; because it is written, "You shall be holy, for I am holy." (I Peter 1:13-16).

As a revivalist this desire to give up the boatload of trash that I have pulled behind me all these years, is deeper and much more auspicious. The words of a dear friend from many years ago have lodged in my memory: *"Bob, remember, you can't lead a revival from a bar stool. Any attempt to do that will make you look silly and brand you as a fool."*

He was right.

6. Those who lead revivals must be at peace with all men:

I know that getting along with people is an astronomical task. We human beings can act like a bagful of angry cats at a moment's notice. To be honest, I can be a cantankerous individual. No one that I know would even try to pretend that I am innocent. I can get upset over perceived slights faster than a speeding bullet. I know this. To even make the attempt to dismiss my guilt by pointing at the other person is a fool's errand. I need to admit my prickly nature and seek the Lord's help.

Daily.

The need to be forgiving toward others is especially important to anyone that is advocating revival. Being the man in the room that thinks a revival is sorely needed will oftentimes draw the ire of many in that room. Sinners hate to be called on their fleshly activities. You will find them calling for security to remove you from that room or worse. It is just that simple.

The only way to face these situations is to plan to forgive before any forgiveness is needed. The heat of the moment is not the time to begin taking those steps. God is calling us to seek revival. Many individuals will come against you. This is a fact. Your only defense is to forgive and move on. Remember, winning an argument is a poor substitute for leading a revival. We, as God's servants, have bigger fish to fry:

Pursue peace with all men, and the sanctification without which no one will see the Lord. See to it that no one comes short of the grace of God; that no root of bitterness springing up causes trouble, and by it many be defiled. (Hebrews 12:14, 15).

7. Those who lead revivals must commune with God through prayer and the Word:

I love to eat. All of my friends that know me will agree to that. The Bible says that reading the Word is tantamount to eating. The Word of God is food—spiritual food:

Therefore, putting aside all malice and all deceit and hypocrisy and envy and all slander, like newborn babies, long for the pure milk of the word, so that by it you may grow in respect to salvation, if you have tasted the kindness of the Lord. (I Peter 2:1-3). (See also, Jeremiah 3:15, 15:16; Psalm 19:7-10. 119:103).

Prayer is also seen in the Word as the way to increase spiritual strength. Prayer is the release of God's potential within any and all situations. Those that pray are literally engaging in spiritual war in the name of the Lord and with perseverance they will see His power and grace.

When they came to the crowd, a man came up to Jesus falling on his knees before Him saying, "Lord, have mercy on my son, for he is a lunatic and is very ill; for he often falls into the fire and often into the water. I brought him to Your disciples, and they could not cure him." And Jesus answered and said, "You unbelieving and perverted generation, how long shall I be with you? Bring him to Me." And Jesus rebuked him, and the demon came out of him, and the boy was cured at once. Then the disciples came to Him privately and said, "Why could we not drive it out?" And He said to them, "Because of the littleness of your faith; for truly I say to you, if you have faith the size of a mustard seed, you will say to this mountain, 'Move from here to there, and it will move; and nothing will be impossible to you. But this kind does not go out except by prayer and fasting." (Matthew 17:14-21).

For those that want to participate in a revival reading the Word and praying is the most important thing they can do. The Word is the foundation of God's plan and prayer is the release of His power to advance that plan. These actions are forever joined as the catalysts for revival. To be more precise, revivals are birthed in the hearts of those that are on their knees reading the Word and praying. Christians that balk at engaging in these two spiritual disciplines will see nothing but business as usual.

8. Those who lead revivals must not be biased or prejudiced:
We are not an island unto ourselves.[77] We all live together and this planet and must learn how to get along. Revival leaders must be sure to reach out to everyone who is seeking God. People are never to be evaluated through the lens of bias and prejudice. All men are equal in God's eyes, regardless of their wealth, societal position, race, appearance, national origin or any other human yardstick.

You shall love the Lord your God with all your heart, and with all your soul, and with all your strength, and with all your mind; and your neighbor as yourself." (Luke 10:27; see also John 13:34, 35).

The 1906 Azusa Street Revival was one of the most influential repudiations of racism that has ever occurred in church history. This landmark revival was led by a black man, William Seymour, who was a

---

[77] "No man is an island," a famous line from Meditation XVII by the English poet John Donne published in 1624

son of slaves. The revival occurred in Los Angeles and was known for its power and focus and its rejection of the Jim Crow laws[78] that buttressed racism in the United States. Blacks and whites worshipped together without bias and fear and were attacked by the culture of the time. Newspapers ran stories about "race-mixing" and threats were issued to the revival participants. The questions concerning black leadership over white congregants was non-existent amongst the revival participants. Although there had been some integrated churches before that time, the 1906 Azusa Street Revival was the first to be on such a massive scale.

NOTE: *In Numbers 12:1-16 the story of Miriam's rejection of the Cushite woman is a fascinating commentary on God's opinion of racism and bias. Miriam, Moses' sister, rejected his leadership and found fault with his marriage to a black woman. God struck her with leprosy and made her as white as snow. The humorous example of this act of judgment should speak volumes concerning God's position on bias and racism.*

Or should.

9. Those who lead revivals must be persons of faith:

A person called to lead a revival will hear many startling revelations from the mouth of the Lord. These messages are designed to give direction, share pertinent instruction, encourage confidence and remove fear. In order for any human being to be able to process these supernatural directives without disintegrating under the pressure, it will require the leader to be equipped with power and exceptional faith.

It was exceptional faith that sent Moses to confront Pharaoh, a suicidal act if not for the leading of God. It was exceptional faith that prompted Joseph to take his wife, Mary, and their newborn son, Jesus, to Egypt. It was exceptional faith that led Sergeant Alvin York to risk his life in order to singlehandedly attack a German machine gun nest, taking 32 machine guns, killing 20 German soldiers, and capturing 132 others during the Meuse-Argonne Offensive in France during WW I. And it will take exceptional faith for a person to lead a revival. Revivals by their very nature are excursions into the unknown. To take this leap into the maelstrom is not for the person weak in faith and trust.

"...for truly I say to you, if you have faith the size of a mustard seed, you will say to this mountains, 'Move for here to there,' and it will move; and nothing will be impossible for you." (Matthew 17:20).

And,

---

[78] **The Jim Crow Laws** were the official laws enacted, mostly in the South, after the Civil War to enforce an official discrimination against blacks. Separate public restrooms, restaurants, schools and hotels were developed to inhibit any socializing between whites and blacks.

And without faith it is impossible to please Him, for he who comes to God must believe that He is and that He is a rewarder of those who seek Him. (Hebrews 10:6).

10. Those who lead revivals must be free of the love of money:

Unfortunately, this truth is oftentimes ignored.[79] It is the main cause of the repudiation of the church by the unchristian world. True revivalists cannot make money and personal wealth a goal. If they do, the power and anointing of the revival becomes questionable. I have attended "revivals" (and churches) where multiple offerings were taken because the first offering was not enough. It does not take a Bible scholar to admit that the hundreds of stories of revivalists, evangelists and ministers that own mansions, drive luxury cars, fly in their personal jets, wear suits costing tens of thousands of dollars and amass treasures of all kinds are a detriment to the gospel. Simply put, greed is sin.

Shepherd the flock of God among you, exercising oversight not under compulsion, but voluntarily, according to the will of God; and not for sordid gain, but with eagerness; nor yet as lording it over those allotted to your charge, but proving to be examples to the flock. (I Peter 5:2, 3; see also Colossians 3:4, 5).

I want to make it crystal clear that serving the Lord Jesus Christ is not a way to earthly riches. I know that many of the popular Bible teachers today say the very opposite, but in my opinion, they are promoting a pipedream that is patently untrue. Jesus Himself put the subject to rest:

Jesus answered them and said, "Truly, truly, I say to you, you seek Me, not because you saw signs, but because you ate of the loaves and were filled. Do not work for the food which perishes, but for the food which endures to eternal life, which the Son of Man will give to you, for on Him the Father, God, has set His seal." (John 6:26, 27; see also I Timothy 6:3-10).

A leader of a revival must be free of greed. This is a given. There is no place in God's kingdom for the greed of man. No place at all…no matter who tries to sell it.

And He who sits on the throne said, "Behold, I am making all things new." And He said, "Write, for these words are faithful and true." Then He said to me, "It is done. I am the Alpha and the Omega, the beginning and the end. I will give to the one who thirsts from the spring of the water of life without cost." (Revelation 21:5, 6, 22:17).

Hear my heart. Greed will not only destroy a revival it will destroy a ministry. The sin of greed has been the snare of many and we who love God and deeply desire to see His gospel go forth in power, must

---

[79] There are many wonderful ministers that do not deserve this criticism. Please realize that I understand this fact and do not wish to accuse them. But for those that forget God's commands to resist greed, I do not want to issue them a pass. They are to be repudiated quickly and thoroughly.

bow the knee and pray for the church. Let us practice the ministry of intercession and pray that the Lord will touch the hearts and minds of those brothers and sisters that have fallen under the control of greed:

My prayer: *Dear Lord, we all must admit that we sin and fail You in many ways. Please help us to live our lives and conduct our ministries with grace, love and freedom from the sin that is crouching at the door. Forgive those in Your church that are led by greed and are consumed by the desire to benefit from sordid gain. Deliver them from this sin and thus allow Your children to experience Your presence and love. Send a revival and let it begin in our hearts. In the name of Jesus.*

Amen.

How does God choose the leaders of revivals?

When choosing leaders, the world seeks for education, work experience, personality, personal contacts, networking, looks, compatibility, and relationship to the owner or boss. Without spiritual insight, the world must do a thorough evaluation for each candidate it is considering.

A supernatural God does not look for His revival leaders the same way that the world seeks its leaders. He does not use internet want ads, unemployment job boards, job seminars, corporate "head-hunters," select his family members[80] or any other way that the world uses to seek leaders. God evaluates His prospective leaders supernaturally by examining their heart. The Lord's words to the Prophet Samuel while he was searching for a king of Israel should suffice:

But the Lord said to Samuel, "Do not consider his appearance or his height, for I have rejected him. The Lord does not look at the things man looks at. Man looks at the outward appearance, but the Lord looks at the heart." (I Samuel 16: 1-7).

An interesting fact is present in this verse: God sees potential leaders completely different than human beings do. We cannot see the human heart and cannot evaluate candidates like God can.

God chooses broken and repentant persons to lead His revivals. Academic degrees have no importance and only relationship to Jesus really matters.

Now as they observed the confidence of Peter and John and understood that they were uneducated and untrained men, they were amazed, and began to recognize them as having been with Jesus.[81] (Acts 4:13).

---

[80] **Nepotism:** The act of choosing your family and/or friends to be a part of the leadership of your ministry or church. Unfortunately, this is done in many churches and ministries of our time. Remember, only God can choose those who lead and not human beings that attempt to take care of their sons and daughters by giving them positions of leadership.

[81] The apostles were ordinary men. There wasn't a PhD in the crowd. Their qualifications for leadership was simple—*they had been with Jesus.* In our modern world churches we look for those

NOTE: In Christianity Today I saw an ad in the back of the magazine that read: *Christian church seeking a senior pastor. Candidate must have graduate degree, at least eight years of pastoral experience, have an infectious personality, possess a winning personality and be able to work with a large staff. Send personal resume, a list of professional contacts and a cover letter to—*

I was speechless. I had just read a secular want ad for a pastor! This was a Christian church seeking a pastor in the exact way as a secular business looking for a CEO! There was no mention of any supernatural giftedness and/or call of God at all! I began to pray and said, "Lord, we're in deep trouble...please send revival..."

I sat in stunned silence, took a breath and then said,
"Please."

In closing

It has been said that Christianity is always just one generation away from extinction.[82] This is because God has no grandchildren, but only sons and daughters that He calls to Himself. Each individual person in every generation must realize their need for God and must act accordingly. A revival is a time when people are called to make a decision. The question is: *Do I choose Jesus Christ as my Lord and Savior and thus pass out of death and receive His life?* This opportunity is only presented when a redeemed human being tells an unredeemed human being how to be translated out of the kingdom of darkness and into the kingdom of light.

Giving thanks to the Father, who has qualified us to share in the inheritance of the saints in Light. For He rescued us from the domain of darkness, and transferred us to the kingdom of His beloved Son, in whom we have redemption, the forgiveness of sins. (Colossians 1:12-14).

Quite literally, the torch is being passed from one human being to another. Revival leaders, pastors, and ordinary Christians must all remember that we will come to the end of our earthly lives. There will be an end. One of the main tasks of a revival leader, pastor (or minister), or even an ordinary Christian is to prepare those who will take over in our stead. I know this is difficult to consider, but it is imperative. We must prepare to pass the torch to the next person(s) in line.

The things which you have heard from me in the presence of many witnesses, entrust these to faithful men who will be able to teach others also. (II Timothy 2:2).

And,

The passing of the torch from Elijah to Elisha:

---

with degrees. This is humorous in light of God's desire to only select persons that qualify through their spirituality and submission to God.

[82] This quote attributed to Dr. George Carey, the Archbishop of Canterbury.

Elijah took his mantle and folded it together and struck the waters (the River Jordan), and they were divided here and there, so that the two of them crossed over on dry ground. When they had crossed over, Elijah said to Elisha, "Ask what I shall do for you before I am taken from you." And Elisha said, "Please, let a double portion of your spirit be upon me." He said, "You have asked a hard thing. Nevertheless, if you see me when I am taken from you, it shall be so for you; but if not, it shall not be so." As they were going along and talking, behold, there appeared a chariot of fire and horses of fire which separated the two of them. And Elijah went up by a whirlwind to heaven. Elisha saw it and cried out, "My father, my father, the chariots of Israel and its horsemen!" And he saw Elijah no more. Then he took hold of his own clothes and tore them in two pieces. He also took the mantle of Elijah that fell from him and returned and stood by the bank of the Jordan. He took the mantle of Elijah that fell from him and struck the waters and said, "Where is the Lord, the God of Elijah?" And when he also had struck the waters, they were divided here and there; and Elisha crossed over. Now when the sons of the prophets who were at Jericho opposite him saw him, they said, "The spirit of Elijah rests on Elisha." And they came to meet him and bowed themselves to the ground before him. (II Kings 2:8-15).

Pray for revival

Chapter Eight

The Top Ten Ways the Church Opposes Revival

"I believe that one reason why the church of God at this present moment has so little influence over the world is because the world has so much influence over the church."
    - Charles H. Spurgeon

    The battle against revival mounted by the world and its corrupt culture should be expected. Unbelievers, firmly entrenched in their carnality and unbelief, will always fight the church and its message of revival and will always pursue ways to discount, minimize and directly attack a genuine revival at every opportunity. The problem becomes disconcerting when some churches join the world's opposition by resisting the biblical call for revival. In my opinion, the church's opposition to revival is akin to any resistance to God's commands. Simply stated, it is an act of rebellion that is only cured by repentance.

    And the LORD said to me, "Faithless Israel has proved herself more righteous than treacherous Judah. Go and proclaim these words toward the north and say, 'Return, faithless Israel,' declares the LORD; 'I will not look upon you in anger. For I am gracious,' declares the LORD; 'I will not be angry forever. 'Only acknowledge your iniquity, that you have transgressed against the LORD your God And have scattered your favors to the strangers under every green tree, and you have not obeyed My voice,' declares the LORD. 'Return, O faithless sons,' declares the LORD; 'For I am a master to you, and I will take you one from a city and two from a family, and I will bring you to Zion.' "Then I will give you shepherds after My own heart, who will feed you on knowledge and understanding (Jeremiah 3:11-15).

NOTE: I must say clearly that not all churches have dropped the ball. Some are greatly supportive of revival and are actively seeking it. My difficulty rests on the simple truth that there has been a definite increase in ecclesiastical resistance to genuine revival in our time. This fact is indisputable and should be explored.

    The importance of this issue is beyond question, especially when the Word of God presents such a serious warning:

    But false prophets also arose among the people, just as there will also be false teachers among you, who will secretly introduce destructive heresies, even denying the Master who bought them, bringing swift destruction upon themselves. Many will follow their sensuality, and because of them the way of the truth will be maligned; and in their greed they will exploit you with false words; their judgment from long ago is not idle, and their destruction is not asleep (II Peter 2:1-3).

With all that said, I present the top ten ways that some modern churches oppose revival. I feel that this issue must be addressed with the honesty needed to stimulate a genuine revival.

The church doesn't experience revival because
10. The church has a tendency to become a human institution:

The Bible is very clear that the church was not meant to be a social club, a circus sideshow or a dating service. The church was designed by God to be a supernatural entity empowered to bring the life-giving gospel to the entire world,

"All authority in heaven and on earth has been given to me. Therefore go and make disciples of all the nations, baptizing them in the name of the Father and the Son and the Holy Spirit, and teaching them to obey everything I have commanded you. And surely I am with you always, to the very end of the age." (Matthew 28:18-20).

The life of the risen Christ was meant to pulsate within the hearts and lives of those who have been grafted into His Body by the supernatural work of the Holy Spirit. Vibrancy, holiness, power, anointing, purpose, biblical foundation and boldness are the marks of the true church.

But when the church becomes just another human institution it loses its connection to the living God and becomes an empty shell of its past glory. Without the Holy Spirit's direct empowering and leading, the church, dependent on human energy, becomes excruciatingly boring and weak. A weak church has no supernatural options and becomes a pawn in pagan society's power game. Gripped by passivity, it will never lead but will only follow that society—making zero impact. A passive church, devoid of any supernatural strength, will abandon its biblical mandate to bring Christ to the world and will never recognize its need for revival and will stand against it if it comes. There are just too many stories that can be told that illustrate that sad truth.

Leonard Ravenhill's latter years included many invitations for him to travel to various churches and speak. Some of these messages can be found on YouTube and are extremely valuable to any person who wants to understand true revival. I am amazed at how Brother Ravenhill spent his time spanking the churches he was visiting. I'm sure that his hosts thought that he was coming to spank the pagans (and other churches) and bring those other groups to task and to elevate the hosting church, but he didn't fulfill their expectations. He was there to put a charge into the Christians (all of us) for dropping the ball when it comes to prayer, evangelism and revival. Brother Ravenhill's main criticism of the church was its propensity to seek a "vacation" from the Holy Spirit's mandate to repent and be filled with God in order to fulfill the commandment to make disciples throughout the world. He was relentless.

And 100% accurate in his criticism.

KEY POINT: *Remember, the church is a supernatural entity and not a social club. Revival will quickly deliver the church of any false understanding of its divine purpose.*

9. The church is often afraid of offending the world:

The Lord warned us that our love for Him would provoke the world. He said,

"If the world hates you, you know that it hated me before it hated you." (John 15:18).

Since it is impossible for our love for Christ to not cause a wedge between us and the world, why do so many Christians fret over the world's negative opinion of God's church? Why is it that there are so many Christians who so desperately want to be loved, hugged and stroked by the world that they reject what they deem as Christianity's "offensive" message of exclusivity in the proclamation of the words of Jesus Christ?

FACT: Jesus Christ said emphatically that He was the only way to God.

Jesus said to him, "I am the way, and the truth, and the life; no one comes to the Father but through Me (John 14:6).

And,

And there is salvation in no one else; for there is no other name under heaven that has been given among men by which we must be saved (Acts 4:12).

With the words of Jesus Christ echoing in our hearts there should be no argument successfully mounted within Christendom against the exclusivity of the Christian church and its message. Without any hesitation the truth is: there is no other religion, faith, belief, etc. that can claim to be divine truth if it denies that true Christianity stands alone as God's message to the world. In other words, Jesus Christ does not share His throne with Buddha, Mohammed, Krishna, or any other false contender.

Period.

Every year during the Christmas season the evening news is filled with the complaints of pagan America against any and all public references to the birthday of Christ. The liberal newscasters, enthusiastically supportive of any criticisms advanced by the enemies of Christ, endorse the invectives against manger scenes or any other public displays of Christ advanced by the offended atheists. The atheist complaint is simple: In their opinion, hearing the name of Jesus will somehow offend their fragile sensitivities and cause them to experience some debilitating emotional effects. The liberal progressives, always ready to support some hair brained cause, join the chorus and demand that the word "Christmas" be omitted from public discourse. The political correctness police, excited by any chance to ridicule God and

His people, leap into action and demand the same oft repeated demands: The renaming of Christmas as a "Winter Holiday," the omitting of Christmas carols from school celebrations and the banning of manger scenes from public property. A liberal church in my hometown, sensing an opportunity to appeal to the carnal rabble, voted to placate the hurt feelings of the offended pagans by deleting any references to Jesus Christ in their holiday celebrations. The liberal progressive pastor standing before the television cameras in his robe and turned-back collar, addressed the viewers, *"Since we are a church that seeks the happiness of all and are not willing to offend anyone, we have decided to celebrate the spirit of the season by omitting any religious references."* Sporting an asinine, self-satisfied smirk, he went on to invite the people of the town to attend a celebration without any added religious overtones. The pastor, thinking his wonderful gesture of ecumenicalism would be praised by the unsaved mob, was shocked when no one came. One astute non-Christian was interviewed by the local television station and asked for his opinion on why no one attended the "Christ free" holiday church service? The man's answers spoke volumes:

"Christmas is Christmas. Pretending that something that is—isn't—is like pretending that the rattlesnake in your tent really isn't there. That sounds like a mental illness to me and anyone in their right mind would avoid any association with those that push that trip into the Land of Oz."

The man was then asked, *"So how did you celebrate the winter holiday?"*

He answered, *"Well, my family and I didn't celebrate some 'winter holiday.' We celebrated 'Christmas.' We had a great meal and sang Christmas carols. My eighty-five year old Dad even read the Christmas story out of the Bible. I guess Christmas should be celebrated like it should be and not ignored or re-engineered by the pack of fools that run that silly church."* The man then applied some salt in the wound by adding, *"Are you going to bleep out my mentioning of the word Christmas to satisfy the morons at City Hall?"*

So out of the mouth of a non-believer we receive instruction? It is a tragedy that some that bear the name "Christian" fail to understand that our allegiance is to the Person of Jesus Christ and His message and not to some shabby political correctness mythology. We should never acquiesce to the bullying tactics of the opponents of Christ but instead speak truth into every situation. Christians need to heed the warning given by Jesus Christ Himself:

"Therefore everyone who confesses Me before men, I will also confess him before My Father who is in heaven. But whoever denies Me before men, I will also deny him before My Father who is in heaven (Matthew 10:32, 33; see also Luke 9:26).

The choice is clear. Any church/and or individual Christian that downplays its/or their relationship with God in order to be accepted by the world is on the road to apostasy and will never see a revival. What they may experience is eternal judgment.

NOTE: *A world accommodating church is not a safe environment for real, Bible honoring Christians. They will stone you before you can find the cloakroom. If you find yourself in one of these liberal, apostate churches you need to flee as fast as you can. To stay in a church that has turned against Christ and His Word will become a destructive element to you and your family. Please forego the excuse that you are there to help them make changes. Your Christian input will only brand you as a fanatic (in their opinion) and you will be in direct violation of the mountain of Bible verses that command believers to never join the lockstep march over the cliff into eternal darkness* (Jude 22, 23; II Cor. 6:14-18). It must be understood that we are God's people and we must remain loyal to His message.

A suggestion: When encountering an offended pagan desperately attempting to erase Christmas, look him or her in the eye and say,

"Merry Christmas..."

Believe me, you will feel better...

KEY POINT: *Never be afraid of the world. The truth is that a Christian is a member of an eternal family that will judge angels and the world* (I Corinthians 6:1-3). *We need to make zero apologies to a world system that has been judged already. True revival will elevate that truth.*

8. Christianity has a tendency to morph into a cultural experience:

Whenever a TV talk show host does a story on Christianity in America you'll hear the stats that indicate that Christians make up a large portion of the country's population. I certainly hope that my readers understand that this is a fallacy. If not, I have a bridge to sell you in Brooklyn.

Any Christian with common sense certainly knows that America is definitely long passed any claim of being a "Christian nation." Take a trip to a local beach or visit a college campus or attend a local schoolboard meeting[83] if you need any proof that we're an apostate, non-

---

[83] I went to an elementary school in Omaha, Nebraska to attend a Christmas pageant (renamed: "The Snow Show"). I sat in the audience and listened to nineteen songs about snowmen and snow. There wasn't a single reference to Christmas, Jesus, or any other Christian connection. It was like attending a Kiwanis Club meeting. When I filed out of the auditorium I was met by the school principal. He asked me the question, "How did you enjoy the show?" I looked him in the eye and said, "Gee, where did you find nineteen songs on snowmen and snow?" He shrugged and said, "It took about two weeks to round them all up. It was a herculean task..." The principal, recognizing that I wasn't a Kool-Aid drinker, took me aside and poured out his heart. He told me that one woman on the school board forced them all to dump Christmas and produce the liberal nonsense. I answered, "Only one woman was able to hogtie all of you Nebraskans? Don't tell me, she must be from California or New York?" The principal's eyes widened and he said, "How did you know that? She's from Los Angeles." I answered, "It's a no-brainer. California and New York are

Christian, country, hurtling toward the gates of hell in a full out sprint. Just check the next election results if you need any more evidence. You'll discover that the majority of candidates that are often supported by the American voters are the most thieving, godless political opportunists that can be dug up and placed on the ballot. The fact is that this country has some dubious individuals that have been placed in charge—and this is not by mistake. A country awash in immorality does not want godly leadership. They want like-minded ringmasters that pave the way to complete moral debauchery. The new chant has become: ***Sex, drugs and rock-n-roll!*** as the nation falls over the cliff into oblivion.

Newsflash! We're not a Christian nation and never were. We may think we were because of the Christian culture of the nineteenth and twentieth centuries, but America was and is a nation with Christians living in it…surrounded by many times more non-believers. Churches that fail to understand this will never see the need for revival. They'll just continue to be surrounded each Sunday by a multitude of pew sitters who speak "Christianeze" but aren't born-again.

"Not everyone who says to Me, 'Lord, Lord,' will enter the kingdom of heaven, but he who does the will of My Father who is in heaven will enter. Many will say to Me on that day, 'Lord, Lord, did we not prophesy in Your name, and in Your name cast out demons, and in Your name perform many miracles?' And then I will declare to them, 'I never knew you; DEPART FROM ME, YOU WHO PRACTICE LAWLESSNESS.' (Matthew 7:21-23).

In John 1:13 we read God's Word concerning those who have become His children. He says, *"Who were born, not of blood nor of the will of the flesh nor of the will of man, but of God."* This passage unequivocally states that each individual person must come to Christ through their own personal decision. Being born in a Christian family, although a good thing is not a guarantee that you will become a Christian. The John verse defined:

Born not of blood: *Christians aren't born that way. To be a Christian you must have experienced a spiritual rebirth. In truth, you can physically join a church and not be born again. This fact should be proclaimed with clarity: No one is physically born a Christian. And more importantly, no one is an automatic Christian because they are an American.*

---

breeding grounds for militant liberals. They spread around the country like a plague, destroying the faith and cultural heritage of America." The principal agreed and then hung his head and shuffled away. I felt bad for him and his fellow Nebraskans. They had been run over by the liberal bulldozer. My last words were, "Good luck and make sure you guard your wallet or you'll be paying for every hair brain liberal scam known to man."

Nor of the will of the flesh: *No one will be saved by being a good person or by performing good works (Ephesians 2:8-10). Attempting to earn your position in Christ by performing good works is a waste of time. Good works are the result of the supernatural act of salvation* (James 2:14-26).

Nor of the will of man: *No priest or pastor, denomination or church can declare you saved. Human beings do not have the power to save anyone. Our job is to declare the gospel and lead people to the Savior, but their response to His invitation must be from them* (Psalm 49:7-8) *and not through some empty declaration.*

But of God: *Only God can save us. He extends His grace and we respond to the gospel. The salvation experience is wholly supernatural.*

An evangelist once said that God does not have any grandchildren—only sons and daughters that He calls to Himself. Another great saying that bears truth: *"Living in a garage does not make you a car. Just as attending a church doesn't make you a Christian."*

Each individual person in each generation must experience the supernatural moment of salvation when that person chooses to serve Christ and then passes out of the dominion of darkness into the kingdom of the Son He loves (Colossians 1:13, 14). Some Christian churches in America have forgotten the requirements of this personal and individual conversion experience, initiating a crisis within their ranks.

NOTE: *The irreducible fact—true Christianity is a supernatural experience that transforms human lives. When it becomes only cultural it becomes deadly. For the record, Al Capone and Adolf Hitler were baptized as infants. Only the most intellectually challenged would consider these satanically inspired monsters to be believers. We must get the clue. Hosing down the baby is not going to cut it. When that child grows up he/she must come to Christ regardless of the initiatory ritual of infant baptism. The facts are that parents still have a responsibility to train their child in the faith so their child can make a real decision on Whom he/she will serve. All Christian parents should take heed and realize that their children are not automatically saved because mom and dad are Christians and the kids have been baptized as infants. Each child must deal with the Lord as an individual person. With this understanding it should be a no-brainer why we need revival in our time. In fact, a failure to recognize the need for revival is what it is—a fatal error that will doom millions...and maybe some of our own children.*

KEY POINT: *Many that claim to be Christians are misguided when they fail to recognize that salvation is completely a supernatural experience. Also, there is no such thing as being partly saved. You are or you're not. A true revival will clear that up in a heartbeat.*

7. Too many churches avoid personal evangelism:

Notice that my statement isn't a blanket one. I am aware that there are churches that evangelize. They are not the majority, but they exist. These churches, because of their desire to evangelize, are often recognized as the most impactful church in their particular location. The reason for their impact: They receive teaching from the pulpits that clearly imparts the truth that Jesus Christ gave the Great Commission (the divine command to evangelize) to His followers just before leaving the earth to return to heaven,

And Jesus came up and spoke to them, saying, "All authority has been given to Me in heaven and on earth. Go therefore and make disciples of all the nations, baptizing them in the name of the Father and the Son and the Holy Spirit, teaching them to observe all that I commanded you; and lo, I am with you always, even to the end of the age" (Matthew 28: 18-20).

The leadership of these obedient churches make it clear that the Lord was specific that we are all to "GO."[84] Their point: *this command from God should cause serious Christians to lay down the excuses, get up off their backsides and "GO" out and bring in the harvest of souls.* Sitting in church staring at the stained glass windows is not going to fulfill the Lord's command. We have to get up and "GO!" Again, those churches that teach and then "do" this will be strong and fruitful. Those that don't will not...they will be meaningless social clubs and not vibrant, spirit-filled churches.

I would be amiss if I did not acknowledge that most Christians (myself included) are not comfortable speaking to strangers about Christ. It is something in our genes. We do not like it and oftentimes we will be stubborn and not do it. It is mind-boggling to consider that the vast number of those who name Christ as their Lord will refuse to witness for Him. I do it, but I still struggle with my fears.

Some reasons for the church's reluctance to witness

One of the reasons we will not witness is that we are afraid that people will not like us or that they will think badly of us. But we are the "seed bearers" who bring Christ to the nations. If we do not "GO" and open our mouths they will not hear the message and may not be saved (Romans 10:8-15). Christians should never be crippled by the fear of man. Remember, there is nothing that man can do to harm us. It is the Lord that we should fear (respect). Our refusal to witness can become a sin of omission. What a dilemma!

Many pastors purposely make the attempt to remove the responsibility of witnessing from their congregants because they know that those congregants are uncomfortable. Uncomfortable? Just when

---

[84] I wish to be clear that "the going" isn't necessarily a call to a foreign mission field. The point is that Christians are to share their faith wherever they are and not push some ridiculous concept that it is okay to be a "secret" Christian.

does are discomfort negate our required response to the Lord's command that we "GO" and make disciples of the nations? Christians need to understand that the Lord has commanded us to witness and make the attempt to lead lost humanity to the Savior. Any pastor that omits this truth in order to extend support for their congregant's decision to detach from their obligations is failing in his/her job. Pastors need to open their mouths and deliver the full gospel (Acts 5:20) and not run some deli where we can have it our own way.

Many Christians don't witness because they have not opened themselves up to receive the Lord's power and anointing. The Holy Spirit will give us what we need if we ask for it. The Holy Spirit in a revival energizes and quickens the hearts of God's people and turns them into witnesses for Christ. The fear is removed when the Spirit falls upon you and you will no longer be afraid of man. The Lord Himself mentioned that His people should wait to receive the anointing of the Holy Spirit to be able to witness effectively,

"This is what is written: The Christ will suffer and rise from the dead on the third day, and repentance and forgiveness of sins will be preached in his name to all nations, beginning at Jerusalem. You are witnesses of these things. I am going to send you what the Father has promised; but stay in the city until you have been clothed with power from oh high." (Luke 24:46-49).

Some Christians view witnessing in a bad light. The efforts of door-to-door cults (Jehovah's Witnesses, Mormons, etc.) are often seen as a reason to hesitate in our witnessing to others.[85] The problem with this position is simple: Bad behavior does not alter truth. Truth is truth no matter how many misguided individuals ruin it for others. The simple answer is to witness in a respectful and Spirit-led manner that gives glory to God. Also, it must be said that a negative response to "your" witnessing is oftentimes directly dependent on the bitter resentment the person has developed toward God and the church and isn't personal. A negative response is no reason to cease your obligation to the Lord. Give the message and let the Lord deal with the results.

The simple fact is that many in Christian leadership have never shared their faith outside the walls of a church. A Christian leader that does not witness outside the "safety" of their church building cannot model the evangelistic mandate given to the body of Christ by the Lord Himself. The Lord made it clear that sheep cannot rise above the experiences and equipping of the shepherds (Matthew 10:24; John 13:16). My point is this: A church led by a pastor that is hesitant to share

---

[85] A point to ponder: Cults, without the Holy Spirit, have led millions to their organizations through door-to-door witnessing. Christians should wonder what they could do when being led by the Holy Spirit. I'm sure the results would be stunning.

his faith will not produce an evangelistic mindset. That church will become a social club instead of a spearhead of evangelism.

I withheld this reason until last because it is probably the most prominent reason that Christians avoid evangelism. Simply put, modern Christianity has morphed into a "gimmie stuff" philosophy that is directly related to liberal politics. If you turn on the TV you will see some "evangelist" telling his/her listeners that if you turn to Jesus He will become your butler and give you free stuff. These religious hucksters sell Jesus like a pyramid scheme.[86] Their message: *Become a Christian and you can expect cars, boats, houses, planes, trips, tons of cash and other golden trinkets that you can horde in your mansion in Beverly Hills.* This "navel gazing" Christianity has become all the rage and is so time consuming that a Christian has little time to witness while playing the Jesus Sweepstakes. This is nothing but pure unadulterated hogwash and needs to be countered by the reality of true revival. Let's clean out the sanctuary and make room for God. A true revival will turn all the false golden trinkets to dust.

KEY POINT: *All Christians are commanded to share their faith whenever the Holy Spirit leads. There is no such thing as the "Chico"[87] argument: "It ain't my job, man..." is not a valid argument.*

6. Too many churches and/or ministries pursue money as the main goal:

The love of money is the root of all evil (not money itself). Many churches today are so in debt that they must spend all their time lobbying for more capital to keep themselves afloat. Cash strapped and facing rising costs, these churches will do almost anything to raise the cash they need to make payroll and keep current on the mortgage. In my opinion, connecting cash to the gospel is nothing but unadulterated sin. There are more than enough Scriptures in God's Word to at least give us pause. I think that Peter's comments to Simon the Sorcerer concerning Simon's attempt to receive God's anointing and power with money are enough to put it all into perspective:

Now when Simon saw that the Spirit was bestowed through the laying on of the apostles' hands, he offered them money, saying, "Give this authority to me as well, so that everyone on whom on lay my hands may receive the Holy Spirit." But Peter said to him, "May your silver perish with you, because you thought you could obtain the gift of God with money! You have no part or portion in this matter, for your heart is

---

[86] This is what most of our modern politicians do 24/7. They sell their candidacies with the promise of free stuff—fulfilling the old saying, "You can't beat Santa Claus in an election."

[87] The "Chico and the Man" comedy series was famous in the 1970s (1974-1978). Jack Albertson was a cranky old mechanic that was trying to understand Freddie Prinze, a twenty something streetwise Chicano with a quick wit. Whenever Albertson attempted to get Prinze to do something extra, Freddie (Chico) would say, "It ain't my job, man…"

not right before God. Therefore repent of this wickedness of yours, and pray the Lord that, if possible, the intention of your heart may be forgiven you, for I see that you are in the gall of bitterness and in the bondage of iniquity." (Acts 8:18-23).

If you want an education on this disturbing trend, make a list of all of the items being sold in the typical church. You can start at the coffee counter where the expensive lattes and mochas are made and peddled. It seems that new money-making schemes are surfacing each and every week. But one scheme especially caught my attention: I passed a church recently with a banner above the church sign. It read—**"Call us for information on our 4%—7% interest on church bonds."** There was a phone number. I was stunned! I stood and stared at that sign and felt my blood pressure skyrocket. After a few minutes I calmed down and prayed. My prayer:

Father, forgive us all for our sins. We have all made mistakes. But Lord, especially keep us from being takers and not givers. Keep us Lord from the love of money...Amen.

KEY PONT: *Greed is the mark of a false prophet and/or false ministry* (II Peter 2:1-3, 14-16). *There can never be any excuse for greed, no matter who is trying to sell it.*

5. Too many in church leadership are not revival oriented:

I watched a football game on TV. The quarterback called a running play. He took the ball from center and turned to his right to give the ball to the passing running back. The only problem was that the ball had slipped from his hands and he had nothing to put in the runner's stomach. The fumbled football was recovered by the defense and they went on to score. I make this point to illustrate a truth: A minister cannot give you what he does not have. A minister with no understanding of revival or does not care cannot give you a desire to experience one. Unfortunately, in twenty-first century America, too many pastors and ministers have no clue about revival, and/or simply do not care. This is not fertile ground for producing evangelists and revivalists.

This is disturbing because of a simple fact: The sheep will follow their shepherd and learn from their model. If the pastor has no interest in revival, it will be very uncommon for a parishioner to have an interest. If that parishioner somehow slips through the defenses and develops a desire for true revival he/she may find themselves at odds with the church and leadership. It can be a lonely experience being the only person in the room that knows what is happening.

I do not know how to say this without sounding callous. But I want to warn you to think twice about submitting yourself under leadership that claim that the old ways to minister do not work and that we must find new ways to reach the world. In my opinion, a leader who says this is covering up for their lack of prayer and communication with God.

They are trapped in a "great disconnect" from the ancient path and are adrift on a sea of speculation. God never changes. Hebrews 13:8 says, *Jesus Christ is the same yesterday and today and forever.* Malachi 3:6 says, *I the Lord do not change.* God is eternal and His ways are eternal. He does not adjust to our world view or our debased culture. We must rise to His level and do it His way. It is His Word that is eternal and not ours. Ministers who do not get this are missing the boat and will not produce the powerful ministries that can change the world. They will just get along.

Maybe.

KEY POINT: *In order to understand God's word concerning revival, a Christian must make the effort to investigate. Professing ignorance is no defense. There was even a sacrifice for the sins performed by mankind in ignorance* (Numbers 15:22-31). *This brings home the old adage: "Ignorance is no excuse."*

4. There are very few models of revival in our time:

How does a blind man describe an elephant? We cannot understand what we have not seen or experienced. Ask anyone about a revival and you will get some very interesting answers. The average Christian has no clue what a revival is and what it does. This is because all that most Christians know is church.

So what do we know about church? If we took a poll we would probably get the following: Church takes place on Sunday mornings; it is an hour long; it is all about meetings; the pastor is in charge; he wears a robe; you drop money into a plate that travels back and forth in the pews; some people wear robes, stand up in little rows at the front and sing for you; kids sing songs on Christmas and Easter; people photograph their kids singing and send the pictures to the family in Christmas cards; it interferes with football; they have potlucks; you dress up; etc. Is this exciting? Well, not really. Church is not revival.

The answer is to let Christians know what revival is. There are videos available that tell the story of many of history's great revivals. Show some videos, hand out some books, bring in missionaries who have experienced revivals overseas and raise the expectancy level within the church. If Christians hear about revivals and understand what they are, they would probably become curious to experience one. A curious person, if directed properly might even start praying for a revival! Then they would know what it is and would probably desire to be on board. It is worth a try. The Lord's Word fits well in this discussion,

Where there is no vision, the people perish. (Proverbs 29:18 KJV).

A personal observation

I came to Christ in California many years ago. During that time I had access to the ministries of some of the most powerful witnesses for Christ that one could find. I could jump in my car and travel a few miles and hear Jack Hayford at the Church on the Way in Van Nuys or Chuck Smith at Calvary Chapel in Costa Mesa or John Wimber at the Anaheim Vineyard or Ralph Moore at Hope Chapel in Hermosa Beach. I could turn in any direction and find myself attending the meetings of great evangelists and teachers. Their testimonies and experience prodded me to seek the Lord with intense resolve. Today, many of those servants of God are gone and we no longer have their experience to draw from. This is a problem, especially when many of our younger pastors have no connection with some of these great men of God and are getting their experience from books on church growth. Christianity is to be viewed as a spiritual relay. The torch is passed and the next leg of the race begins. It can only help when the torch is passed from the great leaders of our time.

Reality check: *Imagine you are organizing a 4x100 relay team for the Olympics. You have three of the fastest runners in the world running three of the first legs. Now you have a choice: Put Usain Bolt, the fastest man in the world, as your anchor leg or me...a fat seventy year old man that has trouble walking to the restroom. Which runner would you choose? I sincerely hope you would choose Usain Bolt. Giving me the baton is a joke. You will never get close to the victory stand. I would most likely lose the baton on the way to the bathroom...*

KEY POINT: *In order to learn anything spiritual it is incumbent that a Christian hang out with other Christians that have understanding and are doing God's will. If you want to experience a revival find people that are praying for one and learn. Hanging out with Christians that ignore revival or minimize it will only ensure that you'll never experience one.*

3. The Word of God is often not preached in power:

In 1965 a Professor Thomas J. J. Altizer from Emory University made startling headlines that read: ***"God is dead!"*** It seems that Professor Altizer was the leader of a group of theologians who embraced a form of "Christian atheism" (a strange, untrue concept). People were aghast to see the headlines, but Altizer was just one of hundreds of seminary theologians whose beliefs had crossed the line into liberal blasphemy.

Entire seminaries have been invaded by radical liberal theology. The effect has been devastating. These apostate schools have become graveyards. Many on the teaching staff have had no conversion experience and see nothing significant and/or supernatural in the Christian faith. They routinely dismiss the Bible as the Word of God and turn Christianity into a mere philosophy that must compete with hundreds of other philosophies. The graduates of these "spiritual dead zones" are sent out to occupy the pulpits of dead churches. Oh, what mockery! Dead ministers speaking dead sermons to dead people! The stench is overwhelming. Once great denominations, awash in this liberal flood, have crashed and burned and are no longer a positive influence within Christendom. It is appalling. Denominations that have embraced the false gospel of liberalism will not experience revival. What they should experience are heresy trials.

I made the acquaintance of a man named Merwin who was an avid Bible reader. Merwin felt called to the ministry and sought the advice of his pastor. The pastor had attended the denomination's bible school before it became liberal. The well-meaning pastor, unaware of the intensity of the liberal shift, recommended the school to Merwin and he enrolled.

Almost immediately, Merwin ran afoul with the instructors and administration at this liberal school. It seemed that they wanted him to put his Bible aside so that he could absorb the poison of the liberal/progressive theology that has destroyed so many denominations and churches. Merwin could not understand their pressing need to dismantle his faith and resisted their efforts. Finally, the staff met and decided to show Merwin the door because of his "intractability." He left with a great hurt in his soul and did not make another attempt to attend a Bible school. A good man was lost to the ministry.

Unfortunately, the above story is far from being unique. I have heard dozens of these stories over the years. My heart aches for the men and women that are shot down by the liberal churches and denominations that have sold their souls for a bowl of rancid soup. The church needs to heed the wakeup call echoing from the throne of heaven. The Prophet Jeremiah wrote down God's feelings toward His people that reject His Word:

"Be warned, O Jerusalem, or I shall be alienated from you, and make you a desolation, a land not inhabited." Thus says the LORD *of hosts, "They will thoroughly glean as the vine the remnant of Israel; pass your hand again like a grape gatherer over the branches." To whom shall I speak and give warning that they may hear? Behold, their ears are closed and they cannot listen. Behold, the word of the* LORD *has become a reproach to them; they have no delight in it... "Hear, O earth: behold, I am bringing disaster on this people, the fruit of their plans, because they have not listened to My words, and as for My law, they have rejected it also"* (Jeremiah 6:8-10, 19).

It doesn't take a Bible scholar to realize that God is adamant that His Word be read and obeyed. Any church or denomination that condemns a person like Merwin that is attempting to obey God's Word because they believe that they (the denomination or church) are now smarter than God and know better are subject to a great judgment. This cavalier attitude is spreading like a plague and only a revival can stem the judgment.

KEY POINT: *God's Word—all of it—Old and New Testament is true and cannot be broken. True revivals will be based on the Word and will elevate the Word to exceptional levels. Anyone touched by a true revival will see God's Word as authoritative and absolute.*

2. Too many churches are not praying:

I know that the reader is aware by now that I feel that prayer is the most important thing we can do. Many churches in the twenty-first century do not share my sentiments. It is far too common to discover that prayer rooms are closed and/or being used as maintenance closets or lunch rooms. Instead of sipping a latte, leadership should be crying out to God for forgiveness for their tolerance of the absence of revival prayer. I will say this again: "Any church that decides to engage in serious revival prayer will experience revival. Those that don't…won't." I believe that this promise is etched in stone.

Some of my readers may think that I am being too cynical concerning my feelings about the lack of prayer in the American church. Well, my only defense is to explain what my personal experiences have been: I have been attempting to start an intercessory prayer meeting in my city of Omaha. The signs are obvious that we are living in dangerous times and that evil is pressing in all around us. Our families are at stake. Sin is exploding across our country. Only a blind and deaf man would not be able to discern the threats that are clearly seen on the horizon. America is under attack, our Constitution is being shredded as we speak, our political leadership is mired in the swamp of political correctness, the Christian community is seen as an enemy to be confronted and a third world war is looming on the horizon. We are in serious trouble and should be swarming into prayer meetings in every corner of our cities to call on the Lord for His intervention. We should, but we are not. Getting even one person to attend a prayer meeting is almost an impossible task. When I suggest a time of prayer I am looked upon as being a deluded fool attempting to drive the church bus over the cliff. I have been taken aback by the depth of opposition. The disdain that I have seen in the eyes of those that I have asked to come and pray for revival disturbs my soul. The facts are too clear to be misinterpreted. Many Christians see prayer as an inconvenience that borders on a personal attack. They simply do not want to pray and will thrash anyone that suggests otherwise. If the reader disputes my conclusions then suggest a prayer meeting and watch how fast you get tossed into the same boat that I am sitting in. Go ahead and try it. And then let me know the results.

NOTE: *When you approach your church to suggest that prayer meeting, remember that I will be saving an oar for you to use in that boat that I am sitting in. Relax and row…*

KEY POINT: *It is an absolute fact that prayerlessness will produce nothing. If we do not pray we will receive zero for our lack of intercession. Revivals are not occurring in our time because Christians are not interceding for one.*

It is that simple.

1. Too many Christians are never instructed that the walk with Christ is only successful when we practice obedience.

Jesus Christ is Lord and we are not. Such a simple fact and yet it is a truth that is often lost in the murky swamp of modern "Churchianity." Even a casual reading of the holy text, both Old and New Testament, will clearly highlight the spiritual fact that obedience to the Word of God is absolutely essential and cannot be re-negotiated.

Many in the modern church have consumed the Kool-Aid dispensed by the psychotherapists masquerading as ministers of the gospel concerning the erroneous concept that Christianity is based on our rights and privileges. True Christians are the bond slaves of the Lord and are expected to obey His commands. We are never given the "right" to consider the church to be a delicatessen where we get our "food" our way. The Apostle Paul had this truth burned into his soul when he was knocked off his horse while heading toward Damascus in order to do things "his way" (Acts 9). Forever humbled he opened his most famous book by saying,

*Paul, a **bond-servant** of Christ Jesus, called as an apostle, set apart for the gospel of God, which He promised beforehand through His prophets in the holy Scriptures, concerning His Son, who was born of a descendant of David according to the flesh, who was declared the Son of God with power by the resurrection from the dead, according to the Spirit of holiness, Jesus Christ our Lord, through whom we have received grace and apostleship to bring about the **obedience** of faith among all the Gentiles for His name's sake, among whom you also are the called of Jesus Christ* (Romans 1:1-6).

Paul was a bond servant to the Lord Jesus Christ. In Greek the word is *doulos* and means a slave without rights. He was called by God and ordered to serve the Lord without question. Now when was that truth preached on a Sunday morning in the typical American church? When did a modern American preacher instruct his hearers that their most important order from God is the demand for their obedience? The following verses should suffice to set the matter in stone:

*The Prophet Samuel said, "Has the LORD as much delight in burnt offerings and sacrifices as in **obeying the voice of the LORD**? Behold, to **obey** is better than sacrifice, and to heed than the fat of rams. "For rebellion is as the sin of divination, and insubordination is as iniquity and idolatry. Because you have rejected the word of the LORD, He has also rejected you from being king"* (I Samuel 15:22-23).

And,

"*Now it shall be, **if** you diligently **obey the LORD your God**, being careful to **do all** His commandments which I command you today, the LORD your God will set you high above all the nations of the earth. All these blessings will come upon you and overtake you **if** you **obey the LORD your God**"* (Deuteronomy 28:1-2).

And,

*For we have become partakers of Christ, if we hold fast the beginning of our assurance firm until the end, while it is said, "TODAY IF YOU HEAR HIS VOICE, DO NOT HARDEN YOUR HEARTS, AS WHEN THEY PROVOKED ME." For who provoked Him when they had heard? Indeed, did not all those who came out of Egypt led by Moses? And with whom was He angry for forty years? Was it not with those who sinned, whose bodies fell in the wilderness? And to whom did He swear that they would not enter His rest, but to those who were **disobedient**? So we see that they were not able to enter because of **unbelief*** (Hebrews 3:14-19).

Pray for revival.

Chapter Nine
Return to the Ancient Path

"This is what the Lord says: "Stand at the crossroads and look; ask for the ancient paths, ask where the good way is and walk in it, and you will find rest for your souls..."-Jeremiah. 6:16, 17

When God commanded Jeremiah to order Israel to return to **the ancient path**, He was not telling them to wear Amish clothes and drive horses and buggies. Simply put, God was warning Israel that they had deviated from His revealed Word and that a return to God was only possible if the people acknowledged their sin of rejecting the true worship of Yahweh. In other words, the ancient path is the pathway of confession and repentance and is the only designated path to God. All other ways are rejected.

I present the message of the return to the ancient path in its basic form: Jesus Christ is God in human flesh that came to earth to die in the place of sinful man. Mankind will die in their sins if we fail to acknowledge our sin, repent of it, accept Jesus Christ as our Lord and Savior and follow the lead of God's Spirit. There are no other options. It is Jesus Christ or eternal death. This message cannot be altered and must be accepted as the full gospel that was "once and for all handed down to the saints" (Jude 3).

The ancient path also includes the blueprint of ministry that is required to be followed by the believing church. Jesus Christ said to Peter after his declaration that Jesus was the Christ, the Son of the living God,

*I also say to you that you are Peter, and upon this rock **I will build My church**; and the gates of Hades will not overpower it* (Matthew 16:18).[88]

The important point in the Matthew verse is that Jesus is the chief builder of His church. Human beings, although a part of the process, are not the chief designers and builders of the church of God. Simply put, we are the servants of God that carry out His plan.[89] Remember, Jesus is

---

[88] The Roman church uses the Matthew verse to buttress their "Peter is the rock" thesis that is seminal in their understanding of Peter's position as "the first pope." It must be said that there are two different Greek words used in this verse that refer to the "rock." The first Greek word is "petros" which means a small stone. This is the word used by Jesus to describe Peter. Many scholars believe that Jesus used this word to describe Peter's bravery in declaring the truth of Jesus' Person. The second Greek word is "petra" that means a large rock. This is the word Jesus used to describe the fact that the church is built upon Jesus Himself. The scriptures bear witness to this truth: (Psalms 118:22; Isaiah 28:16; Matthew 21:42; Mark 12:10; Luke 20:17; Acts 4:11; Romans 9:33; I Corinthians 10:4; Ephesians 2:19, 20; I Peter 2:7). Notice that Peter understood the truth by making the quote in his first letter. Although men may be confused at least Peter knew the truth.

[89] The Apostle Paul made it clear in the Book of Romans that believers are the "bond-slaves" of God (Romans 1:1). This truth is often forgotten in the modern church that attempts to eradicate this "Master—servant" concept by replacing it with a "Jesus is a buddy" understanding. God does use terms such as "friend" when describing His love for His people, but He is still to be served as the

the head and we are His body. The head commands the body and the body carries out the commands. Our task is to obey God and not attempt to direct His steps. We need to resist our attempts to instruct Him and just obey. When we do this we will experience the revival that will rescue us from ourselves.

We as Christians need to return to that fundamental system of the message and ministry that was instituted immediately after the first revival on the Day of Pentecost,

They devoted themselves to the apostle's teaching, and to fellowship, to the breaking of bread and to prayer. Everyone was filled with awe, and many wonders and miraculous signs were done by the apostles. All the believers were together and had everything in common. Selling their possessions and goods, they gave to anyone as he had need. Every day they continued to meet together in the temple courts. They broke bread in their homes and ate together with glad and sincere hearts, praising God and enjoying the favor of all the people. And the Lord added to their number daily those who were being saved." (Acts 2:42-47).

This is the blueprint of the dynamic ministry given by God to His church. Any church that does these things will become a powerful weapon in the hand of God. Unfortunately, you have to search far and wide to find a twenty-first century church doing the following Scriptural activities:

Completely focused on the pure, unadulterated Word of God

The Word of God is spiritual food to the Christian. A failure to take this food into our souls daily will lead to spiritual malnutrition and possible death. True believers know that the Word of God is to be recognized as the infallible and indispensable message from Almighty God to His people. With that fact in mind the true Christian knows that the Word of God is to be studied and obeyed as if our lives depended on it…and it does.

The unfortunate fact: Worldly concepts and messages have seeped in to the message of the twenty-first century church. Modern secular psychotherapy, liberal politics, corrupt and blasphemous Hollywood films, opinions of unprincipled television and radio commentators and comments from biblically unsound liberal pulpits all set forth the classic case of the blind leading the blind. Only a Bible believing church can stand against such menacing opposition.

Fellowshipping at the drop of a hat

Modern fellowship is usually limited to a cup of coffee after a Sunday service and maybe a polite "How are you" uttered as a common

---

Almighty God Who purchased us from the slave-market of sin by His shed blood (I Corinthians 7:22; I Peter 1:18-19; Colossians 1:13-14).

courtesy and not much more. The Christian fellowship described in the Bible is much deeper and can be described in the following manner: True Christian fellowship means being an integral part of a living and vibrant family. It is opposed to isolation, solitude, loneliness and our present-day independent kind of individualism. True Christian fellowship means sharing common interests, goals, feelings, activities, beliefs, labors, responsibilities, goods, and the most important commodity of all—our time.

NOTE: The downward spiral of civilization strongly indicates that the end times are upon us. There will be a time when Christians will be forced to share their homes with other Christians just to be able to eat. In that time fellowship will take on a new and deeper meaning. It will be fellowship…or die.

Praying without ceasing

Any church that resists the call for intercessory prayer will take their place in history alongside the Dodo bird and other extinct entities. Intercessory prayer is the strongest weapon we possess to derail the plans of those that demand that God's church abandon the battlefield and submit to the rule of the apostate world. A non-praying church is nothing but an embarrassment to God and His promises. A non-praying church will only guard the empty ruins of a long past move of God.

The unfortunate fact: The prayer meeting is a forgotten dinosaur—the least attended meeting in the American church. This is not just an error it is **SIN.** In the end times the church that does not pray will cease to exist and will turn to dust. A non-praying church will grease the deceptions that will cause our downfall and bring judgment upon the land.

Experiencing signs and wonders

Signs and wonders are the proof that God is among us and that He is performing acts of power to light a fire under His people in order to prepare the way for His entrance into our reality. A God that can overturn what the world perceives as reality, is a living God of incredible power and promise. A church that accepts the condition of a world devoid of God's almighty power—is nothing but a powerless social club that cannot overturn the darkness of the present reality. The truth is that God can do anything, including healing those who have been consigned to death, to prove that He is the rightful ruler of history. True Christians should expect God to overturn the pronouncements of the "learned" men that fail to see His greatness. A praying church will know beyond a shadow of doubt that God is master of all. A praying church will experience the presence and power of God.

The unfortunate fact: Many twenty-first century churches deny the Holy Spirit's gifts while others overemphasize them producing a stage show. Finding a balance is often "the impossible dream."

Engaging in deep and intense worship

Truth alert: Worship should never be considered an "add on" or just "filler" but what it really is: The principle duty of every believer. Notice the following command from the mouth of the Lord:

Praise the LORD! Praise God in His sanctuary; Praise Him in His mighty expanse. Praise Him for His mighty deeds; Praise Him according to His excellent greatness. Praise Him with trumpet sound; Praise Him with harp and lyre. Praise Him with timbrel and dancing; Praise Him with stringed instruments and pipe. Praise Him with loud cymbals; Praise Him with resounding cymbals. Let everything that has breath praise the LORD. Praise the LORD! (Psalm 150).

NOTE: An end-times church will worship their brains out as God calls them to declare His greatness. Worship is warfare and we should actively embrace the honor to uproot Satan's kingdom by engaging in it. True worship is anathema to Satan and should be offered up by all who truly love God.

Sharing all things in common

Just like the believers in the first century, Christians of today will be called upon to extend their personal resources to those who are in dire need. The obedient Christians of today will be expected to overturn the outcomes ordained by the workers of iniquity by extending their commitment by not withholding their worldly goods.

The unfortunate fact: People will invest in their own family but may have problems with extending those blessings out to others. In the end times the extension of blessings to the extended family—the church—will be required in order to survive.

Evangelizing everywhere they go

Unfortunately, finding modern Christians with a desire to witness to their neighbors is often an impossible task. People are afraid and embarrassed to speak about their faith and easily succumb to the inhibitions that come directly from the enemy. We should never forget that Christianity is always just one generation away from extinction. If we refuse to witness we may find ourselves in an aging church with a smaller congregation each passing year. Remember, the people we bring to Christ will be one person less that will carry out the Antichrist's commands to annihilate the professing church. It is a defensive action against the enemies of truth.

O God, arrogant men have risen up against me, and a band of violent men have sought my life. And they have not set You before them (Psalm 86:14).

New is not always better

I have already said that we live in a "fast food culture." Everything from soap to cereal must be "new and improved" so that consumers, who have already previously purchased the product without satisfaction, will buy the product again and put money in the pockets of corporate America. Billions are made off selling the same old products with new ads and jingles pasted on the box to prompt the American consumers to dump their money on the counter.

But new is not always better. Anyone who has seen some of the old movie stars knows that the new stars of today are severely "talent challenged." Hollywood, realizing the short-comings of many of today's "stars," surrounds them with action scripts with plenty of bang, pop and special effects just to make them look good on the screen and thusly make a buck at the box office. Dragging a no-talent, egotist into stardom is a hard job. Just ask any filmmaker.

When I was a kid, I can remember going to White Castle[90] in Cleveland, Ohio to eat some of their mini hamburgers. It was always a special treat to sit on a grossly stained stool in those drafty, ugly White Castles and eat miniscule square burgers on those mushy white square buns. Lifting the bun and seeing it stick to the "meat," drove everyone to grab that bottle filled with rancid ketchup and drown those pathetic burgers. Okay, I agree entering a White Castle or any other hamburger joint could be a fatal risk, but I didn't care. To my mind, going to White Castle was a visit to the Promised Land. Many years later I found frozen White Castle burgers in a box at the food store. I felt like I had won the lottery. I grabbed a box of those precious little burgers, ran home and put them in the microwave. The results were disastrous. The mushy white bun was even mushier than I remembered and the meat tasted like molded paste. I tossed what was left in the trash and mentally chalked off another myth from my youth.

So what have I learned? Simply stated: No one can take a moment or a product or anything from our lives and keep it hidden away safe and sound for that proverbial rainy day. Things in this created world change, but not always for the better.

Things from God, however, are different. When God says something or does something it takes its place within the realm of the eternal and does not change. With God you can always depend on stability.

"I the Lord do not change." (Malachi 3:6; see also Hebrews 13:8).

Lost in the swamp

The true gospel has been lost in the swamp of modern twenty-first century Churchianity. Each year we lose more of the old Christians who

---

[90] **White Castle Hamburgers:** White Castle was founded in 1921 and became one of the first fast food chains in the world. It is found mostly in the Midwest and on the East Coast. The restaurants look like miniature castles with parapets and towers that look like chess rooks. The hamburgers were square and were very inexpensive, starting out as only five cents and then becoming 10 cents for many years. The Cleveland market closed down in 2014, but White Castles are still found throughout the country.

still remember how the true gospel used to be preached. It was cut and dry in those days—a gospel free of the modern embellishments and still featuring Jesus Christ as the main attraction. People came to church to "see" and "hear" Jesus and not because of the sideshow presented to reel in the carnal rabble. People traveled miles on dusty country roads to attend tent revivals that served as beacons of hope. They spent entire weekends attending meetings that lasted for hours. These hungry people heard the Word of God preached in power, responded to altar calls, got saved and then filled with the Holy Spirit and then went out to find the lost. It was a different world then and the simple gospel fit like old house shoes.

The lies some people say

I have to draw attention to some of the laughable comments made by some around the church today—"I'm tired of fire and brimstone sermons," and "I don't want judgmental sermons I just want to hear about God's love…"

Let us get one thing straight. No one in an American twenty-first century church has heard a fire and brimstone sermon for at least seventy years. Show me a pastor who preaches that way and I will show you a pastor who is bucking for inclusion in a special display case at the Smithsonian. Modern preachers, steeped in political correctness and filled with the seeker friendly dribble, do not give fire and brimstone sermons anymore.[91] Sermons about God's judgment and hell have gone the way of the dinosaur and the Dodo bird and no living parishioner—under the age of eighty—has ever heard one. Sermons emphasizing God's judgment are as rare as hair on a rock—which is baffling since Jesus is coming back to judge the world,

For we must all appear before the judgment seat of Christ, that each one may receive what is due him for the things done while in the body, whether good or bad. (II Corinthians 5:10; see also Revelation 19:11-16).

The fire and brimstone sermons that these "theological experts" are referring to are most likely some parody they saw on a TV sitcom, or some joke told in a back alley. They have never heard one.

And furthermore, hearing about God's love will not do you any good if you do not repent of your sins and embrace the holy God Who is your judge. God's love, although eternal and unchanging, is still only beneficial to those who receive His forgiveness. The fact is that billions of unrepentant and unredeemed human beings will be launched into the

---

[91] David Wilkerson was probably the most famous preacher to preach in the old style. He was a force in the Christian church and lit fires everywhere he went. When he was killed in a car crash in April 27, 2011, the church lost a revival lion. Any pastor or preacher that wants to see his church explode in Holy Spirit power should check out his sermons on YouTube. There was no compromise in this man at all. He was 100% committed to Jesus Christ…without apology.

fires of hell even though they are loved by God. This tragedy would be minimized if God's people would tell the truth—**God's love does not remove the command to repent and accept the gospel. If you do not obey God's command you will die in your sins and be judged. And then you will join the other billions who missed the boat by rejecting the grace of God manifested toward those that repent.**

*Or do you think lightly of the riches of His kindness and tolerance and patience, not knowing that the kindness of God leads you to repentance? But because of your stubbornness and unrepentant heart you are storing up **wrath** for yourself in the day of wrath and revelation of the righteous judgment of God, who will render to each person according to his deeds: to those who by perseverance in doing good seek the glory and honor and immortality, eternal life; but to those who are selfishly ambitious and do not obey the truth, but obey unrighteousness, wrath and indignation. There will be tribulation and distress for every soul of man who does evil, of the Jew first and also of the Greek, but glory and honor and peace to everyone who does good, to the Jew first and also to the Greek. For there is no partiality with God.* (Romans 2:4-11).

Enter the "Political Correctness Police"

You know who they are. Every church today has them—sometimes more than we really want to have. They are the "Political Correctness Police." They lurk about waiting to hear someone, usually a prophet, tell someone the truth about God's judgment and hell, or any other uncomfortable topic. They rush in and throw a mattress down on the floor so that the listener will not hurt themselves when they are driven to their knees because of the Holy Spirit's conviction. In their minds the worst thing imaginable is to make someone uncomfortable. It seems that they will do everything in their power to remove any and all discomfort—even if that discomfort was the result of the Holy Spirit's conviction. The real truth is that the "PCP" only have one group that they dislike and would like to drive out of the church—the prophets or anyone else who tells the truth regarding sin and its destructive abilities. They really do not like prophets and would banish them to Afghanistan if they could.

Christians are commanded to speak the truth by bringing warnings to those who are in questionable places in their lives. Iron sharpens iron, but this is almost impossible when the iron is discarded and we are left with hammers wrapped with sponge rubber to soften any blow. None of this nonsense existed in the first century when the church was following the ancient path. In those days brothers and sisters expressed their intense love for their brethren by warning them of the potholes in the road. In the churches we need to jettison the political correctness of our time and bring back the prophets who have been banished to

Afghanistan. We need to bring them back so that they can take their rightful places as the watchmen on the wall,

I have posted watchmen on your walls, O Jerusalem; they will never be silent day or night. You who call on the Lord, give yourselves no rest, and give Him no rest till He establishes Jerusalem and makes her the praise of the earth. (Isaiah 62:6, 7; see also Ezekiel 22:30, 31).

I wish to speak to those who are the watchmen on the walls. Yes, I know that you are looked upon as being the "Debby Downer" that would ruin a public hanging. Your fellow brothers and sisters most likely will conveniently forget to include you on the party list. You are the ones that the pastor instructs when you are called to make an announcement at church: "Oh, and try not to make them feel that they're being pressured to do—"(fill in whatever information or warning the pastor feels will bring discomfort to the congregation).[92]

Believe me, I know how you feel. Being stared at like you have six noses is not my idea of how to spend your morning at church. We who are called to be watchmen will always be treated this way. There is no escape. If you have a call to speak truth, without compromise, you will be looked upon with disdain. This is a fact. Do not attempt to run away from this assignment, because what you are doing is exactly what every true prophet in the Old Testament and the New have done. This is 100% true. Remember, no prophet is going to be loved in his/her own town. This is the word of the Lord and is the burden you will bear.

My only admonition is to warn you to be careful of how you react to rejection. Your fellow brothers and sisters, including some leadership, will look on you as if you are a cross to bear. Do not give them back their own medicine. You would be wrong to do so. I am not saying that their treatment of you is right…in reality they are as wrong as anyone could be. But they will not admit this and you will pay the cost. Love God and love His people. Give your word and refuse to be angry if and when they dismiss it. Be thankful that they only gave you an eye roll or a contemptuous sigh. I know some watchmen that were faced with an angry mob like in the movie **Frankenstein** that carried torches to the castle in order to corner the monster. Believe me, God wants you to speak His Word and He knows how you feel. Do not give them ammunition by acting angry and dismissive. Be thankful that God has

---

[92] This has happened to me and if you are watchman on the wall I'm sure it has happened to you. The sobering truth is that many of the new twenty-first century pastors have been exposed to the seeker friendly propaganda and consider themselves as the anointed guardians of comfort. Many of the pastors of these seeker-friendly churches believe that telling the truth to erring believers is an embarrassing procedure to be avoided. To many of these leaders, creating discomfort only means a loss of a tithe-paying member.

entrusted you to be a watchman on the walls. Your action may save many lives.[93]

When the church tries to fit in

I have heard Christians bragging about their church and their pastor—"Hey, my church is really cool!" And, "Pastor Billy Bob is not like other pastors, he's really with it." I believe that these Christians are sincere, but I am not sure that they really know what they are saying. Having a church that is "cool" may not mean that your church is God-centered and biblically sound. Frankly, I do not want to be part of a church that is just "cool." I want to be part of a church that is preaching the gospel with power and leading the city to Christ. I want to be part of a church that is expanding the kingdom of God on all fronts, healing the sick and bringing deliverance to Satan's captives. I want to be part of a church that is romping and stomping in its message and ministry for Jesus Christ. I want to be a part of that kind of church. Now, if your church is doing all those things and you still think it is cool, then I would agree with you. That would be a cool church! Or maybe better yet—a hot church!

And Pastor Billy Bob may be considered "with it," because he wears blue jeans, has a ring in his ear, and can talk the cultural jargon of our time. But just because Pastor Billy Bob does those things does not necessarily mean that he is "with it." What truly matters is whether Pastor Billy Bob is doing the following: wrestling in daily, intercessory prayer; leading people to Christ and then making them strong and vibrant disciples; and being a pastor after God's own heart and not just another twenty-first century church ringmaster majoring in the "warm fuzzys." Now if your pastor is doing all those things then I can accept that he is really "with it." I should be clear, however, that it is never a question of whether a pastor is "with it." **It is always a question of "Who" he is with.**

The spiritual smorgasbord of the modern church

Many churches today have set up a spiritual smorgasbord where they pick and choose what commands of God that they will obey. This is another rib-tickling, back slapper when you realize what they are doing.

---

[93] I once traveled to Ohio to see my family. It had been many years since I lived there and I had come to Christ while in California. While visiting at my Uncle Bill's house I spent a few hours with my cousin out in the garage. I witnessed to him and laid out the gospel in a way that should have saved anyone in earshot. My cousin dismissed me and I returned to California feeling defeated. A year later I received a letter from an unknown person in Ohio. He introduced himself and said that he had been in the garage while I was speaking with my cousin. I remembered him as a friend of my cousin that seemed to be working on my cousin's car and not paying much attention. The young man said that he had accepted Christ after hearing my message. I was stunned. I never paid him any mind and only focused on my cousin. The young man sent me Christmas cards for a few years, always sharing his adventures of faith. I lost track of him, but I will never forget. Open your mouth and speak. The Lord will use your words for His purpose. And you may be surprised at who may be listening.

In essence they are telling God that some of the activities that He wants His church to engage in are simply not acceptable to their narrow views of ministry. A church that sets itself up as a "specialist" is not seeing the truth that they are to be "general practitioners" for the gospel. The angel came to the disciples after their arrest and supernatural release and said, "Go stand in the temple courts," he said, "and tell the people the **full message** (gospel) of this new life." (Acts 5:20; see also Acts 4:18-20).[94]

The church of God is to give the full gospel—not portions that we like or accept, but the entire message of Jesus Christ.[95] The Word of God clearly reveals that any attempt to add or detract from the message of God is to be avoided at all costs.

Every word of God is tested; He is a shield to those who take refuge in Him. Do not add to His words or He will reprove you, and you will be proved a liar (Proverbs 30:5, 6).

And,

"Now, O Israel, listen to the statutes and the judgments which I am teaching you to perform, so that you may live and go in and take possession of the land which the LORD, the God of your fathers, is giving you. You shall not add to the word which I am commanding you, nor take away from it, that you may keep the commandments of the LORD your God which I command you (Deuteronomy 4:1, 2; see also Revelation 22:18-20).

We are to minister in power and model the ministry of Jesus in everything we do. It is my opinion that in order to accomplish this we must return to the ancient path before it is too late.

Pray for revival.

---

[94] The full gospel is the complete, unadulterated message of Jesus Christ. It is a message that hasn't been tweaked by representatives of denominations and churches that deny portions of the Scripture in order to support theological biases.

[95] The message of Jesus Christ is to be promoted in its entirety. It is not to be a spiritual smorgasbord where we can pick and choose the parts that we like and omit those we don't like. This is because the message comes from Him and it can never be separated from Him. We human beings do not have the supernatural insight to be judges of His message. We can only present it without amendment. Remember, we are the bond-servants and He is GOD. We have no option. We must do what we are told…

Chapter Ten

Jeremiah's Blueprint for Revival

"The word of the Lord came to me saying, 'Before I formed you in the womb I knew you, before you were born I set you apart; I appointed you as a prophet to the nations.'" –Jeremiah 1:4, 5

Jeremiah is unique. He is the only Jewish Old Testament prophet who was told specifically by God that he was appointed to be a prophet to the "nations." The Hebrew word for nations is *goyim* or "gentiles." This means that Jeremiah was a prophet for the gentiles—an interesting and yet perplexing designation for any prophet in Israel.

Many theologians have attempted to understand this peculiar role for Jeremiah. The one theory that seems to bear the most credibility is based on three points:

First, in the Book of Jeremiah we see many references to God's intervention in the history and affairs of gentile nations and kingdoms. Detailed warnings of judgments directed at Egypt, Babylon, Philistia, Ammon, Elam, Moab, the city of Damascus and others appear throughout the text. This inclusion of the gentile nations, although found in other Old Testament books, is clearly more pronounced in this particular book and presents Jeremiah's unique call to the nations.

Secondly, Jeremiah's unveiling of a promised **New Covenant** that was radically different from the Old. The difference was that it was not likened to the "corporate" relationship with a particular nation based on ethnicity but an individual relationship based on faith with any person that would accept the terms—both Jew or gentile.

*"Behold, days are coming," declares the Lord, "when I will make a **new covenant** with the house of Israel and with the house of Judah, not like the covenant which I made with their fathers in the day that I took them by the hand to bring them out of the land of Egypt, My covenant which they broke, although I was a husband to them," declares the Lord. "But this is the covenant which I will make with the house of Israel after those days," declares the Lord, "I will put My law within them and on their heart I will write it; and I will be their God, and they shall be My people. They will not teach again, each man his neighbor and each man his brother, saying, 'Know the Lord,' for they will all know Me, from the least of them to the greatest of them," declares the Lord, "for I will forgive their iniquity, and their sins I will remember no more."* (Jeremiah 31:27-34).

The new covenant's inclusion of the repentant gentiles was inaugurated by Jesus Christ at the Last Supper. The direct connection with Jeremiah's prophecy of a coming new covenant and the Last Supper is indisputable when reading the text.

*When the hour had come, He reclined at the table, and the apostles with Him. And He said to them, "I have earnestly desired to eat this Passover with you before I suffer; for I say to you, I shall never again eat it until it is fulfilled in the kingdom of God." And when He had taken a cup and given thanks, He said, "Take this and share it among yourselves; for I say to you, I will not drink of the fruit of the vine from now on until the kingdom of God comes." And when He had taken some bread and given thanks, He broke it and gave it to them, saying, "This is My body which is given for you; do this in remembrance of Me." And in the same way He took the cup after they had eaten, saying, "This cup which is poured out for you is **the new covenant in My blood..."*** (Luke 22:14-20).

And lastly, the Book of Jeremiah is a blueprint for revival—not only in Jeremiah's time but also for the ages.

NOTE: Although the people of Jeremiah's time ignored the call for revival and did not repent, Jeremiah's words are still etched in stone for those who seek the real movement of God for our day. **God's promise:** Anyone who reads Jeremiah's blueprint and follows its instructions will light a fire that will change the course of history.

Jeremiah's blueprint explained

God's spoken words to Jeremiah echo throughout time. They are an eternal indictment of all who refuse to call out to God for His deliverance,

This is what the Lord says: "What fault did your fathers find in Me, that they strayed so far from Me? They followed worthless idols and became worthless themselves. They did not ask, 'where is the Lord; Who brought us up out of Egypt and led us through the barren wilderness, through a land of deserts and rifts, a land of drought and darkness, a land where no one travels and no one lives? I brought you into a fertile land to eat its fruit and rich produce. But you came and defiled my land and made my inheritance detestable. (Jeremiah 1: 5-7).

The Lord made His indictment of His people very clear with His description of His miraculous intervention in their deliverance. It is obvious that God is chastening them for not asking "Where is the Lord" when the lack of His power and presence is clearly experienced. To hammer His point home God repeats His statement:

"The priests did not ask, 'Where is the Lord?' Those who deal with the Law did not know Me; the leaders rebelled against Me. The prophets prophesied by Baal, following worthless idols. (Jeremiah 1:8).

In this verse the Lord declared that the rejection by His people is universal—including the leadership. He stated that religion without a personal relationship with God is evil and deceptive. In God's opinion, claiming to be a follower of God without a vibrant salvation experience is nothing but an empty boast. According to God there seemed to be no difference between those who say they are believers and those who have no relationship with God in any shape or form.

Thus says the Lord, "Let not a wise man boast of his wisdom, and let not the mighty man boast of his might, let not a rich man boast of his riches; but let him who boasts boast of this, that he understands and knows Me, that I am the Lord who exercises lovingkindness, justice and righteousness on earth; for I delight in these things," declares the Lord. "Behold, the days are coming," declares the Lord, "that I will punish all who are circumcised and yet uncircumcised (their claim to be believers but are not)—Egypt and Judah, and Edom and the sons of Ammon, and Moab and all those inhabiting the desert who clip the hair on their temples; for all nations are uncircumcised (they are not believers), and all the house of Israel are uncircumcised of heart (not true believers)." (Jeremiah 9:23-26).

Anyone that can read and has any basic understanding of reality must agree that the modern church is literally dropping the ball. We seem to be so easily sidetracked that we fail to zero in on our main task—the evangelism of the world. Let me present a short parable:

The Milk Company

A milk company was created to do a simple task—make milk. The company did this successfully for a number of years until a new owner decided to bring in some "experts" that he thought would improve the business. The experts started devising some new programs after doing a lot of researching, planning and organizing.

The experts developed plans to produce different kinds of milk, and even other kinds of drinks, snack foods, yogurts, ice milks, ice creams, cream cheese, whipping cream and dozens of other new products. They developed fancy packages, slick ad campaigns and designed attractive t-shirts with catchy logos on them that they gave away. The factory workers buzzed with excitement as they cranked out the hundreds of new and interesting products. The experts talked about milk, trained others to talk about milk, and trained others to talk about talking about milk. The years went by and the company eventually failed. The reason for the failure—the company had forgotten about its original mission…to make milk.

The Christian church also has a mission. The Lord of the church explained that mission to His people in His last directive: **Go into the world and make disciples.** It really is a simple plan.

The problem is, like the fictional milk company, the church has brought in "experts" who are trying to make God's original plan…better. These "experts" talk about making disciples, train others to talk about making disciples, write books that talk about making disciples, hold seminars on how to talk about how to talk about making disciples, and talk about talking to others on how to talk about talking on making disciples. But when all is said and done we must admit that we have forgotten the job—to make disciples.

Jeremiah, like us in the modern church, has one simple task. He has been commanded to warn the people of their sins and prompt them to confess their rebellion before the Lord. It is in this context that God calls Jeremiah to present His grace to the rebellious people. It is God's offer of revival. All throughout this great book we see the anger of God balanced by His call of grace. Our God is a good God Who only wants the best for His children. He cannot be diverted from His task and will press His people to obey Him and fulfill the mission.

God will anoint those who are called to lead the revival:

Jeremiah, like us all, made excuses when called by God. He sounds very much like Moses, who mentioned his lack of verbal giftedness as a reason to be given a pass from the Lord's call (Exodus 4:10-12).

"Ah, Sovereign Lord," I said, "I don't know how to speak; I am only a child." But the Lord said to me, "Do not say, 'I am only a child.' You must go to everyone I send you to and say whatever I command you. Do not be afraid of them, for I am with you and will rescue you," declares the Lord Then the Lord reached out his hand and touched my mouth and said to me, "Now I have put my words in your mouth." (Jeremiah 1:6-9).

The servant of God will receive the anointing from the Lord to step out and be the spokesman for revival. We are not to "do" spiritual works in our own frail human strength. We do the things of God by His Spirit and His power,

"Not by might nor by power, but by my Spirit," says the Lord Almighty." (Zechariah 4:6).

The purpose of God's people clearly explained:

See, today I appoint you over nations and kingdoms to uproot and tear down, to destroy and overthrow, to build and to plant." (Jeremiah 1:10).

We are appointed by God **over** the nations. In other words, we are the head and not the tail. (Deuteronomy 28:13). God's people are to lead their culture and not to follow it.

NOTE: God has made it quite simple—only the people that know where they are going are supposed to lead.

We are to **uproot** and **tear down** Satan's plans and kingdom. Uprooting and tearing down? Did God really say that His followers are not to be "peaceniks" expressing compromise at the drop of a hat? **YES!** We are an army and not some gaggle of tourists sitting in beach chairs at Club Med. Real Christians know that compromise is the language of the Devil. If you shake the Devil's hand you better count your fingers. We are not to compromise but are called to defeat the powers of hell on this earth. We are to recognize that we are in a spiritual war and prepare ourselves for it. And then do it...

We are to **destroy** and **overthrow** the works of the flesh. First our own sinful acts of the flesh and then the sinful acts of the flesh in the culture. We do not accommodate the enemy (the flesh and sin) by trying to befriend it in order to secure some semblance of peace. We face the enemy (the flesh and sin), label it clearly and then decisively destroy it without mercy. It is really quite simple.

We are to **build** and to **plant**. After engaging in the war for the control of the earth and for the very lives of humanity, we are to become the healers and builders. We do not leave the battlefield in hopeless shambles, but assist the Lord in His restoration.

NOTE: I believe that the Lord purposely uses people that have been healed by God to be "the wounded healers." The wounded healers are really the only ones that truly understand what hurting people are going through. This truth is easily discovered within the Word:

Blessed be the God and Father of our Lord Jesus Christ, the Father of mercies and God of all comfort, who comforts us in all our affliction so that we will be able to comfort those who are in any affliction with the comfort with which we ourselves are comforted by God. For just as the sufferings of Christ are ours in abundance, so also our comfort is abundant through Christ. But if we are afflicted, it is for your comfort and salvation; or if we are comforted, it is for your comfort, which is effective in the patient enduring of the same sufferings which we also suffer; and our hope for you is firmly grounded, knowing that as you are sharers of our sufferings, so also you are sharers of our comfort (II Corinthians 1:3-7).

The purpose of God does not sound like what we hear today from the compromising modern church. Unfortunately, many churches in our modern culture are fearful of disturbing the status quo and make the attempt to fit in to the culture of the time. Many in today's church seem to be ignorant of the call to spiritual battle that is trumpeted throughout the pages of the Bible. Those who know the truth and attempt to blow the trumpet will be soundly disciplined by those who make up the ignorant mob.[96] This ignorance drives the church to act the fool and roll over when the flood of sin and immorality sweeps through our cities and neighborhoods, taking captive millions of lost sinners. Compromise

---

[96] An evangelist came to my church many years ago and said, "Jesus loves the world, but He is not a peacenik." His meaning was that the Lord's love was not to be used as a shield against repentance and restoration. Today, whenever Christians point out the sins and inconsistencies of our fallen culture they are accused of being loveless. This, in fact, is the exact opposite. What a Christian is really saying is—*Jesus loves you and I love you too much to not warn you that your sins are leading you to death and hell. Repent before you die without Christ and suffer eternal damnation.* This is a real act of love, especially when we all know that the person who utters these truths will be chastised and insulted by the foul, ignorant screaming mob.

has become the universal message and the church becomes a pawn in the march of evil that is drowning the earth. God commands Jeremiah to stand up against sin and embrace the call to attack sin at its roots. This attack against sin is never to be seen as an attack against sinners, but as an impassioned reaching out to the drowning sinner through prayer and evangelism. The weapons of our warfare are never carnal and fleshly, but an exercise of the spiritual weapons that God has given His people.

For though we walk in the flesh, we do not war according to the flesh, for the weapons of our warfare are not of the flesh, but divinely powerful for the destruction of fortresses. (II Corinthians 10:3, 4).

The main weapon is love; a love so powerful that it breaks the chains of despair and hopelessness that keeps our culture bound. This love never winks at sin but drives the Christian to their knees to express their love in a war of deliverance. Because we share God's love we are able to reflect it back toward a culture that is dead while standing on its feet. This is not the squishy, "sloppy agape," that we see in the modern church. This is the love of God that unmasks sin and rescues the sinner by offering a way out—the repentance that restores the soul.

NOTE: Many Christians use "love" as a bludgeon against God's prophets. Their argument: If you correct a sinner and/or refuse to accept someone's sin as a "right" you are a hater with no love. This is complete and unadulterated baloney. A person who truly loves will love so much that they will do their best to save a sinner from destruction by telling the truth. The "do-gooder" that is attacking the prophet is the real culprit that is allowing another human being to be deceived. Just a fact...

Through our intercessory prayers we tear down and uproot, we destroy and overthrow the evil world system. This is not work for the faint hearted. This is the work for on-fire, gospel breathing, and powerhouses of faith. This is the work of revival.

The warning of the coming judgment of God:

The Word of the Lord came to me: "What do you see, Jeremiah?"

"I see the branch of an almond tree," I replied.

The Lord said to me, "You have seen correctly, for I am watching to see that my word is fulfilled."

The word of the Lord came to me again: "What do you see?"

"I see a boiling pot, tilting away from the north," I answered. The Lord said to me, "From the north disaster will be poured out on all who live in the land. I am about to summon all the peoples of the northern kingdoms," declares the Lord. "Their kings will come and set up their thrones in the entrance of the gates of Jerusalem; they will come against all her surrounding walls and against all the towns of Judah. I will pronounce my judgments on my people because of their wickedness in forsaking me, in burning incense to other gods and in worshipping what their hands have made." (Jeremiah 1:11-16).

The branch of the almond tree is a reference to Aaron's staff that was placed within the Ark of the Covenant (Numbers 17). The staff was the symbol of God's authority. God is saying that he is doing these things through his power and authority in order to establish in the minds and hearts of the people that God is not to be trifled with. His authority will not be questioned through the rebellious actions of those that claim to be His spokesmen.

The boiling pots were placed upon the city walls and filled with burning oil. The pots were to be turned over on the heads of an attacking army that was surrounding the city. Notice that God is saying that the pots are to be tilted away from the invading armies (away from the north). This indicates that God is bringing his wrath upon his own people for their sins and not against the invaders.[97] The invaders are in fact the hand of God being used to discipline the rebellious people. This is a clear indication that God does his work with those who count…his own people. The invaders are just "potted palms" on God's stage. They only perform the acts of judgment.

The command to speak for God:

"Get yourself ready! Stand up and say to them whatever I command you. Do not be terrified by them, or I will terrify you before them. Today I have made you a fortified city, an iron pillar and a bronze wall to stand against the whole land—against the kings of Judah, its officials, its priests and the people of the land. They will fight against you but will not overcome you, for I am with you and will rescue you," declares the Lord." (Jeremiah 1:17-19).

Those who speak for God are always a minority in number. Their job is to stand up against the vast majority of those who do not have a clue what God is doing. Being God's spokesman is a lonely job and you will not make friends easily. The people will often not understand your message and will find fault with you. Jeremiah was warned that they will even fight against him.

The sin of mankind will place all humanity in direct rebellion against God and those who speak for God will be lumped in with Him for special resistance. When God tells Jeremiah that He will make him an iron pillar and a bronze wall He is saying two things: As the iron pillar you will hold up my plans and purposes like a pillar holds up a roof. As a bronze wall you will resist all attempts to break my plans and purposes. Iron and bronze are much stronger than plaster and will not be broken down or collapsed by the enemies of God. Those who have been called and sanctified to speak against humanity's sin are a special breed

---

[97] It doesn't take a Bible scholar to see that the Islamic terrorists are acting as the new Babylonians. They are attacking our nation to wake us up to how far we have fallen from God. A revival sent by God that calls this nation back to Him will do more to end the terrorist threat then all the bombs and guns on earth.

that have been internally equipped—by the Holy Spirit—to carry out the assignment. These special people have an inner love for God that allows them to trust Him completely. In love, they will speak against mankind's words that support the world's rebellion.

The failure of God's people:

Chapter two details the litany of sins committed against the God of Israel. The sin came from the top—the priests, prophets and kings—and went all the way down to the lowest person. There was a complete rebellion against the Lord—much like today.

The sins of the people—

They left their first love (Jeremiah 2:1-3).

They became idol worshippers (Jeremiah 2: 5).

They ignored God's power and provision that was extended to the people (Jeremiah 2: 6-7).

They were led by leaders and prophets who did not know the Lord and did not understand his Word. They are the perfect case of the blind leading the blind (Jeremiah 2: 8).

They exchanged the living God for their own gods. In our day the idols we choose can be anything—cars, money, jobs, relationships, sexual perversions, hobbies, our own family and children, our desire to be loved by the world, etc. (Jeremiah 2: 9-12).

The two overwhelming sins:

"My people have committed two sins: They have forsaken Me, the spring of living water, and have dug their own cisterns, broken cisterns that cannot hold water." (Jeremiah 2:13).

The symbol of water is used throughout the Word to represent the Holy Spirit. God is telling Jeremiah that the people have rejected the Spirit of God and His power and have built their own church (the cistern) that cannot hold the Holy Spirit. They have done the most disastrous act imaginable—the attempt to build their own kingdom without God's leadership, power and presence. What a travesty! What insult! How can believers reject God and do their own thing? Welcome to the modern church. This is routine throughout America today. And we wonder why there is no revival?

The plea for God's help from a sin-soaked people:

As a thief is disgraced when he is caught, so the house of Israel is disgraced. (Jeremiah 2:26).

A thief only feels disgrace when he is caught—not when he is doing his sin. God's point is that Israel only calls out when the pressure is too much for them to bear. They do not turn to God because it is the right thing to do. Their repentance is an act of expediency,

...yet when they are in trouble they say, "Come and save us!" Where then are the gods you made for yourselves? Let them come if they

can save you when you are in trouble! For you have as many gods as you have towns, O Judah. (Jeremiah 2:27, 28).

There is an old saying in the military: "There are no atheists in a foxhole." This means that people turn to God when they are in trouble or when great pressure is upon them. God is so angry at their false repentance that He mocks their gods. His point is well taken—when you are in trouble you come to me. Why not go to your false gods that you admire when things are good and the pressure is off? The reason is that people know in their hearts that God is real and that their idols are false. Their reluctance to accept His righteous leadership is just an example of their inner rebellion against truth.

Repentance of our sins is the only way to receive blessing:

"Return, faithless Israel," declares the Lord, "I will frown on you no longer, for I am merciful," declares the Lord. "I will not be angry forever. Only acknowledge your guilt—you have rebelled against the Lord your God, you have scattered your favors to foreign gods under every spreading tree, and you have not obeyed me," declares the Lord. (Jeremiah 3:11-13).

God continued to offer forgiveness and restoration to His people throughout the Book of Jeremiah. It is a great example of the goodness and grace of God. No matter how evil His people become He is still willing to deal with them in a loving and restorative manner. What grace! What love and acceptance! What enduring patience is exhibited by our God!

And all He requires is that we truly repent.

The exceptional promises of revival explained:

When revival comes God pours out His Spirit and brings healing to the land. If only the people of God would believe His Word and repent. Then everything they have prayed for would take on flesh (become real and tangible).

When revival comes—

God will give Spirit-filled and anointed leaders when Israel repents: *"Return faithless people," declares the Lord, "For I am your husband. I will choose you—one from a town and two from a clan—and bring you to Zion.* ***Then I will give you shepherds after my own heart, who will lead you with knowledge and understanding."*** (Jeremiah 3:14, 15).[98]

God will cure backsliding: *"Return faithless people; I will cure your backsliding."* (Jeremiah 3:22).

---

[98] This promise is one of the most sobering truths we can embrace. Quality spiritual leadership is only given to those who have repented of their sins of rebellion. If a church truly desires a godly pastor who will preach and lead through the power of the Holy Spirit, they must prostrate themselves and seek God's forgiveness and restoration. When we do that God will send us His best. If not, we will get leaders that will appeal to our carnal natures.

God will bless the nations through the example and presence of His godly people: *"If you will return, O Israel, return to me...then the nations will be blessed by Him and in Him they will glory."* (Jeremiah 4:1, 2).

God will save His people: *"O Jerusalem, wash the evil from your heart and be saved."* (Jeremiah 4:14).

God will give full restoration: *"**If you repent**, I will restore you that you may serve me; if you utter worthy, not worthless words, you will be my spokesman."* (Jeremiah 15:19).

Jeremiah's challenge to our time

I said earlier in this chapter that Jeremiah was chosen by God to be a prophet to the church. I truly believe that my point is accurate. Jeremiah's blueprint, if followed, will bring the Christian church into a new season of revival that is desperately needed.

It is obvious to anyone who is conscious that the world is heading for the abyss. Without a re-igniting of revival fire in God's church the numbers of lost souls will explode beyond comprehension. It is time to cease our defense of mediocrity and rebellion and seek God's divine intervention. Revival, true revival is the need of the hour.

Pray for revival.

Chapter Eleven
The Point Men and Women that Lead Revival

1. Confess all known sin.
2. Deal with and get rid of anything doubtful in your life.
3. Be ready to obey the Holy Spirit instantly.
4. Confess Christ publicly.

-The battle cry of the 1904 Welsh Revival.

In Vietnam there were men who walked the point for their platoon or company. They were out in front, exposed and ready to protect the men that were depending on them for a safe passage through the jungle. The point men were literally the cream of the crop, fearless heroes who excelled at their task. Many American GIs fondly remember the men who walked the point drawing the enemy fire and leading the way.

In the church we also have point men and women. They are the ones who lead the way and take the incoming fire that is meant to bring down the church and assassinate common sense. Such point men and women have always led the way in the quest for revival.

Ordinary people

Just who are the point men and women of God who seek revival? Are they superstar Christians, powerhouses of faith, famous leaders of great churches or maybe well-known evangelists? The answer is none of the above. It is a matter of historical record that revivals are seldom birthed through the leadership of Christians of renown.

It is the ordinary people whom God uses to seek revival. They are the ones who are willing to spend the time and effort to intercede for the Lord's outpouring of power and majesty. I once heard a famous evangelist make the following pronouncement: *"No PhD has ever led a revival."*[99]

The Lord loves ordinary people. He made an important comment about His love for them when He spoke through the Apostle Paul in his first letter to the Corinthians,

"Brothers, think of what you were when you were called. Not many of you were wise by human standards; not many were influential; not many were of noble birth. But God chose the foolish things of the world to shame the wise; God chose the weak things of the world to shame the strong. He chose the lowly things of this world and the despised things—

---

[99] I am not sure that Martin Luther qualifies as a revivalist since he did not "technically" lead a revival, but instead was instrumental in launching the Protestant Reformation that broke Rome's stranglehold on biblical interpretation in the 1500s. Many historians argue that Luther was a revolutionary whose accomplishments are extraordinary and infinitely important, but he was not a revivalist in the classic sense. Again, I am not completely convinced that he was a revivalist, but definitely was an important man of God.

and the things that are not—to nullify the things that are, so that no one may boast before him." (I Corinthians 1:26-29).

In this chapter I want to highlight five individuals who serve as an example of God's plan to use the ordinary and common people to advance His Kingdom. One was a Sunday school teacher from Wales, two were elderly housebound sisters, one was an African-American pastor struggling against the racism of his day, and one was a hippie singer from 1960 California. They were all ordinary persons who were overlooked by their peers and often dismissed by the established church…and yet they were the chosen ones used by God to light the fires of revival in their generation.

Evan Roberts: Revival's Quiet Man

Most of us have a picture in our minds of what a leader of a revival should look like. If we took a vote my guess is that John the Baptist would win in a landslide. Can you imagine the grizzled John shuffling out of the wilderness and then heading toward a church to blow off the roof? His piercing eyes would burn a hole through your soul and his thunderous voice would pop your eardrums. There would not be a locust safe for miles.

No one would have voted for the young twenty-six year old from Wales who was slightly built, retiring in demeanor and a virtual unknown. His name was Evan Roberts and he appeared on the scene with no fanfare or notoriety.

Evan Roberts was born on June 8, 1878 in Loughor, Wales. He was the only son of coal miner Henry Roberts and his wife Hannah. The Roberts were members of a strict Calvinistic Methodist Church in Loughor called Moriah Chapel. From his earliest days, young Evan was very committed to God and never missed a church meeting. With little interest in normal boyish pursuits, he spent his time in prayer and the memorization of Scripture. He was captivated by his grandfather's stories of the 1859 Welsh Revival and began to pray for God to do it again.

At age eleven he dropped out of school to work with his father in the coal mines where he stayed for twelve years. Being a physically slight young man and obviously ill-suited to the rigors of coal mining, he left the mines at 23 years old to be a blacksmith's apprentice at his uncle's shop. Always careful with his personal conduct, Evan never smoked or drank and no unkind or blasphemous word escaped his lips. He was universally loved by all who knew him.

The spirituality of Evan Roberts was so pronounced that he was chosen to be the superintendent of Moriah Chapel's Sunday school. While in that position he developed close ties with the youth group prodding them to pray with him for revival. Following Evan Robert's leadership, the youth group became a no-nonsense gathering of prayer warriors bent on carrying the banner of revival throughout the land. They loved Evan and wanted to follow his lead.

First and foremost, Evan Roberts was a man of prayer. The concern within his heart was for revival and he spent eleven years praying nightly for it to occur in his beloved Wales. He was so captivated by intercessory prayer that he once was asked to leave his lodgings when he frightened the landlady with his all night groaning and cries to the Lord.

In the spring of 1904, Roberts felt a call to preach and decided to begin studying for the ministry. Concerned about his lack of formal education, he decided to sign up for a grammar school in Newcastle Emlyn to prepare for his entrance into Bible College. On September 13, 1904, Evan Roberts went to Newcastle Emlyn to begin his studies. But God had other plans for this young Welshman and steered him toward a Christian convention being held in Blaenanerch just 2 ½ weeks after starting grammar school. On September 30th Roberts attended a service led by evangelist Seth Joshua.[100] During the service Roberts experienced what he described as a Baptism with the Holy Spirit. This spiritual quickening occurred during a prayer time when he uttered the words **"Bend me O Lord."** It seemed like heaven opened and the anointing of the Holy Spirit flooded his innermost being. It was at this time that God spoke the words into his heart that would forever change Wales and the world—*"Leave the school and return home. Start preaching My message."* Evan put up a brief struggle, but quickly acquiesced to the Lord's commands and headed back home.

On the night of his arrival at Loughor, Roberts captivated the parishioners at Moriah Chapel with his message of repentance and consecration. The quiet and shy young man, freshly empowered by the Holy Spirit, was now a sharpened tool in the hand of Almighty God. For the next month, Roberts stirred the congregation with his fiery appeals for revival. The intercessory prayers for revival went on all night in the youth group. The expectancy was high and the young people stood in faith with their leader.

Commencing on October 31st, a series of public revival prayer meetings were held at Moriah Chapel. On the night of November 6th Evan Roberts prodded the participants to stand and publicly confess Jesus Christ as Savior and Lord. When they did the entire congregation was hit by the power of God and in one accord they fell to their knees in submission to Christ. The message was simple: God was tired of religion and wanted His people to bow the knee and accept His leadership.

---

[100] Seth Joshua was a Welsh Presbyterian minister and evangelist who was a forerunner of the 1904-1905 Welsh Revival. Joshua testified that he had prayed for years for God to raise up a young man to revive the churches. Evan Roberts was that young man.

The word spread and the revival burst forth and saturated the entire Welsh countryside. Hundreds of people surrounded the church twenty-four hours a day pleading with God to save their souls. There was no room in Moriah Chapel so the youth group became Evan's traveling ministry team and they began to share the message of repentance and salvation throughout Wales. The truth was finally allowed to surface— God was not impressed with religion and wanted true revival. Human sin and rebellion was no longer acceptable.

The revival was a tsunami. From the beginning to August 1905, a period of nine months, 100,000+ people came to Jesus Christ. The effects were so stunning that saloons closed for lack of customers. Crime evaporated. Family abuse all but disappeared. Political rallies were unattended. Sports programs stopped for the want of fans and players. The mules in the coal mines were confused when the miners stopped using profanity to direct them. Newspaper reporters flocked to Wales to report on the revival and the news spread around the world. British Prime Minister David Lloyd George was caught up in it and said that God was rocking Wales like an earthquake. Rich and poor alike came to Christ. The entire country was saturated with the presence of God. Revival was on the menu. The fact was finally allowed to surface: God was sick and tired of men's agenda and was loosing His church from the shackles of human deceptions and was bringing His truth to the forefront.

Evan Roberts never ceased being the quiet unassuming man. Instead of demanding to be the leader of the revival, he would sit on a pew like any other seeker and allowed others to give their testimonies. Many times he would not speak at all, but instead allowed the Holy Spirit to have full control of the meeting. It was shocking in 1904 Wales for ordinary people to stand up and give a word or read a Scripture without the oversight of the professional clergy. Nothing like this had ever been seen and the effects were astounding. The Holy Spirit had top billing and Roberts refused to do anything that would interfere with God's leadership. This simple act allowed the revival to reach incredibly high levels of divine presence and power. Many observers said that it was the purest and most anointed revival ever seen. Hundreds of people were drawn into the ministry and kept their call for the rest of their lives.[101] The changes ran deep.

Like a shooting star the leader of the 1904-05 Welsh Revival flashed across the skies and then withdrew from the revival. The reason

---

[101] I met a beloved brother in Christ named Brother Willis. He had been saved through Evan Roberts' ministry in Wales in 1905. Brother Willis was in his nineties when I first met him at a church in Redondo Beach, California in the 1970s. The man was a brilliant preacher that carried an anointing that was so powerful that he was still a force at such an advanced age. When he spoke about the 1904-05 Welsh Revival he would light up the room. Brother Willis was a treasure.

for his withdrawal was simple: Evan Roberts was a gentle man of peace and didn't know how to handle the vicious attacks against him and the revival. The constant criticism occupied page one in every newspaper in the country. The most vicious critics were the established religious leaders that demeaned his character labelling him a dangerous radical that was insane...or worse. Deeply hurt by the attacks from his beloved church, he suffered an emotional breakdown that crushed him beyond remedy.

Broken and depressed, he left the revival and went into seclusion. He spent the remainder of his life writing poetry and tending his garden. He died in 1951 as a virtual unknown in Cardiff. He was 73 years old.

There is an important point that I must repeat: Evan Roberts was not the kind of super star evangelist that we see on our television screens. He didn't write books, make CDs, travel in a private jet plane, receive enormous offerings, own a number of houses, or any of the other accoutrements that seem to be attached to the modern TV evangelists that are so commonplace in our time.

Evan Roberts was an ordinary man called and anointed by an extraordinary God. This fact must never be lost to the "ordinary" Christians of today. God will do His work through anyone with a willing heart. Did you hear what I said? **GOD WILL DO HIS WORK THROUGH ANYONE WITH A WILLING HEART!** This truth must be burned into our souls. The Lord of the church has plans to bring His fire of revival upon the earth. He wants **YOU** to be part of it. To borrow a slogan used to promote education for all children in our country I will say, *"In God's kingdom there are no Christians left behind."*

The story of Evan Roberts is a testimony to the faithfulness of God's ordinary people. Listen to God. Do what He says. Do it with boldness; and you will see revival burst forth like a flood.

The 1904-1905 Welsh Revival is the most studied revival in history. This revival was the igniter of the Azusa Street Revival in Los Angeles in 1906 and all the subsequent moves of God that followed.[102] According to the experts it is the greatest example of the truth that prayer ignites revival. It cannot be ignored that ongoing, persistent intercessory prayer was the catalyst of one of the greatest outpourings of spiritual power and grace ever seen on earth. Millions of people were influenced by it and the cause of Christ has been greatly advanced.

The history of the church was forever changed when Evan Roberts heeded the call of God and gave his life to revival. Evan Roberts will always be remembered as revival's gentle soul.

---

[102] Great Pentecostal denominations like the Assemblies of God and the International Church of the Foursquare Gospel were birthed by the 1906 Azusa Street Revival.

The legend of Peggy and Christine Smith

Many stories have been told about the great revival preaching of the famous evangelist/revivalist Duncan Campbell during the New Hebrides Revival of 1949. His powerful sermons can be found on YouTube for those who desire to hear what God's anointing sounds like when He has control of the speaker. Little is known, however, of the prayer warriors that called down this revival.

In a little cottage in Barvas, Scotland the New Hebrides Revival of 1949 was ignited by the prayers of two elderly sisters, Peggy and Christine Smith. Peggy was eighty-four and blind while Christine was eighty-two and crippled with arthritis so severe that she could not move. Because of their infirmities, neither could attend public worship at their church. Faced with this difficulty they decided to use their cottage as a prayer central. Every night they would intercede for God to pour forth His revival on a land that was barren of spirituality and love for God. The women were tenacious in their intercession and bombarded heaven with tears and cries for the outpouring of God's Holy Spirit.

One night Christine read the Lord's words from Isaiah,

For I will pour out water on the thirsty land and streams on the dry ground; I will pour out My Spirit on your offspring and My blessing on your descendants; and they will spring up among the grass like poplars by streams of water. This one will say, 'I am the Lord's'; and that one will call on the name of Jacob; and another will write on his hand, 'Belonging to the Lord,' and will name Israel's name with honor. (Isaiah 44:3-5).

Immediately, both sisters knew that this was a call for them to press in and claim the promises of revival for their land. A short while later Peggy had a vision—*Revival was coming and the church of her fathers would be crowded again with young people.* Over a period of a few days the messages from God began to pour forth like a flood. During one of their intercessions, the Lord gave the sisters specific instructions to send for their pastor, Rev. James Murray MacKay, and inform him of the coming outpouring.

They sent for Pastor MacKay and told him that God had told them that a powerful revival was coming to the land and that he needed to start preparations for its coming. The pastor, knowing these women for many years, understood that they were speaking for God. He asked them what he was to do and they said, *"Gather the deacons and tell them to consecrate themselves through prayer and fasting. While they are doing this they are to make preparations for the outpouring of God's Spirit."*

Pastor MacKay passed on the message to his deacons and they began to prepare. A small group of young men began meeting in a barn for the sole purpose of praying down God's Spirit for revival. Each night they met and cried out to the Lord. One night one of their number stood up and read from Isaiah,

On your walls, O Jerusalem, I have appointed watchmen; all day and night they will never keep silent. You who remind the Lord, take no rest for yourselves; and give Him no rest until He establishes and makes Jerusalem a praise in the earth. (Isaiah 62: 6, 7).

Knowing that this was a message from God, the young men made a covenant with God that they would not cease until revival fire fell from heaven. From that night on a new, and deeper call descended upon them. Finally, one of the young men began to call for a renewal within them to cleanse their hearts to prepare the way. He stood up and began reading from the Psalms,

Who may ascend into the hill of the Lord? And who may stand in His holy place? He who has a clean hands and a pure heart, who has not lifted up his soul to falsehood and has not sworn deceitfully. He shall receive a blessing from the Lord and righteousness from the God of his salvation. This is the generation of those who seek Him, who seek Your face—even Jacob. (Psalm 24:3-6).

The young man turned to the others and said, *"Brethren, it seems to me just so much humbug to be waiting and praying as we are, if we ourselves are not rightly related to God." The young man lifted up his hands and cried: "Oh God, are my hands clean? Is my heart pure?"* The power of God hit him and the others, causing them to fall upon the floor and confess their sins. The wave of supernatural power filled the barn and they were ready to go forth.

The revival hit the islands like a hammer. Churches were filled to overflowing. Men, women and children all were touched. The Bible became the only guide as everyone sought God's wisdom from its pages. The revival was so strong that people walking alone on a dark road that were not aware of the revival would feel compelled to fall to their knees and ask for God's forgiveness. People without any visible leading or knowledge of where they were going found themselves knocking on the doors of a house where a Bible study and prayer meeting were taking place. The revival became so strong that the Smith sisters called for Pastor MacKay and asked him to contact the famous evangelist Duncan Campbell to come to the islands and be the leader of the revival. At first Campbell refused, but was later drawn by the Holy Spirit to come and meet the two women. Campbell wrote in his memoirs that Peggy's sightless eyes seemed to burn a hole in his soul. She told him to go to a nearby village that was hostile to the revival and preach the Word. Campbell answered her by saying that God had not told him to do that. Peggy then said, *"Well, Mr. Campbell, if you were as close to God as you should be you would be hearing from him right now."* Campbell went and saw the power of God fall upon the village. He stayed and led the revival for two years.

Lord, thank You for giving us Peggy and Christine Smith.

William J. Seymour

The Pentecostal revival that occurred at Azusa Street in Los Angeles, California in 1906 was ignited by the efforts of a black man named William J. Seymour. The story of this man of God is a sterling example of God's sovereign desire to use the ordinary person in His plans to expand the kingdom.

William Seymour was born on May 2, 1870 in Centerville, Louisiana. He was the son of Simon Seymour and Phyllis Salabarr who were both freed slaves who had labored on Southern plantations during the Civil War.

The Seymours endured grinding poverty. William had little formal education and lived under the smothering racism called Jim Crow.[103] In 1895, when he was 25 years old, he moved to Indianapolis, Indiana where he worked as a waiter in that city's restaurants. He had always had an interest in spiritual things and joined the Methodist Episcopal Church.

In 1900 he moved to Cincinnati, Ohio where he applied for membership in the Church of God Restoration Movement which was also called the Evening Light Saints. This group was a part of the Holiness Movement which focused on healing and the blessing of God that they referred to as the baptism with the Holy Spirit. The movement preached the imminent return of Jesus Christ and believed that followers of Christ should be prepared for the coming of the Lord by the pursuit of personal holiness and intense ministry.

While living in Cincinnati, Seymour was struck with smallpox that nearly took his life and caused the loss of his left eye. Seymour wore a glass eye the rest of his life and grew a beard to hide the smallpox scarring that marked his face. His physical afflictions only served to draw him closer to God, compelling him to decide to become a preacher. In 1902 he was ordained as a minister in the Church of God.

After time spent in Georgia, Mississippi and Louisiana, Seymour moved to Houston, Texas in 1905. He served as a temporary summer replacement for Pastor Lucy Farrow at her Holiness Church. It was at this time that he met the man who was to change his life.

Charles Fox Parham was a white evangelist who ran a Bible school in Houston. Parham, although not personally experiencing the gift of "speaking in tongues," was interested in this phenomenon and believed

---

[103] Jim Crow laws were enacted in the South after the Civil War as a control of the freed slaves. These laws designated the behavior of all blacks—telling them where they could or could not go or do. These "laws" were an embarrassment to the South and were only diminished after much struggle.

that it was a sign of the baptism with the Holy Spirit. He impressed Seymour who asked Parham if he could attend the Bible school to learn about the experience. Parham accepted Seymour as a student but applied the restrictions that had become commonplace during that time in America's history. Seymour could attend the Bible school, but was to keep himself separate from the white students. He had to suffer the indignities of racial segregation by staying outside the class and only listening through a window or by sitting in the hallway. These restrictions were intolerable to Seymour and he eventually left the school, but he had learned enough about speaking in tongues to cause a stir in his heart.

While in Houston, Seymour met Neely Terry, a woman who had come from Los Angeles to visit friends in Houston. She told stories about the spiritual stirring that was beginning to occur on the West Coast and prompted Seymour to go and see for himself. William Seymour accepted Terry's invitation to go to Los Angeles to conduct some meetings at a church led by Julia Hutchins.

Hutchins was a holiness preacher who first welcomed Seymour. Seymour's initial preaching stirred the church members, but his preaching on the baptism with the Holy Spirit with the evidence of speaking in tongues so alarmed her elders that they threatened a mutiny if she did not get rid of Seymour. Hutchins, mindful of church politics, locked her church and refused to allow Seymour to re-enter.

Kicked out on the street, Seymour accepted the invitation by a Mr. and Mrs. Richard Asberry to meet in their home on Bonnie Brae Avenue. It was at this home that the Holy Spirit fell on the gathered participants and the revival exploded into reality.

As the excitement spread, more and more people came to Bonnie Brae Avenue to witness the revival themselves. Hundreds stood outside on the street twenty-four hours a day to try and hear the messages preached by Seymour from the front porch. There were so many people that the residents of Bonnie Brae Avenue felt threatened and forced people off their front yards with shotguns. When the front porch collapsed and the city fathers demanded that the meetings cease, the group began to look for a larger venue.

Seymour's group found an abandoned church building at 312 Azusa Street in downtown Los Angeles. The building had once housed a small church but was now a warehouse and livery stable. The people cleared out the building which only measured 40 x 60 feet and began to construct their new church.

The pulpit was two orange crates facing rows of planks laid out as seats. Seymour would spend hours with his head inside the orange crates praying before he would face the people with the message sent by God. The place was cold and drafty and did not have the appearance of a church but was filled with the presence of the Holy Spirit Who brought a beauty that transcended the meager surroundings. The crowds became so large that the services were held throughout the day and long into the night. Thousands came to join in with the excitement. The issues of race were left at the door as whites and blacks joined together to worship. It was one of the first times that whites and blacks had joined together as fellow Christians

Newspapers sent reporters to witness the astounding events. The reporters ignored the spiritual implications and focused on the "race mixing" that was occurring in downtown Los Angeles. The newspaper accounts were usually negative as reporters emphasized the "strange activity" they dubbed as "holy rolling." The negative attacks exploded against the ministry on the pages of the nation's newspapers.

The Holy Spirit's power and presence was so pronounced that miraculous healings became the order of the day. All kinds of diseases disappeared from the sick people who were literally carried into the building. Thousands came to Christ and were baptized with the Holy Spirit and many received the gift of tongues. The neighboring white churches stood against the ministry expressing their dismay concerning the "race mixing" and the appearance of "glossolalia" (speaking in tongues). The animosity from the established church against the Azusa Street Revival was so intense that threats were directed at the members and many even lost their jobs. In spite of the attacks the revival increased until thousands had been touched by God and began taking their experience back to their cities and towns throughout the nation and even the world.

The Azusa Street outpouring lasted until 1915 when the revival ran its course. Seymour and his wife, Jennie, remained in Los Angeles as pastors of a small African American congregation. Seymour died of a heart attack on September 28, 1922. His wife remained until 1931 when the congregation lost the building.

During William Seymour's ministry thousands had been touched by God and many great Pentecostal denominations were launched.[104] The estimates vary but church historians believe that millions were saved and touched by the Azusa Street Revival. The Kingdom of God had been greatly expanded, the Holy Spirit's fire had fallen upon the church and the roots of the "charismatic experience" were planted deep within the church at large. It is important to note that all this was led by God and His chosen minister—a one-eyed, son of former slaves who only wanted to express his commitment to his Lord.

Lord, thank You for giving us William Seymour.

---

[104] The Assemblies of God was established in 1916 and the International Church of the Foursquare Gospel (Foursquare Church) was established in 1923. Other Pentecostal denominations followed.

Keith Green: God's troubadour

Keith Green was a young, rebel rock musician of the 1970s who came to California to immerse himself into the hippie drug culture. He had a Jewish and Christian Science background and was attracted to eastern mysticism and "free love." All this came to an abrupt end when he received Jesus Christ as his Lord and Savior. His wife, Melody, also received Christ and both joined the Vineyard Christian Fellowship in Santa Monica, California that was led by Pastor Kenn Gullicksen.

Keith and Melody experienced powerful conversions that propelled them to seek the Lord's leading for the direction of their ministry. They began having Bible studies in their home that became so packed with God seekers that there was no room to move around the house. Many that attended those studies later testified that the Lord's presence was so thick in the Green house that you could close your eyes and imagine being in heaven

Combining his musical talent with an incredible anointing for evangelism, Keith traveled widely singing and playing his piano while preaching the gospel without restraint. His style was unique—being closely tied to his music. He would play his piano and stop when he had a point to make. The man was a dynamo for Jesus Christ and his penchant for revival was legendary. He was a man of integrity who lived the life of Christ in his daily walk. Being freed from the drive for financial success, he was the first high-profile contemporary gospel artist who gave away copies of his albums for free to anyone who asked—an act that disturbed his record company.

In 1978 Keith and Melody began *The Last Days Ministries Newsletter.* In it they published stories written by their evangelistic friends like Leonard Ravenhill, Winkie Pratney and David Wilkerson. The publication became a well-designed magazine that was renamed *Last Days Magazine.* The magazine was completely dedicated to evangelism and revival and started including articles that had been written years before by famous revivalists like Charles Finney, John Wesley and William Booth. The Greens moved their operation to Texas where they bought a 40 acre plot of land. The location became a Christian training center called The Last Days Ministry. Christians of all ages traveled to Texas to study and prepare for ministries throughout the world.

A Keith Green concert was a happening. He electrified his audiences with his musical talent and his preaching. With intense emotion he explained the importance of evangelism and revival. When he told us to get up off our backsides and take the gospel out of our comfort zones and into the streets, his words resonated like spiritual dynamite. No amount of words could ever describe the impact that he had on those who believe in revival. My heart for evangelism and revival was birthed in my exposure to the ministry of Keith Green.

On July 28, 1982, Keith and two of his children, three-year old Josiah and two-year old Bethany were killed in a plane crash with nine other people. The Christian world mourned the passing of this great point man for God. Keith was 28 years old.

Lord, thank You for giving us Keith Green.

Those who lead revivals are broken before God

Those who lead revivals are those who have been broken before God. This is true because men and women that can withstand the withering attacks of opposition are not born they are made. The "making" occurs within the broken hearts of those who have seen pain and suffering and have learned to survive in the midst of the trials of life.

God will hear the revival prayers of the man or woman who weeps over the sins of the world. Deep, bone-shaking prayer uttered for the plight of mankind is heard on high. Revivals are literally "prayed down" by those who grab onto God and will not let go. In the Old Testament we have a famous story of spiritual tenacity. Jacob wrestled with God all night and declared that he would not let go until God blessed him,

So Jacob was left alone, and a man wrestled with him till daybreak. When the man saw that he could not overpower him, he touched the socket of Jacob's hip so that his hip was wrenched as he wrestled with the man.

Then the man said, "Let me go for it is daybreak." But Jacob replied, "I will not let you go unless you bless me." The man asked him, "What is your name?" "Jacob," he answered. Then the man said, "Your name will no longer be Jacob but, Israel, because you have struggled with God and with men and have overcome." Jacob said, 'Please tell me your name." But he replied, "Why do you ask my name?" Then he blessed him there. So Jacob called the place Peniel, saying, "It is because I saw God face to face, and yet my life was spared. (Genesis 32:24-30).

Jacob's name which meant, "One who supplants" was renamed "Israel," which means "God perseveres." Those who persevere in revival prayer will be blessed by God.

There is no other way.

Those who lead revivals cannot fear man

John the Baptist walked out of the wilderness and confronted Herod, telling the apostate king that he had sinned when he took his brother's wife. Herod was angered at John's reprimand and demanded that he stop. But John did not stop and the rest of the story is very familiar. Through lies and deceptions Herodias, Herod's adulterous wife, manipulated Herod by directing her own daughter to dance a seductive dance in order to trap him into having the Baptist executed. When the executioner's sword fell, John's mortal voice was stilled, but its echo rang throughout the land and is forever enshrined in God's holy Book. John had a message and it could not be stopped by man.

The apostles preached in the name of Jesus throughout the streets of Jerusalem after Pentecost. The Sanhedrin, the rulers of the Jews, ordered them to stop...but they did not stop. They continued to preach the glorious news of Jesus Christ's sacrifice for the sins of the world. It seems that men and women bearing the anointing of God cannot be stopped by the whims and pettiness of mere human beings. The truth is that the opposition of the whiners and naysayers does nothing but make them stronger.

As we ordinary people pray for revival, we must look back toward our elders in the faith who gave their lives to pass us the torch. For we are all part of a "torch relay" that carries the fire of God's Word throughout the centuries. Can you imagine the many hands that have touched the torch that is now in your hand? Can you see their faces? Can you see Paul and Peter, Stephen, Jonathon Edwards, John Wesley, Charles Finney, the Smith sisters, William Seymour, Billy Graham, Keith Green and all the millions of ordinary people who have carried that torch? Can you see how that torch burns in your heart? Do you know that you must pass it on?

Yes, we must pass it on. Revival will come, but it will come only through the tears and travailing of intense, deep prayer. Yes, revival will come, but it will come only through the kind of prayer that no man can stop. The truth is that those who pray for revival cannot fear man. Those who pray for revival can only fear God.

Pray for revival.

Chapter Twelve

The Watchmen on the Wall

On your walls, O Jerusalem, I have appointed watchmen; all day and all night they will never keep silent. You who remind the Lord, take no rest for yourselves; and give Him no rest until He establishes and makes Jerusalem a praise in the earth. -Isaiah 62:6-7

In 2001 I watched a TV series called the "Band of Brothers."[105] It was a World War II drama based on Stephen E. Ambrose's 1993 non-fiction book of the same name. The series chronicled the history of an army unit called "Easy Company" that was a part of the 506th Parachute Infantry Regiment, 101st Airborne Division. These men parachuted into German occupied France on D-Day and met Hitler's armies head-on, becoming a spearhead of the successful liberation of Europe during that turbulent time in world history.

The award winning series featured a number of interviews of the surviving Easy Company veterans. Almost to a man they wept for their comrades that had paid the ultimate price on those frozen battlefields of Europe. Although each of the Easy Company veterans had differing stories to share they all agreed on one important point: the mutual love and respect they had for each other was birthed in the fires of intense combat over sixty years ago.

With a deep sense of veneration, I watched transfixed as these elderly warriors told their stories of valor mixed with pain and suffering. I grasped the filmmaker's major point of the series: the fact that only these men, these survivors of Easy Company, this band of brothers knew what it meant to be part of a campaign that had impacted the history of the world.

Another band of brothers

The Christian church has its own band of brothers. Like the veterans of Easy Company they are bound together by a common mission.

The similarities between Easy Company and this band of Christian brothers are profound: Both were and are called to serve in a war; both endured and endure extraordinary trials and tribulations; both wept and weep over the distress of their brethren; both suffered and suffer suffocating attacks from a malevolent enemy; both had and have a crucial impact on the history of the world. Although the roles are similar there is one important difference. Unlike Easy Company that was formed at one time in history to fight a human enemy, the Christian band of brothers are engaged in an ongoing spiritual war that has continued for

---

[105] The title of the book and series comes from the famous Saint Crispin's Day speech in William Shakespeare's play Henry V. The speech was delivered by Henry V of England to his troops before the Battle of Agincourt.

centuries. Simply put the members of Easy Company are a part of history. But the Christian band of brothers transcend history and exists in the now.

The Christian band of brothers has a name. They are the watchmen on the wall. So what is a watchman on the walls?

A definition: In the ancient world walls of piled stones surrounded the fields planted with crops that were the only source of food for the community. On these walls men were stationed in watchtowers to guard those fields from animals and marauding thieves that would attempt to steal those crops. Those "watchmen on the walls" had to perform their required task of guarding the food supply or the people would starve. The Holy Scriptures expanded the role of the watchmen on the walls to include the task of guarding the city and/or nation. Those watchmen on the walls manned the watchtowers on the city walls to guard against surprise attacks from hostile neighbors and/or armies. If a threat appeared the watchman would blow the trumpet to warn the people to rise up and defend themselves. In both situations the solemn task of the watchman, like the men of Easy Company, had life and death consequences.

The watchmen on the walls mentioned in the Old and New Testaments were the "alarm system" put in place by God to sound the warnings required to bring deliverance to the people. The watchmen on the walls today are the men and women of God that speak prophetic words of warning into the souls of the people of God.[106] They are the thin line that separates God's people from the rabid attacks of a voracious enemy that is attempting to destroy every man, woman and child bearing the name of Jesus on their hearts. The watchmen on the walls are the prophets of God fulfilling the call for revival in a world breathing its last. According to the above mentioned Isaiah 62:6-7 verse the watchmen on the walls fulfill the following:

They have answered the call of God: "I have appointed watchmen…"

NOTE: God Himself has called these persons. They didn't make it up themselves and answer only to God.

They never cease their task of proclaiming God's warnings: "all day and all night they will never keep silent…"

---

[106] I want to be crystal clear that although the term "band of brothers" seems to indicate that women are not included in this group the contrary is clearly embedded in the word of God. Men and women, young and old are all included in the call to be watchmen on the walls. The use of the term "brothers" is simply a way to emphasize that they all experience a camaraderie promoted by God. Male and female can all be members of the called. To pretend otherwise is like drawing your pistol from your holster and then shooting yourself in the foot. In my opinion, any woman willing to answer the call for revival can stand in God's "band of brothers" anytime. Remember, the historical list of prophetic women of God is long and growing.

NOTE: Nothing can silence them. No Devil in hell, no unbelieving world, no organized opposition whether from a governmental decree or even from the established church...nothing can stop them...absolutely nothing.

They are tireless in their resolve to fulfill their divine task: "You who remind the Lord, take no rest for yourselves..."

NOTE: The watchmen on the walls will not go on vacation from their ordained task. They will tirelessly proclaim the Lord's call for revival. There is no quit in them and they will not stop until the job is completed.

They will never cease to intercede for the outpouring of real revival: "Give Him (God) no rest until He establishes and makes Jerusalem a praise in the earth."

NOTE: The fire of revival may be lost in the machinations and daily life of the modern church, but these watchmen on the walls will never allow the quenching of God's holy fire. These hardy souls, these men and women, this band of brothers, will remain true to their call to place the trumpet to their lips and sound the alarm. "Arise church!" they shout in unison. "Wake up! Stand and fight!" Like the survivors of Easy Company they can never forget the crusade that they are leading. And like the Jews of today that celebrate the Passover Seder their closing words will be: "Next year in Jerusalem!"

The watchmen on the walls in Ezekiel

In the Book of Ezekiel we are introduced to the persons called "the watchmen on the walls" that have the task of protecting the city and/or nation from the enemies both within and without.[107] The holy text is very clear that their prophetic job is to warn the nation of Israel of coming disasters and judgments. The Lord solemnly warns His watchmen that their obedience to God's Word is a life and death proposition. Their own lives depend on their obedience.

"Son of man, I have appointed you a watchman to the house of Israel; whenever you hear a word from My mouth, warn them from Me. When I say to the wicked, 'You will surely die,' and you do not warn him or speak out to warn the wicked from his wicked way that he may live, that wicked man shall die in his iniquity, but his blood I will require at your hand. Yet if you have warned the wicked and he does not turn from his wickedness or from his wicked way, he shall die in his iniquity; but you have delivered yourself. Again, when a righteous man turns away

---

[107] The Ezekiel verses are clear that the enemies of the people are to be interpreted both in human terms and spiritual. There are indeed human armies that are descending upon Israel and need to be defended against. But there are also the sins and rebellions of the people that have placed them at odds with God and are bringing God's judgment upon themselves via those armies. The Ezekiel verses reveal that the human armies are nothing but tools being used by God to address the need of confession of sin and repentance. The implication is clear, true repentance will bring God's intervention and the people will be delivered. No repentance and the people perish. It is a simple equation that needs to be recognized in our time.

from his righteousness and commits iniquity, and I place an obstacle before him, he will die; since you have not warned him, he shall die in his sin, and his righteous deeds which he has done shall not be remembered; but his blood I will require at your hand. However, if you have warned the righteous man that the righteous should not sin and he does not sin, he shall surely live because he took warning; and you have delivered yourself" (Ezekiel 3:17-21).

And,

And the word of the LORD came to me, saying, "Son of man, speak to the sons of your people and say to them, 'If I bring a sword upon a land, and the people of the land take one man from among them and make him their **watchman***, and he sees the sword coming upon the land and blows on the trumpet and warns the people, then he who hears the sound of* **the trumpet** *and does not take warning, and a sword comes and takes him away, his blood will be on his own head. He heard the sound of the trumpet but did not take warning; his blood will be on himself. But had he taken warning, he would have delivered his life. But if the watchman sees the sword coming and does not blow the trumpet and the people are not warned, and a sword comes and takes a person from them, he is taken away in his iniquity; but his blood I will require from the watchman's hand.' "Now as for you, son of man, I have appointed you a watchman for the house of Israel; so you will hear a message from My mouth and give them warning from Me. When I say to the wicked, 'O wicked man, you will surely die,' and you do not speak to warn the wicked from his way, that wicked man shall die in his iniquity, but his blood I will require from your hand. But if you on your part warn a wicked man to turn from his way and he does not turn from his way, he will die in his iniquity, but you have delivered your life* (Ezekiel 33:1-9).

The Ezekiel references explained

The watchmen on the walls are appointed by God: "Son of man, I have appointed you a watchman to the house of Israel…"

NOTE: A prophet of God is chosen by God and prepared for the task. There is no such thing as a seminary curriculum that is organized and then completed by the candidate to make that person a prophet of God and/or watchman on the walls.[108]

The watchmen on the walls are to listen for God's word and then give it intact to the people of God with no alterations or

---

[108] In the Old Testament there are a few verses that mention a "school of the prophets" or in other translations "the sons of the prophets" or "the company of the prophets." These verses are in I Samuel 19:18-24 and in II Kings 2 and 4:38-44. These verses are not positing the existence of a school where people could go to learn to be a prophet but instead is a reference to the fact that spiritual gifts are "caught" and "not taught." This means that spending time with a prophet and observing how God uses that person will assist you in your adventure of learning about God and how He works in His ministry with men.

"improvements": "Whenever you hear a word from My mouth, warn them from Me."

NOTE: This truth is etched in stone: God's people are "the servants of God" and not His equals. We are to "do" what we are told and not come up with our own opinions and/or ideas. Trying to "lead or direct" God in order to get Him to do our will is completely fallacious and deserves a robust censure.

The word from God to the watchmen on the walls will be a warning. The obedience to that word will bring deliverance to the hearer and also bring deliverance to the deliverer of that word. The opposite response will bring judgment. There is no middle ground: *When I say to the wicked, 'You will surely die,' and you do not warn him or speak out to warn the wicked from his wicked way that he may live, that wicked man shall die in his iniquity, but his blood I will require at your hand. Yet if you have warned the wicked and he does not turn from his wickedness or from his wicked way, he shall die in his iniquity; but you have delivered yourself.*

NOTE: A prophetic word of warning is exceedingly powerful and requires obedience. To ignore that word is an act of insanity and can cost those who are the hearers and the deliverers everything.

This fact alone makes the ministry of the watchmen on the walls intensely serious.

An implied truth—the watchman on the walls is to blow the trumpet of warning whenever he/she sees the enemy approaching: *"And I set watchmen over you, saying, 'Listen to the sound of the trumpet!' But they said, 'We will not listen.' "Therefore hear, O nations, And know, O congregation, what is among them. "Hear, O earth: behold, I am bringing disaster on this people, the fruit of their plans, because they have not listened to My words, And as for My law, they have rejected it also* (Jeremiah 6:17-19).

And,

It will come about also in that day that a great trumpet will be blown, and those who were perishing in the land of Assyria and who were scattered in the land of Egypt will come and worship the Lord in the holy mountain at Jerusalem (Isaiah 27:13).

NOTE: It is true that many persons in the church will see the trumpet call from the watchmen on the walls as an irritant. But this cannot cause the watchmen to temper their charge. The watchmen must open their mouths and speak truth no matter how it may be received. Remember: People hate going to the dentist but if they don't go they will lose their teeth. There are many things that we do not like doing but we better do them or else.

A word of encouragement to the watchmen

In every generation there are men and women who know what revival is and how much it is needed. They appear at times throughout church history and trumpet God's call for the return of His revival fire. These men and women know who they are and will arise when the time is right.

I would be amiss if I didn't say that the watchmen's obedience to God will have a cost. It is a fact that if you are a member of this special band of brothers you will suffer much.

Those that are not watchmen on the walls may wonder how the following comments can even remotely be considered a source of encouragement. I must be honest and admit that I understand that their question has validity. It is certainly true that being stared at as if you have six noses is a long way from experiencing what most people would deem as an encouragement. But if you are a watchman on the wall you know what I mean.

If you are a watchman on the wall the following may apply
You will oftentimes be shunned:

Bringing warnings concerning sin will not help you win a popularity contest. Sinners do not appreciate warnings and will see any attempts to present those warnings as unwelcome criticism. It will be a definite possibility that you will be removed from the party list when word gets out that you are not open to re-interpretation of the sin question. It is my opinion that the words "enter your rest O faithful servant" as uttered from the mouth of God is worth much more than all the applause the world can give on Oscar night.

You will be misunderstood:

In the popular vernacular of our day if you are a watchman on the wall you will called "a hater."[109] You may be verbally assaulted, possibly physically and you will certainly be talked about when you are not present. A famous comedian once said that people laugh and joke when they are nervous and not confident in the outcome of the events of life. This is certainly true. People get queasy when godly people walk into the room and will oftentimes resort to sarcasm and outright verbal assault to temper the nervousness they feel when one enters the door. The best way to look at this is to remember that you serve God and not man and that any rejection of you is nothing more than a rejection of Him.

"The one who listens to you listens to Me, **and the one who rejects you rejects Me;** *and he who rejects Me rejects the One who sent Me"* (Luke 10:16).

---

[109] Rule of thumb: Whenever you hear some politician, reporter or celebrity calling a person a hater it is more times than not a good reason to listen to the individual they are castigating. The secular world hates God and His people and will do anything they can to minimize their message. The use of the term "hater" is the new buzz word that might mean— " *The person I'm attacking is speaking truth and I want to make sure that myself and my friends can go to Hell without hindrance.*"

The enemies of God will see you as a threat:
In my mind, being disliked by Satan and his minions is not a bad deal. In fact, my biggest desire is that I never win a popularity contest in Hell. Remember what the demons said when attacking the phony exorcists that were trying to use Jesus' name to draw attention to their spiritual con.

God was performing extraordinary miracles by the hands of Paul, so that handkerchiefs or aprons were even carried from his body to the sick, and the diseases left them and the evil spirits went out. But also some of the Jewish exorcists, who went from place to place, attempted to name over those who had the evil spirits the name of the Lord Jesus, saying, "I adjure you by Jesus whom Paul preaches." [14] Seven sons of one Sceva, a Jewish chief priest, were doing this. And the evil spirit answered and said to them, "I recognize Jesus, and I know about Paul, but who are you?" And the man, in whom was the evil spirit, leaped on them and subdued all of them and overpowered them, so that they fled out of that house naked and wounded (Acts 19:11-16).

The point of this is that being popular in Hell is very different than being known as an enemy of evil.

You cannot be comfortable with sin:
Obscene jokes will embarrass you. You will not do well at a family reunion held in a saloon. Watching the newest TV sitcom with the star of the show making off-color jokes about Jesus may cause you to consider turning over the tables on the moneychangers. The stuff of "normal" life may simply not be your cup of tea. If you are a watchman on the walls and discover that what I just said applies to you, don't feel bad. The Word of God is quite clear that we should never be comfortable in a sewer.

Flee immorality. *Every other sin that a man commits is outside the body, but the immoral man sins against his own body. Or do you not know that your body is a temple of the Holy Spirit who is in you, whom you have from God, and that you are not your own? For you have been bought with a price: therefore glorify God in your body* (I Corinthians 6:18-20).

You must be vigilant:
In the Old Testament days the watchman manned the watchtower surrounding the fields and the city. His job was twofold: First to protect the crops from marauding animals and thieves and secondly, keep the city safe from the attacks of rampaging enemies looking for opportunities to pillage and murder. Remember, a watchman on the walls in our day

cannot fall asleep at their post. The enemies of God and His people are awake 24/7 and ready and willing to destroy all in their path.[110]

You must speak openly concerning sin and repentance:

Without true repentance what we call "revival" would be just expecting God to bless what is on our own agenda. This in itself is nothing but an act of utter futility—an act of the flesh that is pointless and fruitless. The Book of John speaks clearly concerning what the Lord knew was in man.

Now when He was in Jerusalem at the Passover, during the feast, many believed in His name, observing His signs which He was doing. But Jesus, on His part, was not entrusting Himself to them, for He knew all men, and because He did not need anyone to testify concerning man, for He Himself knew what was in man (John 2:23-25).

This verse obliterates human pride. It reveals that the Lord Jesus Christ, knowing mankind's proclivity for rebellion and sin, didn't trust mankind. Our Lord knew with absolute assurance that we, in our humanness, are completely and utterly untrustworthy. Everything we human beings touch turns to mud. This is true because all of our righteous deeds performed in our human weakness are worthless.

*Oh, that You would rend the heavens and come down, that the mountains might quake at Your presence—As fire kindles the brushwood, as fire causes water to boil—to make Your name known to Your adversaries, that the nations may tremble at Your presence! When You did awesome things which we did not expect, You came down, the mountains quaked at Your presence. For from days of old they have not heard or perceived by ear, nor has the eye seen a God besides You, Who acts in behalf of the one who waits for Him. You meet him who rejoices in doing righteousness, who remembers You in Your ways. Behold, You were angry, for we sinned, we continued in them a long time; and shall we be saved? For all of us have become like one who is unclean, **and all our righteous deeds are like a filthy garment;** and all of us wither like a leaf, and our iniquities, like the wind, take us away. There is no one who calls on Your name, who arouses himself to take hold of You; for You have hidden Your face from us and have delivered us into the power of our iniquities.* (Isaiah 64:1-7).

Expecting mankind to do the right thing without the leading and control of God is a fool's errand. Human beings are conceived in sin and

---

[110] I must make this observation: It seems that the enemies of God and those that actively deny His existence and right to rule have more energy than many of God's people. Communists that hate God and are confirmed atheists tirelessly work to advance communism. They have taken over entire countries because of their incessant desire to accomplish their task. The legions of criminals, opportunists, perverts and blasphemers work 24/7 to drag America down into the sewer. So why is it that finding a tireless worker for Christ is like finding the proverbial needle in the haystack? I must say that if Christians had one half of the energy and resolve of God haters there would be a revival that would change the world. Just thinking...

are indwelt with a sin nature. We are nothing but creatures of flesh and cannot change without a touch from God. This touch will occur when we experience a true revival.

Behold, I was brought forth in iniquity, and in sin my mother conceived me (Psalm 51:5).

The only hope for mankind is true repentance. Without true repentance we remain in our original state—dead in our sins and completely useless for God's purposes. With true repentance we become new persons equipped with the ability to serve God and expand His kingdom.

*Therefore if anyone is in Christ, he is a **new creature**; the old things passed away; behold, **new** things have come.* (II Corinthians 5:17).

You will have little tolerance for lukewarm Churchianity:

I have already gone on record in my warnings concerning the Seeker Friendly Movement in the church. If you are a watchman on the walls you will have zero tolerance for any attempt to water down God's Word to make it palatable to the church shoppers looking for a church that will fit into their casual lifestyle. The Lord Himself made His opinion known concerning lukewarm Churchianity:

*To the angel of the church in Laodicea write: The Amen, the faithful and true Witness, the Beginning of the creation of God, says this: 'I know your deeds that you are neither cold nor hot; I wish that you were cold or hot. **So because you are lukewarm, and neither hot nor cold, I will spit you out of My mouth.** Because you say, "I am rich, and have become wealthy, and have need of nothing," and you do not know that you are wretched and miserable and poor and blind and naked, I advise you to buy from Me gold refined by fire so that you may become rich, and white garments so that you may clothe yourself, and that the shame of your nakedness will not be revealed; and eye salve to anoint your eyes so that you may see* (Revelation 3:14-18).

NOTE: I would be amiss if I did not warn the watchmen on the walls of the price they will pay whenever they do their job of warning the people of God. Without question, watchmen on the walls are the minority in the American church (by far) and in most cases not allowed to be involved in church leadership. The positions of leadership in the average American church will usually be occupied by the confirmed believers in the seeker friendly style. And they will minimize, marginalize and actively censure any person aflame with the fire of revival. In other words they will do anything they can to keep your hands off the steering wheel.

In summation

The watchmen on the walls are the warriors of God that are indispensable to any church seeking revival. Without the sacrifices and resolve of these valiant persons the call for revival would dissipate across the land.

Pray for revival.

Chapter Thirteen
Revival Power

"For the kingdom of God is not a matter of talk but of power." -I Corinthians 4:23

The empowerment of the church

It doesn't take a Bible scholar to realize that the Christian church is unique. Although there are thousands of religions and philosophies vying for the allegiance of mankind the Christian church stands alone as the only credo that is verifiable by the supernatural presence and power of God.

The biblical proof is staggering.

The Apostle Paul trumpets the truth

The Apostle Paul writing in his first letter to the Corinthians made a statement that must be considered by any serious Christian. He inferred that a ministry without the supernatural power of God is failing to enact a normal ministry,

*"My message and my preaching were not with wise and persuasive words, but with **a demonstration of the Spirit's power**, so that your faith might not rest on men's wisdom, but on God's power."* (I Corinthians 2:4, 5).

And,

*For the kingdom of God does not consist in words but in **power**."* (I Corinthians 4:20).

Paul refused to let the matter rest but pressed his argument with another volley in his letter to the Thessalonians,

*"For we know, brothers, loved by God, that He has chosen you, because our gospel came to you not simply with words, **but power, with the Holy Spirit** and with deep conviction."* (I Thessalonians 1:4, 5).

So what did Paul say? He said that the gospel did not come to the Thessalonians in just mere words but in power. What kind of power? Paul's question to the Galatians holds the answer,

*"Does God give you the Holy Spirit and **work miracles among you** because you observe the law or because you believe what you heard?"* (Galatians 3:5).

According to the Apostle Paul God's power is a tangible and observable expression of God's presence that is described as "miraculous." Paul is stating plainly that when the Holy Spirit falls upon human beings great power is released—and we will see it. In Paul's opinion, supernatural ministry is to be experienced as normative and those who reject the Holy Spirit's power are just speaking words. These are powerful statements and should be soberly considered. Remember the simple truth: **Human beings, no matter how godly and sincere they may be, cannot do the things of God without His power!**

The Lord Jesus Christ's support for the message of power

I had a conversation with a fellow Christian that was a member of a church that actively resisted God's supernatural power because of an anti-supernatural theology. He seemed puzzled when I shared the word with him on the biblical commands issued by the Apostle Paul concerning the church's need for an outpouring of the Holy Spirit (I Corinthians 2:4, 5; 4:20; II Thessalonians 1:4, 5 and Galatians 3:5). He furrowed his brow and thought for a moment and then said, "Well, that's Paul's opinion. I'm a believer in the red letter version of the Bible (Jesus' words printed in red). I only put credence in what Jesus says." He smiled and felt like he had performed an act equivalent to Martin Luther's nailing of his "Ninety-Five Thesis" on the Wittenberg door. I quickly responded with the comments appearing below relating to Jesus' feelings about the need for the Holy Spirit's power in His church.

He seemed deflated...

So what did Jesus say?

Jesus said in the book of Luke that the power of God was absolutely essential and that no ministry should commence without it.

Then He opened their minds so they could understand the Scriptures. He told them, "This is what is written: The Christ will suffer and rise from the dead on the third day, and repentance and forgiveness of sins will be preached in His name to all nations beginning in Jerusalem. You are witnesses of these things. I am going to send you what My Father has promised, but stay in the city until you have been ***clothed with power*** *from on high."* (Luke 24: 45-49).

Jesus' instruction is clear. **Do not move without the power of God.** This power is further identified in Acts when Jesus made His command to the church,

"Gathering them together, He commanded them not to leave Jerusalem, but to wait for what the Father promised, which you have heard of from Me. For John baptized with water, but you will be ***baptized with the Holy Spirit*** *not many days from now. So when they had come together, they were asking Him, saying, "Lord, is it at this time You are restoring the kingdom of Israel?" He said to them, "It is not for you to know times or epochs which the Father has fixed by His own authority; but you will receive* ***power*** *when the* ***Holy Spirit*** *has come upon you; and you shall be My* ***witnesses*** *both in Jerusalem and in all Judea and Samaria, and even to the remotest part of the earth."* (Acts 1: 4, 5).

On the Day of Pentecost God's power fell upon those gathered in the upper room. The result was that the handful of frightened disciples, freshly empowered by the Holy Spirit, exploded out into the streets of Jerusalem and led three thousand souls to Christ. The connection between the empowerment of the Holy Spirit and the power to minister and witness is undeniable.

In the Book of Acts we read the Apostle Pater's comments about Jesus' equipping for His ministry. Peter's reference was a response to the story of his visit to the house of Cornelius. In these verses we learn of the work of the Holy Spirit in the ministry of Jesus:

Opening his mouth, Peter said, "I most certainly understand now that God is not one to show partiality, but in every nation the man who fears Him and does what is right is welcome to Him. The word which He sent to the sons of Israel, preaching peace through Jesus Christ (He is Lord of all)—you yourselves know the thing which took place throughout all Judea, starting from Galilee, after the baptism which John proclaimed. ***You know of Jesus of Nazareth, how God anointed Him with the Holy Spirit and with power, and how He went about doing good and healing all who were oppressed by the Devil, for God was with Him.*** *We are witnesses of all the things He did both in the land of the Jews and Jerusalem..."* (Acts 10:34-39).

It should be noted that if Jesus Christ, God in human flesh, needed to be equipped with the power of the Holy Spirit in order to conduct His ministry any attempt by human beings to conduct a ministry without that empowering is ludicrous.

NOTE: The empowerment of the Holy Spirit should be expected by any Christian that obeys the Lord's call to evangelize the lost. A problem arises when some in the church use this power as a show that is held inside the walls of the church. God's power is real. His spiritual gifts are real, but the power and gifts are not for a show. God's supernatural power and gifts must be understood as weapons/tools used by God's people to advance the gospel throughout the world.

How does God use His power to advance His kingdom?

If the work of the church was to be performed by human effort alone we would have some sorry excuses for churches. The only ones still open would be those that could put on the most glitzy and garish show in town. Of course, there would be no supernatural power, no miraculous healings, no "anointed" preaching, and no Spirit-filled worship. Desperate pastors without God's divine anointing would be compelled to have trained elephants, jugglers and door prizes just to bring in some spectators. Left to our own tired human devices, there would be no end to the gimmicks that men would stage just to survive the church competition. We can only imagine hearing about the shameless concoctions engineered by a powerless church to draw attention to their human message: New churches would arise like "the church in the trees," "the bungee jump church," "the computer game fellowship," and "the Twitter Church," as men desperately maneuvered to sell the gospel.

But praise God, we don't have to "sell" the gospel. The gospel has advanced across the earth for two thousand years in ways beyond human understanding. The Lord purposely uses the foolish things, weak things, despised things and the things that are not to shame the ways of men (I Corinthians 1:16-31). A supernatural God never stoops to peddling His wares or begging people to get involved in His program, and yet, every generation, no matter how resistant to the gospel, will see sinners come to Christ (Acts 8:18-24; John 6:66,67). It is a phenomenon that will never be understood by the carnal unbelieving world (I Corinthians 2:14).

So how does God purposely use the foolish things, weak things, despised things and the things that are not to advance His kingdom? How does He promote the gospel without embracing mankind's shabby human methods?

The Holy Spirit is the irreducible fact

The Holy Bible, both Old and New Testaments, cries out with one unified voice:

The gospel of Jesus Christ is a supernatural message advanced by a supernatural church filled with the empowerment of the Holy Spirit. God performs all of His miraculous deeds of ministry, renewal, salvation, restoration, healing, and sanctification through the Person and power of the Holy Spirit. The Holy Spirit, the third Person of the Holy Trinity, is the most powerful force in the universe.[111] He cannot be controlled by the whims of puny mankind and is the catalyst of true revival. The Holy Spirit breathes power into the message and into the church. The results are astonishing. Ordinary men and women and children, filled by the power and presence of the Holy Spirit, become spiritual dynamos that turn entire nations toward the Lord. The simple truth is that God's Holy Spirit directs the church and then provides the power for His church to follow those directions.

This leads me to present an inexorable fact: **Human beings cannot do the things of God without His power.** Let me say it again with a slight expansion: **Human beings, no matter how godly and sincere they may be, cannot do the things of God without His power.**

---

[111] The Bible teaches that the Holy Spirit can speak, think, feel, grieve, act on His own initiative, select ministers and lead the church. These are attributes of personality. Faced with the fact that the Holy Spirit has a real personality, the Christian church acknowledges that He is a real Person. The Christian church also believes that the Holy Spirit is God because of the following three reasons: 1) He is called God in various Scriptures (Acts 5:1-4; I Corinthians 3:16; II Corinthians 3:17), 2) He bears the divine Name—no one is permitted to bear the divine Name except God Himself (Isaiah 48:11), and divine attributes are attributed to Him: Eternal (Hebrews 9:14); Omniscience (John 14:26; I Corinthians 2:10); Omnipotence (Luke 1:35); Omnipresence (Psalm 139:7); Creator (Job 33:4); Holiness (Ephesians 4:30); etc. Faced with these facts, the Christian church proclaims the Holy Spirit's Deity.

Then he said to me, "This is the word of the Lord to Zerubbabel saying, 'Not by might nor by power, but by My Spirit,' says the Lord of hosts. (Zechariah 4:6).

This is such a simple statement and yet it is by far the most controversial statement that can be made in the Christian church. So why do I say that this is such a controversial statement? Isn't the importance of God's power a universal truth embraced by all Christians?

Simply put, no.

What causes the dismissal of the importance of God's power?

Many in the Christian church deny God's power by rejecting outright His supernatural spiritual gifts, or by re-defining them to fit into their theology that is constructed to "sanitize" those spiritual gifts to make them fit into their anti-charismatic presentation. This is tantamount to ordering a soldier to advance toward the enemy lines with nothing but good intentions and no effectual weapons.

Some Christians reject outright the premise that the power of God is absolutely essential for operation within His kingdom. This unfortunate fact is true because of a number of inhibiting factors:

Anti-supernatural theology: This is far and away the major reason for the rejection and/or re-definition of God's power. Entire theological constructs have been developed over the centuries that deny the reality of God's power. Various descriptive names have been attributed to this theological position:

Cessation theology: (spiritual gifts and the expression of the Holy Spirit's power ceased with the deaths of the Apostles). This theological position is taught in many seminaries and is firmly cemented in the churches that embrace this doctrinal position.

Dispensationalism: (God works differently in varied eras).[112] This theological position posits the theory that God works differently in many eras. This allows the adherents to have a solid reason for why God is not supernaturally active in their time. A position like this creates an excuse for why miracles and supernatural gifts are not occurring in the adherents' church. The obvious benefits of this theological position: 1) The adherents can claim to believe in God's power and still have a reason for why they are not experiencing it; 2) The adherents can claim that when God begins another era of miraculous intervention they will actively welcome it. 3) It removes the obvious reasons that they are not experiencing God's power—a fear of the unknown, a lack of faith and/or no desire to engage in the difficulties of ministry..

Anti-charismatic opposition not associated with a doctrinal position: The Christians that support this attitude may or may not embrace the above two positions. Their aversion to God's power is just a

---

[112] To be honest there are parts of dispensationalism that are true and deserve consideration.

result of fear and other reasons. Some, in fact, simply just do not want anything to do with anything supernatural.

NOTE: The average church goer, faced with a theological argument opposing the Holy Spirit's spiritual gifts from a pastor/teacher sporting a degree from some prestigious university, will find it almost impossible to question that leader's premise and seek God's Spirit for the reception of those maligned supernatural experiences. In other words they will just simply give up and do nothing.

The fear of losing control and/ position:

Many of today's leadership have "earned" their positions of power through the hard work of political expediency—in a word: **church politics.** Through the machinations of "palace intrigue" the "lords of the manor" have insured their positions by recognizing and then opposing any pretenders to the throne. Unfortunately for them, the expression of God's power through ordinary people makes shambles of this human concept of leadership. Instead of academic degrees, seniority earned through hard work, and political maneuvering, anyone open to God's Spirit can rise to leadership through the supernatural gifting that only comes from God. God's words to Samuel as he was seeking the chosen king of Israel serve as an example:

When they entered, he looked at Eliab and thought, "Surely the LORD'S anointed is before Him." But the LORD said to Samuel, "Do not look at his appearance or at the height of his stature, because I have rejected him; for **God sees not as man sees, for man looks at the outward appearance, but the LORD looks at the heart"** (I Samuel 16:6-7).

NOTE: Those that guard the halls of power and have no experience with God's equipping through the Holy Spirit, will almost invariably have a problem with God's methods and find it necessary to block what they see as a usurping of their rights. An entrenched leader, with no knowledge of God's supernatural methods of ministry can do nothing else but inhibit the power of the Holy Spirit through the acts of biblical re-interpretation. Hence the imposition of the anti-supernatural theology.

A rejection of struggle:

No one wants to be subject to ridicule, innuendoes, insults and outright rejection. The pain can be almost unbearable. Anyone who has spent any time around the body of Christ knows that oftentimes those who step out to act for God may suffer pejorative censure. Jesus Himself said that those who do His work will suffer rejection and persecution. This truth has certainly played out in the arena of spiritual gifts.

These things I have spoken to you, so that in Me you may have peace. In the world you have tribulation, but take courage; I have overcome the world" (John 16:33).

NOTE: You cannot escape controversy when experiencing the supernatural power of God. This is because we have a supernatural enemy that will marshal his forces against any and all that he deems as a threat. And it must be understood that anyone allowing God to use them in the area of the spiritual warfare through the use of spiritual gifts will be recognized by the enemy as a threat.

Church traditions:

First I want to state clearly that I have no problem with church traditions when they do not inhibit a healthy expression of body ministry. I have met many exceptional Christians that attend traditional congregations that freely minister with the direction and power of the Holy Spirit. Some of my closest friends have pastored those churches and have strong prayer ministries that have greatly benefited the body of Christ. With that said, I must say that sometimes traditional churches may find it difficult to include opportunities for the exercise of spiritual gifts when church services are constrained by the structures of centuries of tradition. Rituals, oral recitations of creeds, traditional observances of holidays and special days on an ecclesiastical calendar, are all competing for the allotted time of a traditional church service. Unfortunately, after fulfilling all the obligations of that church's traditional responsibilities there may not be much time for seeking the Holy Spirit. Because of the obligations of following a strict ecclesiastical calendar many attendees of those churches have never seen the power of the Holy Spirit and only have their traditions to depend on.

Then some Pharisees and scribes came to Jesus from Jerusalem and said, "Why do Your disciples break the tradition of the elders? For they do not wash their hands when they eat bread." And He answered and said to them, "Why do you yourselves transgress the commandment of God for the sake of your tradition? For God said, 'HONOR YOUR FATHER AND MOTHER,' and, 'HE WHO SPEAKS EVIL OF FATHER OR MOTHER IS TO BE PUT TO DEATH.' But you say, 'Whoever says to his father or mother, "Whatever I have that would help you has been given to God," he is not to honor his father or his mother.' And by this you invalidated the Word of God for the sake of your tradition. You hypocrites, rightly did Isaiah prophesy of you: 'THIS PEOPLE HONORS ME WITH THEIR LIPS, BUT THEIR HEART IS FAR AWAY FROM ME. 'BUT IN VAIN DO THEY WORSHIP ME, TEACHING AS DOCTRINES THE PRECEPTS OF MEN'" (Matthew 15:1-9).

NOTE: Again I must state my position clearly: Traditions in themselves are not a bad thing. The problem arises when traditions push out the full gospel that is required by God in order to develop a healthy and balanced church.

But the high priest rose up, along with all his associates (that is the sect of the Sadducees), and they were filled with jealousy. They laid hands on the apostles and put them in a public jail. But during the night *an angel of the Lord opened the gates of the prison, and taking them out he said, "Go, stand and speak to the people in the temple **the whole message of this Life (the full gospel)**." Upon hearing this, they entered into the temple about daybreak and began to teach...* (Acts 5:17-21).

Poor models:

Turn on the TV and you will see a "faith healer." Many of these people are flamboyant in dress, theatrical in presentation, mystical in demeanor, affected in speech and, unfortunately, desperately seeking your money. It is unfortunate that there is so much to overcome before you can hear and evaluate their message. It seems to be true that many of the people on TV are "strange" in behaviors and appear very questionable. But the obvious solution seems to be overlooked by the stable and balanced people that point the fingers—stable and balanced people need to start assuming their responsibility to minister in power. If stable and balanced people would step up and minister in power the supernatural ministries would no longer be in the hands of the "strange people."

NOTE: God is going to get the job done. There are too many people in need of ministry for Him to sit back and do nothing. Remember, if the stable and balanced people refuse to obey God and minister in power the strange people will grab the steering wheel.

Just a thought…

Lack of knowledge:

The Apostle Paul, recognizing that spiritual gifts must be modelled and examined in order for Christians to want to seek them, said the following: Now concerning spiritual gifts, brethren, I do not want you to be unaware (I Corinthians 12:1). This opening statement penned by the great Apostle is clear evidence that Christians need to investigate spiritual gifts and not just reject them out of hand when presented with some theological argument. Too often, Christians, when influenced by their Holy Spirit resistant friends, will forego the investigation required to understand the truth of spiritual gifts and power. Having no viable experience with God's supernatural power they may be forever stifled and not able to offset such intense opposition.

My people are destroyed for lack of knowledge. Because you have rejected knowledge, I also will reject you from being My priest. Since you have forgotten the law of your God, I also will forget your children (Hosea 4:6).

NOTE: The things of the Holy Spirit are "caught" and not "just taught." If you want to understand spiritual gifts hang around people that are doing them. If you hang out in a church that doesn't accept them or denies them altogether you will never learn about spiritual gifts and will get bludgeoned if by some miracle you learn on your own and then try to do them.

Fear of excess:

I fully support the ministry of God's power but must admit that there are incidents of misuse of spiritual gifts. Too often pastors of charismatic churches hesitate to exercise pastoral oversight over a church service and ignore any obvious abuses. The carnal abuse of spiritual gifts manifested by the attempt to elevate fleshly acts of "power" needs to be addressed. Yes, this will cause some consternation from the individual or individuals promoting their particular brand of fleshly excess, but pastoral ministry was never supposed to be a smooth walk in the park.

NOTE: God never said that he would withdraw His ministerial office gifts when a revival appears. In fact, revivals will elevate these pastoral gifts and make them even more indispensable. Remember, a revival must be pastored.

Fear of the unknown:

I get it. Supernatural events can be fearful. This is why any angelic visitor when showing themselves to a human being usually prefaced their appearance by saying, "Be not afraid." But even though the supernatural can be a challenge to our limited experience it should never be dismissed because of fear. God Himself challenged His people to investigate the deep truths of His kingdom:

O taste and see that the LORD is good; how blessed is the man who takes refuge in Him! (Psalm 34:8).

NOTE: When faced with the fact that supernatural displays of God's power are oftentimes frightening it may help Christians if they are reminded that Satan is probably more frightened than they are when he sees the power of God. Remember, the demons saw the power of God and cowered in fear.

And He came down to Capernaum, a city of Galilee, and He was teaching them on the Sabbath; and they were amazed at His teaching, for His message was with authority. In the synagogue there was a man possessed by the spirit of an unclean demon, and he cried out with a loud voice, "Let us alone! What business do we have with each other, Jesus of Nazareth? Have You come to destroy us? I know who You are—the Holy One of God!" But Jesus rebuked him, saying, "Be quiet and come out of him!" And when the demon had thrown him down in the midst of the people, he came out of him without doing him any harm. And amazement came upon them all, and they began talking with one another saying, "What is this message? For with authority and power He commands the unclean spirits and they come out." And the report about Him was spreading into every locality in the surrounding district (Luke 4:31-37).

The debilitating effect of the seeker friendly church:

I have made my opinion known concerning the weakness of the seeker friendly church. Again I will state the obvious. Any attempt by a

Christian church to produce a sanitized and acceptable gospel that can appeal to the lowest common denominator will only produce a glorified social club. Some of my readers may resent my "truthing" but I can read the Bible and know what God says about the truth:

So Jesus was saying to those Jews who had believed Him, "If you continue in My word, then you are truly disciples of Mine; and you will know the truth, ***and the truth will make you free"*** (John 8:31-32).

Any church and/or denomination that is embarrassed of the hard hitting plain truth of the gospel and then embraces the sanitized seeker friendly version in order to appeal to the church shopper is pushing for the removal of their church from the Yellow Pages section for churches and inclusion with the Elks and Eagles Clubs in the Yellow Pages section on social clubs.

FACT: A powerless church is handicapped. A powerless church is no threat to the Devil. A powerless church has no other option but to make the attempt to talk the Devil to death.

The overwhelming proof of God's power

It is a fact that there has been an age old struggle between the people of God and non-believers. For countless generations the battle has raged unabated

To be honest this struggle, although real, is in no way equitable. Finite human beings, armed only with a shabby argument and an attitude, are no match for an almighty, omnipresent and omniscient God. It is no stretch of imagination to recognize how pitiful and ridiculous the non-believers appear when questioning the existence of the eternal God and especially His miracle working power. The Psalmist said it best:

The fool has said in his heart, "There is no God." They are corrupt, they have committed abominable deeds; There is no one who does good (Psalm 14:1).

And,

For the wicked boasts of his heart's desire, and the greedy man curses and spurns the LORD. *The wicked, in the haughtiness of his countenance, does not seek Him. All his thoughts are, "There is no God"* (Psalm 10:3-4).

Always merciful in His actions, God has presented the world with many proofs of His existence and His miracle working power. Any human being that genuinely seeks the Lord will find Him. The following are some of the unavoidable proofs that God advances to prove His case.

Only God alone can point to fulfilled prophecy as a pillar of support of His existence and power:

God made it clear that fulfilled prophecy was and is an infallible proof of His existence and power in both the Old and New Testaments:

"I declared the former things long ago and they went forth from My mouth, and proclaimed them. Suddenly I acted, and they came to

pass. "*Because I know that you are obstinate, and your neck is an iron sinew and your forehead bronze, Therefore I declared them to you long ago,* **Before they took place I proclaimed them to you, so that you would not say, 'My idol has done them, And my graven image and my molten image have commanded them.'** *(Isaiah 48:3-5).*

And,

"*Present your case,*" *the* LORD *says.* "*Bring forward your strong arguments,*" **The King of Jacob says. Let them bring forth and declare to us what is going to take place; as for the former events, declare what they were, that we may consider them and know their outcome. Or announce to us what is coming; declare the things that are going to come afterward, that we may know that you are gods** (Isaiah 41:21-23).

And,

From now on **I am telling you before it comes to pass, so that when it does occur, you may believe that I am He** (John 13:19).

NOTE: No other "holy" book contains verifiable prophecies. The Bible alone contains hundreds of these "truth capsules" that have all come to pass with 100% accuracy.[113] To even make the attempt to deny the Bible's uniqueness is nothing but an act of desperation carried out by those who would also waste their time denying the existence of the sun, the moon and the stars.

God has historically revealed His power and majesty when faced with mankind's futile attempts to resist His dominance and efficacy:

The prophets of Baal stood against Elijah and learned the hard way that God and His servants are not to be trifled with. Those pathetic "prophets" called upon their god in their desperate struggle against the true God and discovered too late that he was nonexistent and thus unable to hear their pitiful rantings (I Kings 18:20-46).

NOTE: The glaring facts stare the unbelieving world in the face: **God has shown His indisputable power before the collective eyes of an unbelieving mankind.** There have been billions of human beings healed of cancer and other terminal diseases in response to the prayers in the name of Jesus.[114] Billions of miracles have taken place throughout

---

[113] Theologians may debate the exact number but there are at least three thousand prophecies within the Christian Bible (Old and New Testaments). These prophecies are not like the ones seen in the popular magazines found in the corner market but are very specific and precise and are 100% accurate to the smallest detail. The 300+ prophecies concerning Jesus Christ stand out as an irrefutable proof of His reality and are extremely useful in evangelistic efforts. The charge that Jesus and/or His followers fabricated such astounding prophetic revelations is nothing but a fantasy conjured up by desperate enemies of Christ.

[114] I was diagnosed with throat cancer in November 2014. The tumor was at the base of my tongue and was as big as a tennis ball. My doctors prescribed radiation as my treatment and I began the process the first week of December. Before treatment began I asked for prayer from my prayer group. They interceded for me and continued to intercede every day. Within three weeks of the beginning of radiation the tumor was gone. My doctors were stunned and said that such a response

human history (ten of them, duly noted in the Book of Exodus, punished the ancient land of Egypt), entire cultures and nations have been affected by the power of God—and again, all this has taken place in the public arena for all to see. History is rightfully called "His Story." There is no place to hide from the display of God's power.

The infinite number of answered prayers offered up in the name of Jesus Christ throughout history is undeniable:

Only the most apostate and carnal human beings can be faced with the infinite number of answered prayers over thousands of years offered up in the name of Jesus Christ and still make an attempt to discredit the obvious conclusion—the biblical God is alive and well and engaged with planet earth and it is all done in the name of Jesus. With so many answered prayers verified through countless testimonies these naysayers can be accurately defined:

The fool has said in his heart, "There is no God," they are corrupt, and have committed abominable injustice; there is no one who does good. God has looked down from heaven upon the sons of men to see if there is anyone who understands, who seeks after God. Every one of them has turned aside; together they have become corrupt; There is no one who does good, not even one (Psalm 53:1-3).

Only Christianity can point to the universal fact of the changed lives of its adherents as a proof of its clear dominance over all competing religions and dogmas:

The competing philosophies and religions in this world, devoid of any supernatural power, can only point to their "supposed knowledge" as a way to verify their truth and reality. Although true biblical knowledge is definitely a desired goal in God's kingdom, it must be said that God points to a much larger proof of His existence—**the changed lives of His followers.** Billions of former murderers, liars, thieves, sexually promiscuous, unforgiving and vile human beings all have one thing in common. They all make the claim that the risen Jesus Christ has entered their hearts and souls and has transformed them by a supernatural act of divine grace and power. All arguments arrayed against God's existence and power must dissipate when faced with such a vast army of transformed humanity. It is no stretch that Christianity alone sees changed lives as an important evaluative tool when assessing God's reality.

It's just that simple…

---

to radiation was impossible and that I needed to continue the treatment. I did continue, but the cancer had indeed disappeared after only three weeks. This was verified by a battery of tests. This miracle of God continues to be discussed each time I return to meet with my doctors. They all say the same thing: *"Cancer that large and advanced cannot disappear after only three weeks of treatment."* Obviously the Lord believes it can…

NOTE: When dealing with an atheist I challenge you to ask them one simple question: "How does your atheism make you a better person?" While they are pondering that question you can then add, "If it could be possible to transport all the people that would answer my next question there would be little room for the billions that would respond. And that question is: How has Christ changed your life?" After the atheist's jaw drops down and he/she begins to mumble you could then ask them the following: "Oh and by the way, how would it make you feel to be standing in the midst of those billions of people all by yourself?"

In closing

The truth cannot be ignored. Christians are commanded to minister in the power of the Holy Spirit. It is an eternal law of God and must be observed. True revivals have always been advanced through the power of God and always will be. This fact should never be obscured by the theology and traditions of man.

Pray for revival.

Chapter Fourteen

Count the Cost

"Suppose one of you wants to build a tower. Will he not first sit down and estimate the cost to see if he has enough money to complete it? For if he lays the foundation and is not able to finish it, everyone who sees it will ridicule him, saying, 'This fellow began to build and was not able to finish.'" –Luke 14: 28-30

Jesus spoke the above words to His disciples to underline the solemnity of the call to discipleship and its required obedience. I believe that Jesus' command to "count the cost" is a universal and timeless directive that includes not only all human decisions, but the command to seek revival in our time.

Serious Christians submitted to God's headship should spend no time defending the lack of revival in their lives and churches, but should instead take steps to obey the Lord by bringing the spiritual famine to an end. It should be noted that throughout the Word of God we are confronted with God's demands concerning human obedience. The following verse emphasizes that call for obedience:

"Whoever has my commands and obeys them, he is the one who loves me. He who loves me will be loved by my Father, and I too will love him and show myself to him." (John 14:21).

We need to stop promoting our excuses that encourage spiritual mediocrity and ask for God's fire to fall upon us. Obedient Christians should "do" the following: **count the cost of revival and then embrace that call for revival.**

A good place to start is to ask ourselves the questions that will prime our spiritual pump and get us walking in the right direction:

The questions we should ask

Do we really want to see revival in our time? I know that on the surface this sounds like a silly question, but I feel that it is a good question to ask. Many Christians may think that they would climb on board with revival, but when the chips are down and the enemies of God are gathering at the gates history has shown that many have succumbed to fear and retired from the battle field.

The fact is that revivals are serious expeditions into the unknown and not for the faint-hearted. No finite human being will find it easy to embrace a supernatural move of God that requires a deep trust of a God we cannot see—an exercise we call faith.

Faith is what leads us to take our place on God's operating table and allow Him to perform surgery within our souls. It is faith that prompts us to seek revival against what seem to be impossible odds. It is at this time that my astute readers will ask, "How much faith do I need…and where do I get that faith?" We must turn to the Word of God to find our answer:

And the Lord said, "If you had faith like a mustard seed, you would say to this mulberry tree, 'Be uprooted and be planted in the sea'; and it would obey you (Luke 17:6).

In Mark 4:30-32 Jesus explained that a mustard seed, although small, would eventually grow into a very large plant. His point was that we only need a little faith joined with a big God to accomplish the things that God wants done. If we couple that knowledge of the smallness of faith that accomplishes God's purposes with the fact that God purposely uses ordinary people to do His kingdom works we should be encouraged to step out and exercise our faith (I Corinthians 1:26-31).

The example of Moses

Moses is considered a sterling example of a man of faith, but as we read the holy text we learn that he was a simple man with fear and doubt like all of us. The great example of this fact is his first meeting with God at the burning bush in the third chapter of Exodus when he expressed his doubts and asked for a confirmation concerning the incredible call to become Israel's deliverer. Moses' attempt to deflect God's call by trumpeting his excuses for not embracing the Lord's commissioning should be required reading by all who are considering the call for revival. When challenged by Moses to prove Himself, God's answer spoke volumes,

And God said, "I will be with you. And this will be the sign to you that it is I who have sent you: When you have brought the people out of Egypt, you will worship God on this mountain." (Exodus 3:12).

God's answer to Moses was twofold: First, He said that He would be with Moses. Can you grasp the profound truth of that statement? God Himself would be with Moses! With those simple and yet compelling words God is stating an astounding fact: **Every human being who has ever lived and ever will live if placed on a scale cannot outweigh the one man who is with God.** As the Apostle Paul said, "If God is for us who can be against us?" (Romans 8:31). Those simple words make all the difference and should encourage any Christian with a pulse. **A man and his God is a majority. A man and his God can usher in revival. A man and his God will win.**

And the outcome is not in doubt.

Secondly, God said that Moses' receiving of "proof" was contingent on his accomplishment of the massive task placed upon him by God. In simple interpretation—Moses would only receive his proof after he had completed the task—the introduction of the definition of true biblical faith: **Risk precedes result.**

Think of the turmoil in Moses' heart while considering this task. Moses, a lowly, insignificant sheepherder from the land of Midian, was being ordered by a voice coming from a burning bush to confront Pharaoh, the most powerful man on earth. Consider these orders: Moses, armed only with a shepherd's staff, was to show up unannounced at Pharaoh's door, demand obedience to God from this godless king, demand the release of thousands of Hebrew slaves who were this king's personal property, lead them through a wilderness with little food and water, and then deliver them to the holy mountain to meet God before he would then know for sure that it was God Who had issued him these orders.

This is staggering.

This extraordinary disclosure makes it crystal clear that true faith is an expedition into the unknown that is only confirmed by the result. We can never have a total assurance from God that removes our need for faith and we must step out of the boat and walk on the water before we realize how limitless He is.

Quite simply, in order to experience revival we must "do" what God has said. Our assurances are based upon the integrity of a God we cannot see and will always require trust. There is really no other way.

Can we do that?

Are we willing to give up our fleshly tendencies to resist God?

To pretend that we have never engaged in resistance to God is a waste of time, because we have all resisted God at one time or another. The human struggle with God is a sad fact of life.

God has spoken many times on the seriousness of human rebellion. Continued rebellion in the non-believer brings death and judgment that leads only to the pit of hell. Rebellion in the believer brings discipline and pain that disrupts relationship with God and leads to the loss of blessings and honor and on to the possibility of apostasy.

In the mid-1970s there was a Broadway musical based on the Book of Matthew called "Your Arms Too Short to Box with God." The show was a smash hit labeled, "A soaring celebration in song and dance." The musical highlighted the utter futility of all human attempts to circumvent God and/or attempt to use Him to accomplish our questionable purposes. For a secular show it had some good lessons that we could learn: Stop trying to box God! Cease your rebellion and throw in the towel and allow Him to fix your wounds!

When God issues His call to revival believers must give heed to that call and lay down their resistance. This is not an easy task as I have already explained. Revival is a mighty outpouring of fire from the altar of God that will either burn us or cleanse us. There is no middle ground. It is a complete surrender to God or certain judgment.

Can we do that?

Are we willing to pray for revival?

Revival only comes through prayer. The pertinent verses are too numerous for anyone to mount a serious argument against that fact.

Like Moses, many of us will feel the need to know for sure that our prayers will prompt the manifestation of God's presence and power. We seem to need the "proof" before we even engage in the warfare. But God has called us to pray and He will bring about the results. Faith tells us that the result will occur. Simply put, prayer is an exercise of faith that covers the time between God's command to pray and the completed and tangible result. We must pray and then trust God to experience revival.

With that said I will state the obvious: Revival prayer is long and laborious and will exact a cost—physically, spiritually and emotionally. Satan hates revival and he will direct his attack against any who make the attempt to advance God's kingdom on earth. I can absolutely guarantee that any Christian that seriously engages in revival prayer will experience the brutal and naked attack from Hell itself. But let this truth flood your soul: **God is with you and will see you through to the successful conclusion.**

Are we willing to spend the time and effort to engage in this kind of prayer? Are we willing to pay the price?

Can we do that?

Are we willing to face the possible resistance from our churches and leadership?

Some churches and/or leadership may not be open to revival. Instead of seeing this as an insurmountable barrier it may be the call to intercessory prayer that may light a fire within your church. We may be the first in our churches to receive the Holy Spirit's prompting to seek revival. This will place a serious call upon us to pray for our churches and leadership to experience that call. Remember that prayer is the key. If we pray for our churches and leadership the chances of our brethren being open to the call are greatly enhanced.

Remember, successful Christianity is a team effort. We need our brethren to hear the call of God in order for them to be open to the exciting task of igniting revival in our nation. Being the only person in the room that is aflame with revival fire may prompt your forced exit from the room.[115]

The enemy of our souls will attack revival whenever the opportunity presents itself. Perceptive Christians need to acknowledge this truth and prepare.

---

[115] History has proven that in many cases a person aflame with God's fire when no one else is experiencing it may find themselves and their fire moved to a central location—like the wooden stake at the center of the town square. In these cases praying that revival fire is spread amongst others takes on the nature of a self-defense action.

For though we walk in the flesh, we do not war according to the flesh, for the weapons of our warfare are not of the flesh, but divinely powerful for the destruction of fortresses. We are destroying speculations and every lofty thing raised up against the knowledge of God, and we are taking every thought captive to the obedience of Christ (II Corinthians 10:3-5).

The fact is that all of us will need help from God and His people during our struggles on this besieged earth. I want to stress this point: We will always need prayer and we will always need our brethren. With that in mind we need to seriously embrace our responsibility to intercede for the saints.

With all prayer and petition pray at all times in the Spirit, and with this in view, be on the alert with all perseverance and petition for all the saints, (Ephesians 6:18).

Mankind's propensity to resist God is legendary and took the sacrifice of God's Son to overcome. We who are called to pray for revival will be tested to the upmost by our churches and leadership. We must ask ourselves if we are open to assume this responsibility.

Can we do that?

Are we ready to follow the Lord's leading?

I would be amiss if I attempted to downplay the difficulties that a believer will encounter when seeking revival. Revival is a call for war against Satan's destructive attempts to inhibit the church in its divine command to advance God's kingdom. Anyone that asks the Lord to pour out revival upon His people must be ready to follow God's lead. This is extremely important because of two facts:

First, only God is able to guide us through the mysterious realm of the supernatural. We are finite human beings and do not have the experience and the understanding to discern all that we will need to successfully navigate the pitfalls and barriers presented by Satan against God's church. We must pray for the wisdom to conduct ourselves and our brethren safely through the spiritual warfare we will encounter.

Be of sober spirit, be on the alert. Your adversary, the devil, prowls around like a roaring lion, seeking someone to devour. But resist him, firm in your faith, knowing that the same experiences of suffering are being accomplished by your brethren who are in the world (I Peter 5:8-9).

Secondly, we must follow wherever our Lord leads. This truth was clearly revealed in the Old Testament story of the cloud and pillar of fire: The Hebrews, escaping from Egypt and heading to the Promised Land, were ordered to follow the cloud and pillar of fire. By day and night the cloud and pillar of fire served as a symbol of God's presence that led the Hebrews in their quest. When the cloud and pillar of fire moved the Hebrews broke camp and followed. When the cloud and pillar of fire stopped the Hebrews stopped and set up camp. There was no movement except the movement ordered and directed by God (Exodus 13:21-22; Numbers 9:15-23). The spiritual truth is unavoidable—God's people are to follow Him wherever He takes them...without question. God will tell you when to leave a church and when to stay. This is God's prerogative and not the prerogatives of finite human beings. Remember, we serve the living God and not some earthly agenda.

NOTE: Throughout Christendom churches and denominations attempt to use various methods to keep or draw people back to the fold. This would be a good thing if the person being drawn back had left his/her relationship with God. In fact, any church or denomination worth its salt should attempt to retrieve backslidden former members whenever possible. But oftentimes the church or denomination is simply making the attempt to draw the person away from the new church that they are now attending for reasons other than the betterment of the person. The value of the new church and its ability to minister to the person is not the question, but only the fact that the person has left the old church (which is often perceived as an affront to the old church and its leadership). Let me say this: **Churches or denominations do not own people.** If there is a good reason for a person to move on to a new church then so be it. It may be a good reason—the old church or denomination isn't doing the job, they may have lost their direction and focus, the ministry has ceased to be a vibrant community of faith and has embraced the poison of liberalism, the youth ministry is non-existent, leadership is ignoring blatant sin in the church or many other reasons. I truly believe that any church that is trying to retrieve old members that have moved on better have something positive to offer that can contribute to the spiritual growth of that person and their family or leave them alone. If we (the church) aren't doing the job we have no right to use a guilt trip to regain control over people and keep them in our dead churches. Again, if you aren't presenting a vibrant, biblical, faith filled and Holy Spirit equipped church don't attempt to draw people to it. **My suggestion:** Seek God and allow Him to straighten out your ministry and then He will draw all the people that you can handle.

It is that simple.

Are we willing to face our fears concerning revival?

Most of us have fears concerning revival. The fears are many so I will list just a few:

We may fear that the "acts of the flesh" will be so pronounced during revival that we will look silly surrounded by people rolling on the floor. I have never seen a "holy roller," but like most people I have heard the stories that are routinely trotted out to dismiss any serious pursuit of revival. In my opinion, someone wiggling on the floor, although strange, is not enough to keep me out of God's throne room. In fact, you would think that non-believers that attend the various rock concerts would truly fit in if there was a bunch of wigglers on the floor. It's amazing to me how much tolerance is extended by non-believers to questionable behaviors when those behaviors have no connection to God. Just a thought...

We may fear that our Christian friends will think we are crazy and even some of our leaders may question our sanity. I think both of these events could indeed happen, but I am not sure that either is enough to keep a serious believer from embracing revival. If the truth be known, receiving censure for embracing the promises of God and doing what He has said is not a bad thing. Being criticized for obeying God puts you in great company. You will stand with the likes of Daniel, Ezekiel, Isaiah, Jeremiah, Zechariah, John the Baptist, Peter, Paul, John, Matthew, Martin Luther, John Calvin, Charles Finney, Jonathon Edwards, Zwingli, David Wilkerson, Leonard Ravenhill, Billy Graham, and hundreds of others that have carried God's torch. In my opinion, criticism directed at a servant of God is a badge of valor granted by God to those who follow His lead.

We may be afraid that God will call us out of our comfort zone to witness to strangers. Unfortunately, I cannot argue against that fear by saying that it will not happen...because it will. The major point of revival is to fill believers with power to go out and find the lost.

FACT: During a real revival you will be led by God to "go" and seek the lost. And you will find them.

We may even fear that praying for revival will make us look like fools. My response to this fear is that the world will always think that praying to God is for fools—unless they are in a tough spot and need prayer (like in a fox hole).

NOTE: When someone who is questioning your love for Jesus says "you are a fool" you may consider answering: "Yes, I am a fool for Christ. Whose fool are you?"

Personally, my greatest fear is that unscrupulous men will attempt to highjack a God-sent revival for their own personal agenda. My concern is real because this very thing has happened in many revivals throughout history. Although this problem is real and must be guarded against, the benefits of true revival are so great that we must not give in to our fear of human distortions and abuse.

FACT: I must admit that I have entertained all of those fears at one time or another, but I must say that I truly feel that they are not enough to derail my desire to experience revival.

True revival is not a walk in the park. A revival will call on us to share our monies, our time and our giftedness. In revivals we will be called to interact with some challenging people whom we would normally shy away from. In essence we are to give ourselves completely and without hesitation.

Can we do that?

God is always primed for revival

There have been many theologians throughout the history of the church that have taught that God sends revival only when He wants to and is never prompted by human prayer requesting revival. I have always seen this position as a "mechanized" approach to God and not the "relational" experience that God desires to foster in His children. Human involvement with God in seeking revival is chronicled within the Word of God.

The Spirit and the bride say, "Come." And let the one who hears say, "Come." And let the one who is thirsty come; let the one who wishes to take the water of life without cost. (Revelation 22:17).

The Word of God is filled with the prayers of God's people calling out to Him for revival. Only unconfessed serial sin and intentional disobedience causes God to consider revival prayer as being of no consequence.

O God of hosts, turn again now; we beseech You; Look down from heaven and see, and take care of this vine, even the shoot which Your right hand has planted, And on the son whom You have strengthened for Yourself. It is burned with fire, it is cut down; they perish at the rebuke of Your countenance. Let Your hand be upon the man of Your right hand, upon the son of man whom You made strong for Yourself. Then we shall not turn back from You; **Revive** *us, and we will call upon Your name. Lord of hosts,* **restore** *us; cause Your face to shine upon us, and we will be saved.* (Psalm 80: 14-19)

And,

O Lord, You showed favor to Your land; You **restored** *the captivity of Jacob. You forgave the iniquity of Your people; You covered all their sin. You withdrew all Your fury; You turned away from Your burning anger.* **Restore** *us, O God of our salvation, And cause Your indignation toward us to cease. Will You be angry with us forever? Will You prolong Your anger to all generations? Will You not* **revive** *us again, that Your people may rejoice in You? Show us Your lovingkindness, O Lord, and grant us Your salvation.* (Psalm 85).

God is an all-consuming fire. The Word of God indicates that He is always ready to send revival to His penitent children. This is a sharp contrast to us human beings who are cold, sinful and shallow and inclined to avoid the presence and power of God. In our natural state we are captive to sin and evil and may resist our loving Father until we surrender to His will,

There is no difference, for all have sinned and fall short of the glory of God. (Romans 3:22, 23).

And,

I know that nothing good lives in me, that is. In my sinful nature, for I have the desire to do what is good, but I cannot carry it out. (Romans 7:14).

We desperately need God's fire to ignite our souls and burn away the dross that clogs our spiritual arteries keeping us from fulfilling our callings as ambassadors of the great king.

Therefore, we are ambassadors for Christ, as though God were making an appeal through us; we beg you on behalf of Christ, be reconciled to God. (II Corinthians 5: 20).

God's fire is the indispensable, missing ingredient in all of us. A true revival is the conduit that God uses to send His all-consuming fire down on our thirsty souls. Those that seek revival must apprehend this truth and press it to its successful conclusion. As the ominous signs of judgment appear on the horizon, it is revival or death. We have no other options.

True Christians have been wired by God to seek revival. Like Moses we may attempt to deflect that call, but deep inside our hearts we know the answer: We must seek revival. It is our calling. The human involvement in the quest for revival is a genuine act of obedience. If we resist we will perish. If we accept the call and press on to the answer we will see God's deliverance.

Pray for revival…

Made in the USA
Monee, IL
16 March 2021